Needs Asses
Post-16 Edu

Needs Assessment in Post-16 Education

Tim Packwood

and

Tim Whitaker

The Falmer Press

(A member of the Taylor & Francis Group)

London • New York • Philadelphia

UK The Falmer Press, Falmer House, Barcombe, Lewes, East Sussex, BN8 5DL

USA The Falmer Press, Taylor & Francis Inc., 242 Cherry Street, Philadelphia, PA 19106-1906

First published 1988

Library of Congress Cataloging in Publication Data

Packwood, Tim.
  Needs assessment in post-16 education/Tim Packwood and Tim Whitaker.
      p.   cm.
    Includes indexes.
      1. Education, Secondary—Economic aspects—Great Britain.
  2. Teenagers—Education—Great Britain. 3. Education and state—Great Britain. 4. Educational planning—Great Britain.
  5. Needs assessment—Great Britain. I. Whitaker, Tim. II. Title.
  LC67.58.G7P33 1988 373.41—dc19 87-34911
  ISBN 1-85000-291-6
  ISBN 1-85000-292-4 (pbk.)

Jacket design by Caroline Archer

Typeset in 10½/12 Caledonia by
Imago Publishing Ltd, Thame, Oxon

Printed in Great Britain by Taylor & Francis (Printers) Ltd, Basingstoke

Contents

Content

Preface and Acknowledgements

Although we had made frequent use of the idea of 'needs' in studying and teaching various aspects of social administration, the chance for a detailed study came from a research project sponsored by the Department of Education and Science. We are grateful for this opportunity and for the support provided by the DES. Our particular thanks must go the Project Steering Committee, namely: John Hedger, Anthony Woollard, Pat Curran, Stephen Williams, Tony Wilshaw, Simon Lambert, John Cooper, Lyn Huggins, Basil Murphy, Alan Crispin, Ron Letch, Jeff Reynalds, Anne Fort and Jack Chapman. They provided expertise, encouragement and critical comment throughout the research.

Maurice Kogan, the Project Director, has also given constant support and encouragement: in devising and implementing the research, in analyzing the results and in producing this book. Our special thanks are also due to Lisa Warr who, as Research Secretary and Administrator, played an enormous part in helping to make the research and writing as smooth and efficient as possible.

But inevitably any success of the research is a result of the help and encouragement given by individuals within the local education authorities and institutions we studied. There is not space to list names, but we are grateful to all those who, from an interest in education, gave us their time and cooperation. We hope that this product from the research will prove useful to them and other practitioners.

In this book we have tried to place what we learned in the field within a wider context of policy and government. Our intention in writing was to address a wide audience. We believe that the issues and ideas considered have relevance for those engaged in the day to day delivery of post-16 education, as well as those who manage and plan the provision. They are also relevant for those with a more general interest in the nature of current education and, wider still, in the operation of social institutions and the application of social constructs such as 'need'.

The book has been written as a continuous narrative, although the two authors each took responsibility for different chapters. Tim Whitaker, who was the Convenor of the research project, wrote Chapters 1, 2, 4, 8 and 9, and Tim Packwood wrote Chapters 3, 5, 6, 7, 10 and 11. Both authors, however, take collective responsibility for the whole work.

The presentation of ideas and argument in the book has benefitted immensely from the advice and criticism of Tony Bush, Simon Lambert, Alan Lambourne and Steward Ranson, who commented upon, and improved, a preliminary version. We are also indebted to Sally Harris for all her skills in typing and presentation in the final stages of production.

Finally, we are grateful to the DES for permission to use the statistics in Table 1 (page 35).

Glossary

ADVISERS	Local Education Authority Advisers
AS	Advanced Supplementary
BTEC	Business/Technician Education Council
CBI	Confederation of British Industry
CEE	Certificate of Extended Education
CELP	College Employer Links Project
CGLI	City and Guilds London Institute
COS	Certificate of Office Studies
CPVE	Certificate of Pre-Vocational Education
CSE	Certificate of Secondary Education
DE	Department of Employment
DES	Department of Education and Science
FE	Further Education
GCE	General Certificate of Education
GCSE	General Certificate of Secondary Education
HE	Higher Education
HMI	Her Majesty's Inspectorate
ITB	Industrial Training Boards
ITEC	Information and Technology Centres
LEA	Local Education Authority
MSC	Manpower Services Commission
NAFE	Non-Advanced Further Education
NTI	New Training Initiative
RAC	Regional Advisory Council
SATROS	Science and Technical Regional Organizations
SCIP	Schools Curriculum Industry Project
TVEI	Technical and Vocational Education Initiative
YTS	Youth Training Scheme

1 The Agenda for 16–19 Education

Post–16 Education

Education and training for the 16–19 age group have seen rapid change in the past ten years. Until then they had remained relatively quiescent as a policy area, despite the problems and deficiencies that were acknowledged to exist. Policy and public attention was occupied with the compulsory stage of education and comprehensive schemes of reorganization. In the mid-1970s a number of interrelated forces — changes in educational thinking, financial stringency, falling rolls, youth unemployment, demands for work related education and training, the advent of Manpower Services Commission (MSC) training schemes and other government initiatives — all combined to place post-16 provision at the forefront of the education policy agenda.

Yet occupation of the centre of the policy-making stage has not been accompanied by a consensus about its goals and direction. The purpose of education is contested; should provision be directed at the fulfilment of individual development or to prepare students for future economic roles in society? Following from this, there are issues regarding the curriculum for this age group; the skills that should be developed and whether provision should be broad or specialized. Related to these themes is the further issue of *how* post-16 education should be provided. Should it be a continuation of the education provided by schools or are there benefits from a break to attend a separate institution that caters for all post-16 education?

These issues have been debated at all levels of the education system for some time. In 1980, the Macfarlane Report on Education for 16–19-Year-Olds (DES, 1980) recommended that authorities should evaluate their existing institutional provision in order to assess how far it allowed for diverse needs and how effective it was in terms of economy. But changes in provision are not easily secured. All education is provided against a background of past thinking and ways of working which constrains attempts to introduce change. The large number of recent initiatives in the post-16 field, including the introduction of the Technical and Vocational Education Initiative (TVEI) and the Youth Training Scheme (YTS), have made the field all the more complex and uncertain. The growth of YTS means that only a quarter of 16-year-olds do not continue with some form of full or part-time education. There has also been criticism from different quarters that existing education for the 16–19s is inappropriate to the changing needs of this age group and the expectations of society.

The last decade has also been characterized by wider uncertainty and change in English society. It has seen deepening economic recession and an emphasis on value for money and cost effectiveness in public services. It has also seen a questioning of the role that public services, and particularly local government, should perform. These wider uncertainties cannot help but affect post-16 education.

For these reasons 16–19 education is highly political. It is marked by entrenched interests with views about needs and how they should be met, and by a growing involvement from central government in developing the curriculum and new forms of provision. Local education authorities and institutions have to attempt to reconcile these conflicting pressures.

But the difficulty still remains of how to determine the provision that should be made available for this age group and how best to satisfy their needs. This is all the more important given the distinctive nature of post-16 education, with specialization and diversification of needs and provision. In this context what is meant by the concept of need and how far is it applicable in the process of determining provision?

Needs and Education

The term 'need' is widely used in discussions of the nature of public services including that of education. It has become accepted as one of the key concepts of social policy, carrying with it normative implications about what services should be provided and for whom they should be available (Bradshaw, 1972; Smith, 1980). This thinking carries a strong acceptance that public services should respond to the recognized needs of the populations they serve. Need becomes used as the dominant principle for the distribution of these services rather than other principles, such as political choice or the ability to pay. The argument continues that once needs have been identified then they can also serve as statements of service priorities. In post-16 education the concept of need appears frequently in discussions on provision. Different views have been advanced about the changing needs of particular categories of students and it has been assumed that education should meet these identified needs.

Yet the term 'need' lacks precision and is used in different ways by different participants (Clayton, 1983). The definitions of need that are used are outlined and reviewed later in this book, but at this point it is sufficient to state that commonly 'need' refers to a view of the discrepancy between what is currently the state of an individual or group and the state that is believed desirable. It contains a judgment of whether this state should be altered and how an alteration can be achieved. For example, an individual student may be judged to 'need' a particular type of course in order to develop the necessary skills to enter a particular sector of employment or to prepare for further or higher education.

Assessments of needs are made at different levels of the education system involving many different participants. In the institutions students' needs have to be assessed in order to determine the courses that they should follow and what the institution itself ought to be providing. LEAs have to make some form of assessment of needs in order to be clear about the basic provision of staff, buildings, equipment, and the level of finance required. In distributing finance to local authorities central government makes an assessment of the resources necessary to meet their needs. Needs assessment, then, is performed in different parts of education systems, for different purposes. An examination of how needs are assessed requires identifying the various activities that contribute, who participates, the criteria that are applied and how different assessments affect educational provision.

The Purpose of the Book

The two preceding sections set the agenda for the book, which seeks to analyze how local education authorities and their institutions assess the needs of the 16–19 age group. This has two interrelated aspects. First throughout the book we describe, in some detail, how needs assessment is currently performed. But, second, we are concerned to move beyond what is, to suggest explanations and point out the implications that result. In other words, the book attempts to capture some of the detail of current educational practice and to interpret this practice by applying theories and ideas developed in the social sciences. This entails a combination of the language and approaches of both the educational practitioner and the social scientist.

The Research

The research on which the book is based was sponsored by the Department of Education and Science and carried out from 1983 to 1986. It had four complementary objectives. The first was to discover the range of information that local education authorities possessed about the activities and needs of the 16–19s including the knowledge derived from students, practitioners in the LEA, the Careers Service, local authority departments, the Manpower Services Commission, local employers and other interested groups. The second objective was to analyze how and why this information was collected and how this influenced the formulation of different concepts of educational needs. The third was to investigate the effect of such statements of need and their relationship with other factors in the planning of provision and corresponding institutional arrangements for this age group. The final objective was to explore the processes by which the LEA evaluated its provision and its ability to meet the identified needs.

The research was carried out in two stages. The first comprised two national surveys of LEAs regarding their policies and their planning for 16–19 year olds. The second, and major part, was case studies in six LEAs across England, three of which focused on the whole authority while the other three explored the roles of particular providers. The methodology of the research is explained more fully in the Appendix. The prime method consisted of a series of semi-structured interviews with the key staff in the LEA and institutions, focusing on how they went about assessing the educational needs of the post-16 age group. The case studies allowed the different opinions of participants to be tested against each other. The findings, from the fieldwork were written up in the form of case study documents which served as a database for the research and were also used to test emerging analyses with the participants in the research. This book uses the findings from case studies to illuminate discussion but also attempts to be more global in analyzing the way that needs are assessed in local education systems and the forces that influence this process.

The Plan of the Book

The main elements of our approach in studying the assessment of the educational needs of the 16–19 age group are depicted in Figure 1. Various levels of analysis have been used to understand the processes involved in needs assessment and how and why this takes the form that it does. Central to our analysis is the dynamic relationship between the contextual and structural influences and the actual processes involved in the determination of needs and provision. Understanding these processes involves understanding the influence exerted by the context of post-16 provision (social, demographic and economic circumstances, national political definition of needs and priorities, existing types of provision and the characteristics of the clients) and by prevailing structural conceptions of what need implies, how it should be identified and how education should be organized and delivered.

FIGURE 1 — THE PLAN OF THE BOOK

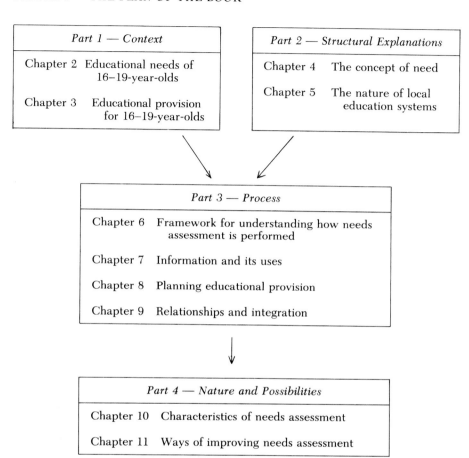

Part 1 of the book covers the contextual factors that influence the nature of 16–19 educational provision and limit the ways in which the needs of this age group are assessed. Chapter 2 outlines some of the forces that shape post-16 provision and in particular the way that central government has sought to modify the aims of the curriculum towards greater vocational relevance. The chapter goes on to discuss some of the main responses to these challenges. Chapter 3 analyzes the complexities of the system for providing 16–19 education in terms of the characteristics of the clients, the sources of guidance that are available to them in determining the use they make of education and the choices between the different forms of institutional provision that are available.

Part 2 moves to the structural explanations that determine needs assessment in post-16 education. Chapter 4 discusses the assumptions underlying the definition of need, showing its many uses in the field of social policy and outlines the way that various public services, including education, have attempted to define and measure need. The analysis shows that needs are defined in different ways by various participants, through the use of different criteria. Chapter 5 considers a number of theoretical perspectives that offer insights into the way in which education is organized and provided.

Part 3 of the book deals with the processes involved in needs assessment in the local educational system. It directly applies the results of our empirical work, while also employing ideas and analyses presented in the two preceding parts. Chapter 6 begins by defining a framework for understanding the processes of needs assessment. This identifies the activities by which needs are assessed and analyzes their contribution according to location, specificity, purpose, form, type of information generated, participants and the type of definition made. The three following chapters take up key areas of process. Chapter 7 reviews the information about needs that is available in the local education system and examines its characteristics and the way in which it is used in schools and colleges, by the careers service and by local education authorities. The chapter concludes by drawing attention to significant issues arising from the way that information is obtained and applied. The next chapter shows the main methods of planning post-16 provision within LEAs and institutions, and the contribution made by needs assessment amongst other factors in determining provision. In Chapter 9 attention is directed to the different relationships within the local education system, between providers and between clients and providers and to how these influence the way that needs are assessed. The analysis shows that the interaction between clients and providers is dynamic, being shaped by the different power and resources that they each possess. This chapter also considers the different methods developed at LEA and institutional levels to aggregate the various assessments of need and coordinate provision.

Our main findings concerning the way that assessments of need are made and the effect they have in planning are drawn together in Chapter 10 of the final part of the book. This analysis is carried out separately for the three components most involved in needs assessment — institutions, LEAs and the careers services — before turning to the general features that pervade local systems of education as a whole. The last chapter offers suggestions that we believe could improve the process of needs assessment as it is currently practised. These reflect our own analysis of the processes of needs assessment as well as evidence from the research of what was felt to constitute good practice. A glossary of the main terms used throughout can be found at the beginning of the book.

References

BRADSHAW, J., (1972) 'The concept of social need', *New Society*, 30 March.
CLAYTON, S., (1983) 'Social need revisited', *Journal of Social Policy*, 12, 2, April.
DES, (1980) *Education for 16–19 Year Olds* (The Macfarlane Report), London, HMSO.
SMITH, G. (1980) *Social Need: Policy, Practice and Research*, London, Routledge & Kegan Paul.

Part 1
The Context of Needs Assessment

2   The Changing Educational Needs of the 16–19 Age Group

In order to analyze how educational needs of the 16–19 age group are assessed in local educational systems it is necessary to outline the main characteristics of this stage of education. The chapter starts by examining the distinctive characteristics of 16–19 education and reviews how these have developed, before turning to discuss the challenges which have occurred in recent years.

The Traditional Pattern of 16–19 Provision

1985 figures show that roughly three-quarters of 16-year-olds were in some form of education and training, of which just over 44 per cent were in full-time education (DES, 1985c). Chapter 3 outlines the different characteristics of these students in post-16 education and the main forms of provision. Holt (1980) notes it is difficult to be clear about the distinctive nature of this stage of education or indeed to devise an adequate terminology to describe its boundaries. At its simplest, this stage marks the transition between childhood and full adulthood. Yet there are a number of different views of the purpose of the education and training that should be provided.

The major characteristic of this stage of provision is the dichotomy between the academic education provided in the schools sector and vocational education found in the further education colleges. The origins of this divide lie in the way that education for the 16–19 age group has developed.

The development of academic education in state school sixth forms was modelled on the type of provision that was characteristic of the public schools. Reid and Filby (1982) have traced the antecedents of this traditional notion of the sixth form and show how the state sector took on and incorporated the features of the public school sixth form. This academic tradition was marked by a specialized curriculum with an emphasis on specialist and intensive study. The Crowther Report of 1959 highlighted what it saw as the entrenched features of this academic route which 'catered for the education of our brightest children' (Central Advisory Council for Education, 1959). The hallmarks which the report endorsed were: the close links with the universities; subject mindedness; independent work; intellectual discipleship and social responsibility. Traditionally the academic student in the school sixth form has followed a small number of subjects in depth; the content and standards of the curriculum were dictated by the universities.

But, as early as the 1950s this form of provision was criticized, both for its aims and for its failure to cater for all the needs of this age group. The Crowther Report criticized the main weaknesses of the sixth form curriculum: overspecialization and the overburden of content which were judged to have a detrimental effect upon the rest of the secondary school curriculum, and the narrow range of provision. The concern at this stage was how to increase the opportunities available for students to undertake courses in the sixth form. Attempts were made to broaden the 'A' level curriculum such as the Schools Council proposals for the introduction of a two level examination (N & F) but this was rejected by the Secretary of State (Goacher, 1984). More recently there has been the introduction of Advanced Supplementary (AS) levels as a way of broadening sixth form education. Despite the numerous attempts to change the nature of 16–19 education, the traditional characteristics of this academic route have persisted. For example, the vast majority of those students that stay on in the sixth form for two years take the same nine 'A' level subjects as those which produced 80 per cent of entries in 1960 (Edwards, 1983). As Edwards and others have commented, the focus of sixth form education has been upon a narrow specialized curriculum for an academic elite intending in the main to enter higher education.

Vocational education developed from a different tradition and exhibits different characteristics. The 1944 Education Act required LEAs to provide adequate facilities for 'further education'. This was to be provided under separate regulations from those in the schools sector. Between 1951 and 1965, the number of full-time FE students grew from 55,000 to 202,000 with a smaller rate of increase for part-time students. The demand for vocational skills expanded during the 1960s and FE colleges responded by providing a broad range of courses, but marked by a greater complexity of provision for the potential student (Cantor and Roberts, 1979). There have been a number of attempts to rationalize the many different qualifications in the vocational sector. The increase in the number of FE students in the 1960s was particularly important for the nature of 16–19 education, as there had been a 40 per cent increase in students taking 'A' levels in colleges under FE regulations compared with only a 20 per cent increase in the schools sector. The overlap between the two sectors was narrowed with the increase of 'new sixth formers' in schools whose needs were being met by the development of pre-vocational courses. The FE sector has had to cope with changes in its market; a shift from traditional manufacturing industries to new technologies; an increase in vocational education; an increase in general and continuing education and in vocational preparation courses (Hollyhock, 1982).

Despite this tendency for overlap the two sectors providing 16–19 education have developed in different ways and possess alternative outlooks about the nature and delivery of education. Students in the school sector follow a subject-based programme supplemented by some form of general studies, whereas the FE college students tend to follow a course-based programme. As Holt (1980) states, 'In schools, the organizing device is the conceptual structure of each separate subject; in further education, the contributory subjects are subordinate to a unifying purpose or theme.' In further education there is a tendency for the curriculum to be concerned with the application of the knowledge gained and its relationship to employment requirements, which creates a more utlitarian setting for the education providers (King, 1976).

The characteristics of these two patterns have persisted although, as will be shown later in this chapter, there have been a number of different challenges to both types of curriculum offered. These have influenced the ability of LEAs to determine the type and arrangements for education in their localities.

The Challenges to 16–19 Education

Provision for the 16–19 age group has witnessed a number of far reaching changes in the past decade. Neave (1980) in reviewing similar developments across Europe argues that in all educational systems the 16–19 sector is highly dynamic, in terms of structural change and curriculum development, as well as of fluctuations in student behaviour. This sector is sensitive to short-term influences. He also maintains that there has been a change in the balance of power away from the traditional educational policy making and administrative bodies towards new agencies with remits from central government. The purpose of this chapter is to outline these main challenges, analyze their likely implications, and document the way that the education system has responded to them. These changes are interrelated and act in different and even conflicting ways upon the education system. The various challenges act as forces upon the system but their exact influence depends on the balance between their strengths and the existing interests within the system.

Political Challenges

The first set of challenges to the traditional pattern of 16–19 educational provision has come from the changing political context. A number of commentators have pointed to the way that the political assumptions surrounding the aims and purposes of education have altered. In the 1960s there developed a distinct pattern of political beliefs which persisted until the early 1970s (Ranson, 1984, Kogan, 1985). Education during this period was characterized by the desire to expand equality of opportunity so as to foster individual development and a more open society. It was believed that these expanded opportunities would act to enhance economic growth. There was considerable political support for the expansion of education throughout the 1960s. As discussed earlier, 16–19 educational provision increased in schools and FE colleges but against a context of buoyant employment opportunities for school leavers which is different from the present state of employment.

The political challenge to these beliefs came with the Callaghan government and his speech at Ruskin College in October 1976, although the seeds were sown earlier in the decade. This challenge focused on the lack of relationship between education and the world of work. The major criticism was that this relationship had been neglected in favour of emphasizing social development of the individual student. An administrative memorandum produced by the DES in 1976, known as the *Yellow Book*, commented that, 'The time may now be ripe for change, as the national mood and government policies have changed in the face of hard and irreducible facts' (Ranson, 1984). It noted the lack of basic skills possessed by school leavers and emphasized that priority must be given to developing the skills of the 16–19-year-olds and particularly the less able. The government was expressing concern at the quality of secondary education and was being more proactive in its definitions of the needs of students. As Ranson (*ibid*) notes, political attention was being directed at the 16–19 sector for two important reasons. First, this period of education represented the interface between formal secondary schooling and the world of work and, secondly, it was less bound by statutory constraints and therefore more susceptible to policy initiative and change by the DES. This was also part of the wider changing relationship between central and local government, which many commentators have interpreted as an attempt to weaken the autonomy of the local education authority in shaping local educational· provision (Stewart, 1986; Ranson *et al*, 1985b; Jones and Stewart, 1983).

Education and the Economy

The second set of challenges resulted from the drastically changed economic circumstances surrounding education, particularly the economic crisis as it developed in the 1970s. The economy suffered a collapse of the traditional manufacturing industries and the emergence of youth unemployment as a national problem. By 1984, 17 per cent of the 16–19 age group were unemployed (DES 1985c). The employment structure was undergoing rapid changes, with a wholesale restructuring of work and greater rigidity and segmentation of the labour market. At the same time there has been growth of new technologies, with implications for the vocational skills required and requiring greater flexibility in the attitude to work (Watts, 1983).

The major thrust of the political criticisms related to the relationship between education and employment opportunities. The view of employers and the Thatcher government was that education had to shift its priorities and seek to provide the skilled and flexible workforce required by the economy. Rather than being seen as an individual right, education must also be justified in terms of economic returns. Jonathan (1983) notes that the presumption that the education provided by the state should serve the interests of the state viewed as an economic collective has grown in importance. This view has been strongly expressed in several government reports. The government's White Paper, *Better Schools*, emphasized that, 'it is vital that schools should always remember that preparation for working life is one of their principal functions' (DES, 1985b). And in the 1985 White Paper, *Education and Training for Young People*, there was the statement that, 'above all else they (the young people leaving school) must be given both a firm foundation and a flexible approach to their working lives. Upon this depends our future prosperity and growth'. These views were further reinforced by the report *Competence and Competition*, commissioned by the Manpower Services Commission and the National Economic Development Council which examined the vocational education and training provided in Britain and compared it with that found in the Federal Republic of Germany, the United States and Japan. This Report concluded that, 'The UK is in danger of falling behind and faces deep rooted problems' (National Economic Development Council and MSC, 1984). The main problems were seen to lie in three areas: the standard of basic education; deficiencies in initial provision of education and training; and in the social climate which was seen to lead individuals and employers to look to public provision rather than take responsibility for meeting their own needs. All these challenges highlight different elements of the role of education in relation to the economy.

Demographic and Financial Challenges

The third challenge to the traditional structure of educational provision has come from the related effects of the decline in school rolls and the reduction in public expenditure on education. The national contraction in the number of 16-year-olds between 1977–78 and 1990–91 was projected to be about 25 per cent, although this concealed local variations. The main implication of this decline lies in the threat it poses to the ability of educational institutions and particularly the schools, to provide an adequate range of courses. The government's White Paper, *Better Schools*, (DES, 1985b) suggested that the minimum size of a school sixth form should be 150 students if it is to provide the necessary range of curriculum; it also stated that schools with sixth forms of less than 100 students would be increasingly vulnerable in the future. Yet even in 1976, 40 per cent of traditional sixth forms in comprehensive schools contained less than fifty pupils and 60 per cent of all classes had less than ten students. The enforced reduction in LEA expenditure meant that LEAs had to be concerned with the economic efficiency of their provision. This demographic decline and financial restraint served to induce LEAs to introduce radical organizational changes such as sixth form and tertiary colleges, with a view to creating more economically efficient institutions. In those areas where there have been no organizational changes, there is likely to be intense competition between the institutions providing 16–19 education.

The Macfarlane Report on provision for 16–19 year olds was produced against this background of demographic decline and financial restraint (DES, 1980). It started by stating that the variety of 16–19 provision by LEAs was to be welcomed but, 'it must not merely reflect special interests, nor must it lead to diseconomies or distortion of purpose'. The Report did not come forward with a firm proposal about what pattern of institutions should be recommended. It reaffirmed the importance of the sixth form to the school but recognized that it was educationally desirable for students to be educated in large groups, thus accepting that there would have to be some form of cooperative arrangements between schools and schools and FE. The message was that no absolute statement about institutional arrangements could be made but rather that LEAs should review their 16–19 provision from the standpoints of educational effectiveness and resource management. The report also urged LEAs to assess the costs of providing 16–19 provision with more precision than hitherto. The significance of the Report lay in its concern that LEAs should take a more directive line in reviewing their 16–19 provision. The underlying message was of cost effectiveness and efficiency in provision (Edwards, 1983). Moreover it prompted the LEA to play a greater role in planning 16–19 provision in its locality, with the assumption that the age of the autonomous educational institution was over. The same ideas are also contained more recently in DES Circular 3/87 *Providing for Quality: The Pattern of Organization to Age 19*. This again stated that LEAs should review their 16–19 provision.

The Responses to these Challenges

It should be noted that some of these changes have been apparent for some time but they have intensified in recent years and become increasingly interrelated. The question is how far the educational system has responded and in what ways.

Vocational Education

The concern that education should respond more effectively to the employment market by developing curricula which satisfy the requirements of employers has been reflected in a number of initiatives in the post-16 field, as well as in other sectors of education. Underlying this concern is the issue of what should be the appropriate curriculum for the 16–19 age group. Pring (1980) has defined this as the questions of, 'generality versus specialization, of education versus training, of balance, of relevancy, of breadth versus depth, and of integration versus subjects'. There have been a number of attempts to broaden the traditional academic curriculum in the schools but these have not brought about significant changes (Holt, 1980). More recently, the government has introduced 'AS' levels as a way of expanding the breadth of the traditional range of subjects taken at 'A' level.

The most significant change in 16–19 provision is the growth of courses aimed at the student wanting one year in the sixth form. The 'new sixth' had been identified as early as the late 1950s in the Crowther Report but this client group assumed a greater significance when more students began to stay on in the sixth form as employment opportunities lessened. For many of these students the only offering from schools was to retake 'O' levels and, as many studies showed, the success rate of these courses was low (Vincent and Dean, 1977). This raised the question of what other types of provision could be made for these students. During the 1970s a number of such courses were developed as alternatives to the academic 'A' and 'O' levels. These included new, more vocationally oriented, courses such as CEE, CFE, COS and the foundation courses of the City and Guilds of London Institute. The apparent value of these courses was that they provided a balance between vocational and general education, gave a chance for students to defer a specific vocational choice and were more likely to prepare school leavers for a job. In the FE sector there were a number of low level courses but the relationship between them was frequently confusing for students (Pratley, 1980).

In the late 1970s the Keohane and Mansell committees were deliberating on separate reviews of vocational courses for the 17-year-old. The former, set up by the Secretary of State for Education, was specifically concerned with reviewing CEE courses and its relationship with similar courses provided in FE colleges. The Mansell Committee, set up by the Further Education Unit (FEU) at the DES, was to review comparable non-advanced courses in the college sector. Ranson (1984) has documented the way that these two committees reached their conclusions. They both agreed about the vocational purposes of these courses but disagreed how they should be designed and assessed. The two committees therefore reflected their different interests. As Ranson states, 'In short, Keohane's CEE proposed separate courses leading to exams, while Mansell's ABC proposed a one-year course leading to profile assessment'. After considering both reports the government came down in favour of the Mansell Report and therefore accepted the FE orientation. The CEE courses which had developed in schools on a pilot basis were to be ended because they were insufficiently vocationally oriented. This decision provoked varied responses from the different interests in the educational system. Eventually a new course was intended to cater for a wide range of interests and abilities and would provide broad general education with a vocational orientation and an opportunity to sample a variety of possible work areas before making a specific choice.

The Technical and Vocational Education Initiative (TVEI)

The development of vocational courses was also paralleled by other changes in the provision of education for the 16–19 age group but most notably by the advent of the Manpower Services Commission (MSC) in the field of vocational education. The MSC was set up in 1974 with the brief to be involved in training both for adults and young people. Its functions in the training of young people are reviewed later in this chapter. It departed from this concern with the setting up of the Technical and Vocational Education Initiative (TVEI). This occurred in November 1982 to the surprise of the education world, and marked a departure from the traditional consensual style of educational policy making (Moon and Richardson, 1984). TVEI was to be experimental, financed until 1988, and took the form of a specific number of schemes to be run under the auspices of the MSC, but administered by the LEAs chosen after a competitive tendering process. The scheme was to cater for the 14–18 age range, thus spanning traditional schools/college divide. Its objectives were to bring about a change in the curriculum so as to make school leavers better prepared for the world of work.

Initially, TVEI was provided on a pilot basis. From 1987 it became a national scheme (DE, 1986). The introduction of TVEI has not been without its critics (Chitty, 1986). First, MSC intended TVEI to be selective so that only certain students follow the scheme. This has been criticized for leading to divisions between students which are seen to be incompatible with principles of comprehensive education. Concern has also been expressed that the effect of introducing TVEI in particular schools will lead to disparities between schools and even between departments in the same school. A final, and broader, criticism is that TVEI is part of a drift towards vocationalism in education imposed by the Conservative government and of a parallel move towards greater central control of the funding and content of education and training.

New Forms of Guidance and Assessment

The development of new curricula for the 16–19 age group has involved new forms of guidance and assessment. New forms of assessment have been introduced because of a widespread disatisfaction with the existing pattern of public examinations and the extent to which they adequately measure student performance. The first feature of these new forms of assessment is the attempt to identify individual attainment more closely. Some of the new initiatives such as CPVE rely on the profiling of achievement to aid student performance and to help employers in selecting potential employees. A second feature is the principle of progression, to allow skills and experiences to be built up in successive courses. Some of the new courses have modular structures to allow students to accumulate a series of credits. The third feature is that students have a greater responsibility for their own learning.

Guidance and counselling for 16–19-year-olds has been felt to be important in allowing students to take responsibility for their own decisions and choices. Concern that students were not always best able to make choices about which courses to take was expressed in government reports. Attention has been directed to improving both guidance within educational institutions and an increased involvement by careers services.

Relationships with Employers

The concern that education was too remote from the world of work has been tackled by fostering better contacts with employers at all levels of the educational system. At the school level this included specific initiatives of a curricular nature such as the Schools Curriculum Industry Project (SCIP). Most schools have also introduced work experience schemes to give students an appreciation of the work context. In the FE sector there have been attempts to make colleges more responsive to the needs of employers such as the College Employer Links Project (CELP) run by the DES and other initiatives (Theodossin, 1986). There is also evidence that teaching staff in both schools and colleges have begun to foster links with employers and use the careers service as an intermediary with employers. Also some of the new initiatives such as TVEI require collaboration with employers in the validation and planning of courses.

The Youth Training Scheme

The MSC has been involved in training young people since its creation. The Youth Opportunities Programme (YOP) was initially set up to provide unemployed young people under the age of 19 with training and work experience and to help them gain permanent jobs. This was born of the increase in youth unemployment and its emergence as a political issue. The YOP was extended in 1980 with the aim that young people not in education or a job would be able to have the chance of vocational preparation.

The Youth Training Scheme (YTS) was created as a consequence of the MSC New Training Initiative of 1981. This proposed a Youth Training Scheme, guaranteeing from September 1983 a full year's foundation training for all those leaving school at the minimum age without jobs. From 1986 it has been expanded to provide two years of training for 16-year-olds and one year for 17-year-olds.

The introduction of YTS has inevitably attracted different responses. Criticisms have been directed about the way the scheme has evolved: the main ones being that Mode A (employer-based projects) have attracted or selected 'better quality' trainees; the varied quality of the schemes; the lack of integration of off the job training and work experience; and the difficulties of ensuring equal opportunities. A more fundamental problem is whether YTS can meet different purposes. It has been attacked as being cosmetic, in that it reduces youth unemployment statistics without creating new employment opportunities; exploitive, using young people as a cheap source of labour; employer dominated and anti-educational, stressing an instrumental view of learning (Finn, 1985). Against this, some see MSC as demonstrating an ability to act rapidly and secure change without becoming too enmeshed by existing interests and arrangements (Pearce, 1986).

Implications for the Education and Training of the 16–19 Age Group

The challenges to the educational system and the ensuing responses have a number of important implications for the way that 16–19 education is planned and delivered.

The first set of implications relates to the involvement of the different participants in policy making. Ranson (1984 and 1985a) has documented the way that central government is playing a stronger role in education vis a vis local government. The drive for new vocational policies has been promoted by central government, rather than emerging as a response to local developments. He shows how central government believed that a redirection of education was necessary as part of a broader review of economic and industrial strategy. The DES was responsible for initiating this change (Salter and Tapper, 1981). As Ranson (1984) notes, 'The policy of reconstructing the education service has been led by the department who have championed the initiative of strengthening the ties between school and work, between education and training in order to improve the vocational preparation of the 14–19 age group'. In particular this action meant more control by central government over the curriculum and this was vividly shown by the way that CPVE was introduced amidst competing interests. Also, the DES is making more use of its powers in stimulating change at a local level through the setting of national curricula guidelines and the use of specific grants, thus altering the balance of power between central and local government.

The development of vocational policies has also been promoted through the creation of the MSC which can both purchase the type of educational and training provision it requires and also sponsors its own training in the form of YTS. This is shown by the decision to allow MSC to control 25 per cent of Non-Advanced Further Education (NAFE) provision, which is seen by some to be a strategy for the government to use MSC to bypass the traditional relationship between the DES and LEAs and implement its policies on training. The LEA itself has had to develop relationships with the MSC in the planning of YTS (Challis *et al*, 1984). The production of Non-Advanced Further Education Work Related Development Plans by LEAs has involved them in closer relationships with the MSC.

The combination of these pressures has also led many LEAs to exert a stronger role in relation to the institutions. On the one hand the curtailment of resources requires LEAs to ensure that provision is cost-effective and so institutions have been urged to cooperate more in the planning and delivery of courses. The same pressures result from initiatives such as TVEI and CPVE which require schools and colleges to work together. This means that LEAs are more likely to monitor and review their patterns of provision than before. The implication for the work of institutions lies in the possible reduction of their autonomy. The current initiatives in the curriculum and the uncertainties they generate also mean that institutions may require help from the LEA in planning their provision. The onset of vocationalism promoted by these initiatives also means that employers are likely to be more actively involved both in promoting training and in working with the educational institutions to influence the curriculum.

The second set of implications emanate from the way that provision to meet educational needs has been framed. The traditional provision for the 16–19 age group catered for distinct narrow client groups, either those who were academically inclined or those pursuing specific training routes. This provision developed at a time of low youth unemployment, and the age participation rate in post-16 education remained low in comparison with other countries. The increase in youth unemployment and the development of ideas about vocationalism have led to a concern that post-16 education should cater for a broader client group than hitherto. There is now a greater national and local concern with the needs of the 'less academic' and with the development of greater vocational skills of use in enhancing employment opportunities. This highlights the difference in aims between education and training. Taylor (1985) distinguishes the values underlying the two concepts. In his view education can be characterized as, 'soft, person-centred, moralized, academic, critical, contemplative, radical in attitude but traditional in form, theoretical, norm referenced, enclosed, a consumption good rather than an investment'. In contrast, training is viewed as, 'hard, task centred, materialistic, practical, oriented towards action, criterion referenced, pragmatic, innovative in structure but conservative in substance, unselective, open, a valuable national investment'. The difficulty is how these two concepts can be brought together through government initiatives.

Ranson (1985a) argues that underlying these developments has been a policy of stratification which has led to a restructuring of education that occurs at the age of 16 rather than at 11 as before. This new system is curriculum-led. In Ranson's words, 'How much education (the question of access and opportunity or the desirable levels of participation) should be offered is then a matter that is decided "internally" by the curricular paths which people get locked into' (Ranson, 1984). Farmer (1982) also notes that there is a tendency for the 16–19 curriculum to be differentiated into four discrete groups: the 'A' level route for those going on to higher education; the technician route for those of above average ability; residual craft studies and vocational preparation for the average and below ability in employment or full-time education, and MSC-sponsored vocational preparation programmes for the young unemployed. This differentiation also results in a disparity in financial support for different categories of students. The implication of this for the assessment of the needs of the 16–19 age group is how changing values about the aims of provision shape the manner in which the needs of these students are defined.

If there is a new system of post-16 education developing as a result of these pressures, it is characterized by uncertainty over the form it will take. Despite the forecasts of 'a revolution in education and training' (Ranson and Travers, 1986) the different aims — vocationalism, cost effectiveness, and relationship with employment — are not necessarily in unison and may even be in conflict. This will influence the capacity of LEAs and the institutions to plan their 16–19 provision.

The next chapter discusses the forms of 16–19 provision that are available, the types of students within the 16–19 age group and the way that educational choices are made.

References

CANTOR, L. and ROBERTS, I., (1979) *Further Education in England and Wales*, London, RKP.

CENTRAL ADVISORY COUNCIL FOR EDUCATION, (1959) *15 to 18*, (The Crowther Report), London, HMSO.

CHALLIS, R., MASON, C., and PARKES, D., (1984) *The Local Authority and YTS*, Interim Report, Sheffield, MSC.

CHITTY, C., (1986) 'TVEI: The MSC's Trojan horse' in BENN, C. and FAIRLEY, J. (Eds), *Challenging the MSC*, London, Pluto Press.

DE, (1986) *Working Together: Education and Training*, Cmnd 9823, London, HMSO.

DES, (1980) *Education for 16–19 Year Olds* (The Macfarlane Report) London, HMSO.

DES, (1985a) *The Technical and Vocational Education Initiative: Early Developments*, London, HMSO.

DES, (1985b) *Better Schools*, Cmnd 9469, London, HMSO.

DES, (1985c) *Digest of Statistics, England 1985*, London, HMSO.

DES, (1987) *Providing for Quality: The Pattern of Organization to Age 19*, London, HMSO.

EDWARDS, A.D., (1983) 'An elite transformed: Continuity and change in 16–19 educational policy', in AHIER, J., and FLUDE, M. (Eds), *Contemporary Education Policy*, Beckenham, Croom Helm.

FARMER, C., (1982) 'The impact of the new FE' in PARKES, D. (Ed) *The Changing Face of FE*, London, FEU.

FINN, D., (1985) 'The Manpower Services Commission and the Youth Training Scheme: A permanent bridge to work?' in DALE, R., (Ed), *Education, Training and Employment: Towards a New Vocationalism*, Oxford, Pergamon.

GOACHER, B., (1984) *Selection Post 16: The Role of Examination Results*, Schools Council Examinations Bulletin, 45, London, Methuen.

HOLLYHOCK, B., (1982) 'The college in its environment' in PARKES, D. (Ed) *The Changing Face of FE*, London, FEU.

HOLT, M., (Ed) (1980) *The Tertiary Sector*, London, Hodder and Stoughton.

JONATHAN, R., (1983) 'The manpower service model of education', *Cambridge Journal of Education*, 13, 2.

JONES, G.W. and STEWART, J.D., (1983) *The Case for Local Government*, London, Allen & Unwin.

KING, M., (1976) *School and College*, London, Routledge & Kegan Paul.

KOGAN, M., (1985) 'Education policy and values', in McNAY, I., and OZGA, J., (Eds), *Policy-Making in Education: The Breakdown of Consensus*, Oxford, Pergamon.

MOON, J. and RICHARDSON, J., (1984) 'Policy making with a difference? The Technical and Vocational Education Initiative', *Public Administration*, 62, Spring.

NATIONAL ECONOMIC DEVELOPMENT COUNCIL and MSC, (1984) *Competence and Competition*, London, NEDC/MSC.

NEAVE, G., (1980) 'The changing balance of power: Recent developments in provision for the 16–19 years of age range in Europe', *Comparative Education*, 16, 2, June.

PARKES, D. (Ed) (1982) *The Changing Face of FE*, London, FEU.

PEARCE, B. (1986) 'MSC and FE', *Educational Management and Administration*, 14, 2.

PRATLEY, B., (1980) *Signposts*, London, FEU.

PRING, R., (1980) 'General education and the 16–19 sector', in HOLT, M., (Ed) *The Tertiary Sector*, London, Hodder and Stoughton.

RANSON, S., (1984) 'Towards a tertiary tripartism: New codes of social control and the 17+', in BROADFOOT, P., (Ed), *Selection, Certification and Control*, Lewes, Falmer Press.

RANSON, S., (1985a) 'Contradictions in the government of educational change', *Political Studies*, 33, 1.

RANSON, S. *et al* (Eds), (1985b) *Between Centre and Locality*, London, Allen & Unwin.

RANSON, S., and TRAVERS, T., (1986) *The Revolution in Education and Training*, London, Longman.

REID, W. and FILBY, J., (1982) *The Sixth: An Essay in Education and Democracy*, Lewes, Falmer Press.

SALTER, B. and TAPPER, T., (1981) *Education, Politics and the State: The Theory and Practice of Educational Change*, London, Grant McIntyre.

STEWART, J.D., (1986) 'A local service: Strengthening the LEA', in RANSON, S. and TOMLINSON, J. (Eds), *The Changing Government of Education*, London, Allen & Unwin.

TAYLOR, W., (1985) 'Productivity and educational values', in WORSWICK, G. (Ed), *Education and Economic Performance*, Aldershot, Gower.

THEODOSSIN, E., (1986) *In Search of the Responsive College*, Bristol, Further Education Staff College.

VINCENT, D. and DEAN, J., (1977) *One-Year Courses in Colleges and Sixth Forms*, Windsor, NFER.

WATTS, A.G., (1983) *Education and Unemployment and the Future of Work*, Milton Keynes, Open University Press.

3   *The Provision of 16–19 Education*

The previous chapter discussed views of what is needed from 16–19 education. Before examining how needs are assessed it is necessary to show whose needs are involved and the guidance and provision that are available for their satisfaction. This chapter commences, then, by considering who education is provided for — students, their parents, employers, the MSC and local community interests — and some of the factors that affect their choice of provision. It then considers the services that assist clients in reaching educational decisions — careers guidance and pastoral care in schools and colleges, industrial liaison mechanisms, careers services and youth and community services. Next, the chapter outlines the forms of provision that are available. These include the familiar choices, school sixth forms and FE colleges, and the newer developments, sixth form colleges, tertiary colleges and consortia arrangements. The chapter concludes by examining the role of LEAs and central government in determining what choices are to be offered and briefly describes how the different elements concerned with 16–19 provision are contained within local education systems.

Education for Whom?

For Students

The age of 16 is a watershed in English education. The legal obligation to accept education as a full-time occupation ceases. In 1984 783,000 16-year-olds had to decide just what their full-time occupation would be; a decision which was likely to have significant, and perhaps irrevocable, effects upon the rest of their lives. One possibility was to continue with education but others included gaining employment, joining a MSC-financed training scheme or being unemployed.

Any of the choices can include some further education. Young people who are employed or unemployed may engage in education on a part-time basis and education is an important component in MSC programmes. Obviously, the choice of full-time occupation does determine the type of education that will be available. Employed students attending a college on a day release basis do not generally follow the same courses as those attending a school or college full-time.

Students' decisions are subject to a number of different influences. Veness (1962) distinguished between decisions which are: 'tradition directed', where choice is determined by family or neighbourhood tradition; 'inner directed', where choice is made according to the student's own interests and aspirations; and 'other directed', where choices follow external advice or the student's desire to achieve a particular position in the social order. Examining career choice in the early 1960s, in a context of near to full employment, Veness found that 'inner directed' choice was most common. This was confirmed by Maizels' study towards the end of the 1960s, although the author questioned whether this would be so if there was significant unemployment (Maizels, 1968). Interests might then fail to find outlets and their match with ability would become more crucial. Today with 44 per cent of 16-year-old boys and 35 per cent of girls unemployed or attending an MSC training course, these reservations have some force. With limited opportunities 'other directed' choice becomes more important. Students require advice regarding what is available and how to make the most of their abilities. An NFER study of 16–18-year-olds remaining in full-time education found that their motives were primarily 'other directed'. More education would improve their career prospects, gain them entry to higher education or qualify them for a particular job. Education was not pursued for its own sake (Dean *et al*, 1979).

Career choices are rarely clear cut. It is not the case that students always know what they want and pursue this with single minded determination. Rather, occupational choice develops over time (Ginzberg, *et al*, 1951). First, a lot depends on circumstances; on what is available and known at the time when 16-year-olds are reaching decisions, and on their attitudes and those of their peers towards education. Second, choice at 16 will be conditioned by earlier experiences, such as those gained from part-time employment or work experience, and by earlier educational choices, such as subject options at 14 or selection of schools at the beginning of their secondary education. The choice of academic subjects at 14, for example, may lead naturally into full-time academic education at 16.

The importance of earlier decisions emphasizes the importance of families and particularly parents, in determining students' career choices. In the National Survey of Health and Development, 40 per cent of young people believed their parents the most useful source of help and encouragement with careers (Clarke, 1980). The Youthaid study found a similar picture (Sawdon *et al*, 1981). Most students who continue in education, do so with parental approval and support (Dean *et al*, 1979). Yet parents frequently lack relevant knowledge or leave career decisions to their children.

Parental attitudes reflect broad social class differences towards continuing with education, as well as parents' own experiences and judgments (Gordon, 1983). Financial considerations are likely to be important. Different forms of post-16 education impose different costs on the family. Students in full-time education are dependent upon parental support, although often boosted by part time earnings. Those in part-time education are likely to be earning a wage and to receive assistance from their employers with the costs of education, although the amount of support given varies (DES, 1984). The MSC covers the costs of YTS programmes and trainees receive a weekly allowance. Much, therefore, depends on the material circumstances of the home and how far immediate earning power can be discounted against future prospects. Any decision made at 16 may well be conditional on achieving other choices. Thus a 16-year-old may continue in full-time education or join a YTS programme only until such time as he, or she, can gain full-time employment. Failure in academic education at 16 may direct a student towards employment and part-time study. Reviewing the research into the transition from school to work, Clarke (1980) concluded that the proportion of school-leavers realizing their ambitions varied between one-third and two-thirds. However, whether 16-year-olds are seeking to enter employment or education, those who can show some ability do best in achieving their choices. Ability may be in terms of personality, academic achievements or practical skills. Early findings from the England and Wales Youth Cohort Study show that 40 per cent of those who leave school without qualifications are unemployed a year later, compared with 10 per cent of those possessing at least one graded examination result (MSC, 1986). Those who can offer least are least likely to realize their ambitions.

For Employers

The above is particularly true for 16-year-olds seeking to enter employment. Jobs for the unskilled and low-skilled are disappearing (Wallace, 1985). Employers' requirements from education are of two kinds; to provide recruits of the desired quality and to provide assistance with training and retraining the workforce. As to the first, the CBI has suggested that schools should provide the following: some mastery of core subjects, so that school leavers are numerate, can communicate and apply their knowledge and skills; an awareness of the requirements of industry and technology and of the contribution these make to society; and, opportunities to develop those personal attributes which are valued by employers, such as self-discipline and self-development. Schools should avoid early vocational specialization (NEDC/MSC, 1984). On the second requirement, employers can organize their own training and some do. Most, however, rely on the FE provided by LEAs. Vocational qualifications have been developed with the participation of industrial representatives and with the needs of industry in mind. The mix of vocational courses that are available in colleges is strongly influenced by the demands of local companies.

Obviously employers vary in the extent to which they wish, or are able, to influence educational provision. They have been criticized for the small industrial and commercial contribution to education and training, and for their passivity. Employers make use of what is locally available if this is convenient and meets their current requirements, but in general they do not seek to make connections between work and education and training (*ibid*). A study by HMI of part-time education and training found that employers were vague about their requirements and often deficient in their own training provision. There was little evidence that they had much impact on the curriculum (DES, 1984). Indeed, in total the communication between industry and education is seen as limited. Forums to evaluate the worth of training and employment or to apply such evaluations in industrial or educational decision-making are not common. As a consequence individuals, including both students and employers, are seen as poorly placed to take decisions regarding their own futures. But as Theodossin points out, 'in the world of the market place there is no necessity for customers to be articulate, reasonable, consistent, or even particularly rational' (Theodossin, 1986).

Although vocational education has a long history of liaison with employers, the previous chapter indicated how education has come in for a share of the blame for the poor relationship. As part of its strategy to improve economic performance by increasing the post-16 participation rate in education and training, central government has sought ways of making education more responsive to employers' needs (Kedney and Parkes, 1985). 'Public sector provision for training and vocational education must become more responsive to employment needs at national and local levels' (DE, 1984).

Employers' links with schools and colleges have been strengthened by initiatives from the DES, the Department of Employment and the Department of Trade and Industry. The devices commonly used will be considered later in the book.

For the MSC

As was discussed in the last chapter, one of the central government's major initiatives to improve training has been the creation of the YTS which is now regarded as a permanent feature of education and training (DES/DE, 1985). The YTS is organized through regional and area offices. The provision is arranged on a local basis within each area, with programmes reflecting the occupational structure and economic opportunities. Provision is through managing agents or sponsors. These include small and large companies, voluntary organizations, chambers of commerce and local education authorities, as well as specialist firms set up to run the YTS. The agents run courses which include work experience with a training element and at least thirteen weeks 'off the job' training away from the workplace. All trainees receive a weekly allowance.

The scheme has two different modes depending on where each programme is based. Mode A schemes are run predominantly by employers, singly or in combination, from the private sector or private training agencies. In 1986 there were over 5000 managing agents (*The Times*, 1986). Mode B schemes are provided by a mixture of local authority, central government and voluntary organizations. The planning of YTS is carried out by MSC on an area basis, in conjunction with the LEAs and managing agents. The schemes provided are monitored by the area boards and trainees are assessed.

In most cases the 'off the job' provision for YTS is purchased from LEAs and provided in FE colleges, which are increasingly dependent on MSC money (Cantor and Roberts, 1983). The MSC is concerned to provide a young work force that is better equipped for industrial needs. It has its own ideas of what this entails and how it should be provided. The curriculum of YTS stresses work-based learning. It is expected to include integrated work experience, vocational training and education, the encouragement of individuals to take responsibility for their own development and the creation of a record of individual achievements. The services required from LEAs will increase with the extension of YTS, as one of the aims is to provide all trainees with the opporunity of gaining recognized vocational qualifications. The YTS has meant that colleges must provide for the 'forgotten third' of school leavers who otherwise might never have entered their doors (Mason, 1984). College staff are not necessarily accustomed to teaching those of low academic ability, or to teaching them in the manner required by the MSC.

The MSC has been concerned with other initiatives that make use of LEAs' provision to help meet education and training needs. The most widely known is the TVEI. TVEI projects have their own steering committees which include: MSC officers, councillors, senior officers and advisers from the LEA; representatives from the careers service; governors, teacher representatives and the headteachers/principals from the participating institutions; and local employers. The work of designing and implementing new courses is typically overseen by a smaller executive committee drawn from the participating institutions, together with the LEA officers and advisers most directly involved. The curriculum is reviewed by academic advisory committees made up of teachers and employers. Individual schemes must satisfy a number of critieria which are similar to those required for YTS. They include: equal opportunities; access by the full ability range of pupils; a balance between general and technical/vocational elements; planned work experience; and regular assessment, guidance and individual profiling. The teaching style involved is characterized by a personal involvement by pupils in establishing individual goals and by an emphasis on activity-based learning. MSC expects to spend an average of £90 million per year on TVEI up to 1996, approximately £30,000 for each school that takes part. It is up to individual LEAs to decide whether or not they wish to participate in TVEI but if so, their proposals must be consistent with MSC aims.

For the Community

Local community interests, such as churches, clubs and associations for ethnic minority groups, may have particular requirements that they wish education to meet. Although these requirements may include the participation of 16–19-year-olds, they are unlikely to be specific to this age group. Mainstream education has been education for the young. It is organized to cater for individual needs, categorized by age and educational achievement, and by academic or vocational courses that have a currency wider than the local area. So, although there is a demand for education that specifically meets local interests, it is frequently regarded as an extra, staffed by part-time teachers and short on resources. And although means exist for local groups to express their particular interests to education, as through the Education Committee, governing bodies or educationalists' own contacts, they are not generally influential as clients and their affect on the nature of provision is marginal. The extent of responsiveness to local interests depends on how far educational managers see providing for them as a legitimate or cost effective activity. And even where this feeling is positive, it seems that local interests are not striving to obtain their own particular forms of provision. As with employers, the expression of their interests calls for much prompting and encouragement from education.

Put simply, the point to stress from the above discussion is that there are a number of different clients for 16–19 education. Inevitably their needs will be different, and will be expressed to education and interpreted by educationalists in different ways. Students will be seeking to realize different values in their education from those sought for by employers for their employees. And the values ascribed to students and employers by educationalists will likewise differ. This means that local education systems must accommodate to diverse interests. But this is nothing new. Education is a individual attribute and categories of clients are made up of individuals with their own needs. Indeed our research suggested a similarity between different categories in demanding an education that was more directly instrumental and work-related than in the past.

Providing Advice

The provision of advice to pupils and students is an integral part of the education process. It has long been recognized that education has a function in preparing pupils for the transition from general schooling to employment or more specialized study, although there have been long-standing criticisms regarding the way in which this has been done (Paul, 1962). In recent years, and stimulated by pressures of youth unemployment, advisory mechanisms have become more explicit and broader in their scope and operation. Advice regarding future choices has been built into educational programmes and seeks to include parents, potential employers and institutions providing post-16 education. This should help identify needs and ensure their satisfaction.

By Schools

During their time at school, pupils and their parents should receive guidance on the choice of occupation at 16. Much of this is implicit and cumulative. Choices are narrowed and refined by the courses that the pupil has chosen. That is why pupils' fourteenth year is such an important stage in careers choice, for they have to decide which subjects to continue until the end of compulsory schooling and which to abandon. Choices are also determined by teachers' assessments of pupils' abilities, as expressed in the marks given for work and in reports. According to Peck (1980), 'careers education is the concern of all teachers (and) they should be involved in, rather than excluded from, the process of career choice which each one of their pupils must make'.

Peck's comment refers to the fact that schools generally make some specialist provision for careers guidance. A member of staff may be designated as careers teacher and a programme of careers education provided for one or two periods a week from the third year onwards. Pupils are likely to have a tutor or form teacher who is concerned with their overall progress rather than that achieved in particular subjects. And even if there is no careers teacher, secondary schools will have a teacher or teachers who are responsible for helping pupils to sort out the possibilities. It is usual for schools to arrange careers evenings when pupils and their parents can come and hear about the educational provision that is available at 16 and some of the local employment opportunities. Visits by college staff to schools can provide an important way of informing pupils about FE (Dean *et al*, 1979). Some schools provide short work experience schemes for their older pupils, which can help the latter in deciding their future careers. Schools generally are increasing the contact with employers, which provides them with some insight into their needs.

Schools are an important source of knowledge regarding the choices available at 16. But they vary in the attention given to careers education. What is provided has been criticized as inadequate in helping students make the transition from school to working life or further education (DES, 1984) and as routine and automatic (Peck, 1980). LEAs have attempted to improve the quality of careers education, this generally being one of the responsibilities of the careers service (Peck and Robinson, 1986) but there are problems. Teachers do not necessarily possess relevant knowledge and may not see providing careers advice as part of their role. Opportunities for full and part-time courses available in FE colleges are not always widely publicized (Dean *et al*, 1979; DES, 1984). If a school has a sixth form, it is likely to regard it as the pinnacle of its educational provision. It is understandable, then, if it encourages recruitment to its own sixth form and plays down other possibilities.

By Careers Services

Advice from the schools on careers choice is supplemented by that of the careers service. Careers services are provided by LEAs under the guidance of the Department of Employment. While resources have been limited by restrictions in local government expenditure, some authorities have seen the local careers service as a priority area because of its role in promoting youth employment.

Careers services are organized in different ways. They normally have a headquarters unit which is located in the LEA department, and a number of local offices which serve the schools within their areas. They vary in the extent to which they are centralized or decentralized (Ranson *et al*, 1986). The broad aim of careers services is stated as helping those leaving full-time education make a satisfactory transition into employment (DE, 1980). This involves: informing pupils, students and staff of the demands of working life and on the scope and range of opportunities available; guiding pupils and students as to their choice of vocation; and, placing school and college leavers and the unemployed within employment, education or training or special schemes. The traditional role of careers services has emphasized the second and third function, guiding pupils and placing them in employment or further education.

The extent to which careers services influence students' choices is uncertain. The Youthaid study found them second to the family as a source of information for jobs to which pupils aspired. They were the chief source of information for job applications, although their importance varied between different schools and they were not seen to be as useful as personal contacts for actually gaining a job (Sawdon *et al*, 1981). Generally a careers officer will be designated to work at a particular school. It may not be the only school the officer serves, so averaged across the year he or she might be working there for one day a week. The careers officer would probably assist with the careers education programme and attend, and help arrange, careers evenings. Most of the officers' effort would go into guidance, either on an individual or group basis. Careers officers commonly work with pupils from 14 onwards, with a concentration in the final year of compulsory schooling. In some cases particular categories of pupil may be advised by specialist officers; for example, those with special needs or who are thought academically more able. It is common practice for guidance to be facilitated by the use of computer-based systems and backed up by a variety of careers information services.

Ranson and his colleagues noted how the changing context of their work is changing the nature of careers services. With high youth unemployment, vocational guidance and placement work loses some of its relevance. The careers service can become no more than a booking agency for YTS. Thus some careers officers have emphasized the role of providing information about employment opportunities, which necessitates less time in schools and more time in making contact with employers. As a result, the careers service is better able to inform employers of the available educational opportunities and help them to define their educational needs. Others emphasized counselling and outreach work; helping clients towards self-perception and focusing on those with particular problems, such as the unemployed (Ranson *et al*, 1986).

After 16

Both educational institutions and careers services continue to give advice to young people after the age of 16, when they have made their initial choices or have had decisions forced upon them. Schools provide pastoral care and a measure of careers guidance to students in their sixth forms. Colleges do the same for their 16–19-year-olds, although support is far more in evidence for those taking full-time than part-time courses. Members of HMI described the guidance given to part-time students on enrolment as minimal and perfunctory, leaving students uncertain as to whether they had made correct choices (DES, 1984). The Macfarlane Report also passed on the judgment by HMI that careers provision for those taking general or pre-vocational courses was rudimentary (DES, 1980). Colleges, in particular, are likely to have established relationships with local employers. These can be used to keep employers aware of the education that is available and may help them in deciding their needs. Knowledge gained from these relationships can also be passed on in advising students.

Although resource restraints may force careers services to regard assisting 16-year-old school leavers as their first priority, they also serve older students. Specialist officers are frequently used to advise those aiming at higher education or taking YTS programmes, and careers services commonly have a specialist to work with the unemployed. But there is a change after sixteen. A decision has been taken and although it is not seen as irrevocable, it does condition the way in which needs are regarded. Generally young people have to take some initiative in subsequently seeking help, admitting that they may have made a mistake in selecting a course or facing up to the fact that their training scheme is not working out. For some this is no problem. As young people gain in age, so many gain in self-confidence.

By the Youth and Community Service

The available assistance is also weighted towards those who are continuing with their education and training on a full-time basis at school or college, or through a YTS programme. There are some young people who find it impossible to relate to education and see it as irrelevant to their interests. Perhaps this is because they feel that they have failed educationally or because their chief interest is in some activity that is not valued by educational establishments. They can receive support and advice from youth and community services. LEAs make these services available to young people from 14 to 21, although they tend to be used by only a small percentage of the total age group. They are typically organized around youth centres which may be attached to schools. LEAs also provide financial support for youth work performed by voluntary groups. Youth and community services have been hit hard by the economic recession (Taylor, 1983). Schools and colleges represent compulsory and mainstream areas of provision and have been given a measure of protection by LEAs. Youth provision does not carry the same priority. But it may be the only public agency that is in contact with unemployed and poorly educated young people. Youth workers see themselves as helping to counter some of the deficiencies in the way that schools treat the less academic or the 'rebels', and as helping to engender community feeling. To get to the unattached, youth workers undertake outreach work with young people in their own environment; meeting them in the pubs, the shops or the streets (Macdonald, 1980). They can provide them with support; such as information and guidance, contact with other welfare agencies and provision of simple social skills. The Youth and Community Service can act as a sponsor for MSC provision and thus be directly involved in providing education and training.

The Choices Available

Table 1 below indicates the career choices made by 16-year-olds in England for 1984/85. It will be noticed that if YTS is included, the majority, 77 per cent of the boys and 79 per cent of the girls, were continuing with some

TABLE 1: *OCCUPATIONAL CHOICE OF SIXTEEN YEAR OLDS 1984/85 (Provisional Figures)*

	Boys	Girls
Number	402,000	381,000
Full time education — (percentage)	39	50
schools (including sixth form colleges)	28	31
FE establishments (including tertiary colleges)	11	19
Employment — (percentage)	17	15
with part-time day study	6	3
without part-time day study	11	12
YTS — (percentage)	32	26
Unemployed — (percentage)	12	9

Source: DES (1985) *Digest of Statistics — England 1985*

form of education and training. In addition, the DES estimated that 10 per cent of the total population of 16-year-olds were attending evening classes and some of those in employment who were not undertaking part-time day study at public facilities, would receive some formal training from their employer. The table indicates the substantial contribution made by YTS, which catered for 32 per cent of boys and 26 per cent of girls.

The concern here is with educational provision. The majority of those continuing with full-time education continued at school, and were receiving their education in a sixth form or sixth form centre, or sixth form college.

Sixth Forms

In 1984/85 29.7 per cent of 16-year-olds in England were at school. The vast majority of these, 78.5 per cent of the boys and 74.4 per cent of girls, were taking GCE 'A'level courses which were generally two years in length (DES, 1985(b)). These courses would enable them to continue with higher education or provide them with qualifications for entry into employment. This is the 'traditional sixth' and school sixth forms are best known for their role in providing specialist academic education. But around 20 per cent of those attending schools were taking one-year CSE or GCE 'O' level courses, endeavouring to improve the qualifications they had gained at 16. Success could lead to their moving on to an 'A' level course or gaining employment. The minority, below 5 per cent, were taking other courses. These would include commercial courses, that were particularly popular for girls and other pre-vocational courses that had been introduced by schools (*ibid*). These latter two categories, 25 per cent of school attenders, represent the 'new sixth', that started to increase in numbers as sixth forms drew on comprehensive rather than selective schools (Watkins, 1982). They are a mixed group of students and take a mixed bag of courses. Nonetheless the NFER study of sixth forms found that students taking vocational and pre-vocational courses were the most satisfied. They found their education relevant (Dean and Steeds, 1982). However some commentators believe the opportunities for the 'new sixth' are restricted by the traditional sixth (Reid and Filby, 1982) and there is a danger that their courses are stigmatized as 'second best'.

School provision for the post-16s can take a number of different forms and reflects the way in which each LEA organizes its secondary education. The conventional sixth form represents the senior years of secondary schools. Some LEAs have allowed all their secondary schools to provide sixth forms, whereas others have a 'mushroom' pattern of secondary education with some schools providing a sixth form and others terminating their secondary education at 16. It is claimed that sixth forms provide an attractive and supportive ambience for continuing with education. Students work in a familiar environment with teachers who know their strengths and weaknesses. They also have an opportunity to exercise a leadership role in the school community. This may provide a motivation for continuing with education and is held to develop attributes of leadership and responsibility. Sixth forms are thought to benefit from the recruitment of well qualified staff, both because of the additional posts of special responsibility allowed under Burnham pay scales and because of the attractions of advanced teaching. This has a spill-over effect on the quality of teaching lower down the school. Schools are readily identifiable institutions and it may be that parents prefer their children to continue with their education at a place which they know. Schools also have an ethos of control and discipline and parents may prefer this to what is seen by some as the greater licence and anonymity of FE institutions. These feelings appear to be particularly evident in respect of sixth forms in voluntary schools, where the education may be provided within a particular moral framework. Schools are known and valued by local communities and the continued existence of sixth forms of proven merit is supported by the present central government.

There are also disadvantages and these have become clearer with falling rolls and financial restrictions. If sixth forms are small they are unable to provide an adequate range of academic courses, let alone the new work-related courses for the less academic that are urged by current policies. Although small classes may have some benefits in terms of teaching, they mean that the quality of the educational experience is diminished for the students and the sixth form is possibly being maintained at the expense of the rest of the school. There is some evidence that examination results are worse for small than for large sixth forms (DES, 1981). In an area with a 'mushroom' sixth form pattern, where one school only has a sixth form, the benefits will accrue to this school only and there is little or no advantage to the schools which contribute their 16+ pupils. It has also been shown that pupils dislike moving to another school at 16 and participation rates may suffer as a result.

Consortia and Sixth Form Centres

One solution to these difficulties has been to develop arrangements for collaboration between schools in providing post-16 education. Such arrangements enable all schools to provide the more popular subjects, while provision of minority subjects that attract few students or of courses requiring specialist skills and facilities that are not widely available can be limited to one or two locations. A particular form of collaboration is where a number of schools combine to provide a sixth form centre.

Collaboration may be by mutual agreement, although some LEAs are showing an increasing interest in creating formal collaborative arrangements between schools through such devices as consortia. This is discussed in more detail in Chapter 8. Collaboration has advantages in that schools can retain their own identity. Subject options, including minority subjects, are retained but the number of uneconomic small classes, with restricted educational opportunites, is reduced.

There are problems. Collaboration depends upon the goodwill of the collaborators. With falling rolls and greater opportunities for student and parental choice, the educational environment has become more competitive. Schools, understandably, may put their own interests first and be unwilling to relinquish control over their own sixth forms. If students have to travel between different institutions it is expensive, and time consuming, and difficult to provide a clear educational identity or to provide the care and support which is the hallmark of the 'good sixth form' (Briault and Smith 1980). A sixth form centre avoids these disadvantages because arrangements are more formalized. The sixth form centre represents a discrete physical entity, with its own director. This helps create a clear identity for the students and general public. But it does mean that sixth form education is divorced from the sites of the majority of the constituent schools, and the staff and equipment engaged in advanced work are less easily available for wider use in the schools.

Sixth Form Colleges

The sixth form college is one step on from a sixth form centre. Secondary schools cease providing education at 16 and all sixth form work is concentrated in one institution. The majority of sixth form colleges are open to all 16-year-olds, with some priority given to those moving from secondary schools in their catchment areas. They provide the traditional two year academic 'A' level courses and also the one year 'O' level repeats plus the limited range of vocational and pre-vocational courses that FE examining bodies are prepared to validate because the colleges are legally schools. Sixth form colleges appear to be popular institutions, maintaining academic traditions and providing more for the 'new sixth'. Staying-on rates have risen wherever they have been used for post-16 provision. In 1985/86 there were 108 colleges in England (PQ, 4 March 87), provided by about a third of LEAs. In January 1986 they were catering for 21 per cent of all sixth formers in maintained secondary schools. Their advantages are provision of a wide range of subjects economically, including those for one year pre-vocational courses. They can respond flexibly to individual requirements and emphasize breadth through general studies programmes (Macfarlane, 1978). They have fewer small classes and can fully utilize the specialist skills of the staff. Students benefit from the opportunity of making a fresh start in a new institution and from the more adult and less rigidly controlled environment. They gain socially from mixing with greater numbers of their peers. Attendance at college identifies students as adults whereas at schools they are part of what is regarded as a child population (*ibid*). Their presence at college owes more to their abilities rather than, as is argued for school sixth forms, the sponsorship of their teachers (Reid and Filby, 1982). On these arguments sixth form colleges are more democratic and less paternalistic institutions than schools sixth forms.

On the negative side, some students are felt to do less well in colleges. They cannot cope with the change, with the larger numbers and the need to create new relationships with the staff. Sixth form colleges are unable to provide a wide range of vocational and part-time courses because they operate under School Regulations. General studies courses designed to give breadth are not seen as worthwhile by the instrumentally minded students (Dean *et al*, 1979). Their emphasis remains, like the sixth forms in schools, academic. A change between institutions need not necessarily break educational progression, but continuity requires close links between sixth form colleges and the secondary schools that provide their intake in terms of curriculum planning and student guidance. Links can be forged and made systematic but this may prove difficult because of traditions of institutional independence and freedom.

FE Colleges

The FE colleges contain about a third of the 16–19-year-olds in full-time education. When account is taken of those receiving part-time education, participating in YTS schemes or attending evening classes, the majority of 16–19-year-olds participating in education do so by attending a college. Colleges are administered under FE Regulations and are thus able to cater for part-time students. Staff employed under FE Regulations have different pay scales and conditions of service from those applying to schools. Because the colleges need to employ staff with industrial experience for their vocational work, qualified teacher status is not obligatory although the majority of staff in FE colleges are teacher trained.

In 1984 there were 437 colleges in England (DES, 1985(a)). It is difficult to generalize about them. They exhibit a variety of titles: colleges of FE, colleges of technology, technical colleges, tertiary colleges. Although many commenced life with a vocational emphasis, providing work related education and specific occupational training, they have evolved to provide academic and a wide range of recreational and leisure courses. Many have become active in providing opportunities for continuing education and they are also likely to offer some advanced, higher education courses. The advent of YTS has brought a new clientele into colleges for 'off the job training', compensating for the decline in part-time students on vocational courses caused by the recession. The majority of colleges are broad in their provision. They provide a range of academic subjects and their vocational courses reflect the breadth of the local manufacturing and service sectors. There are also some specialist institutions, such as colleges of art and agriculture.

This diversity is seen as a strength. Colleges can potentially cater for a wide range of needs. Because of their size they can offer a greater choice of subjects than are available in most school sixth forms. Because of their range of provision they can cater for students whose requirements cross the traditional 'A' level, 'O' level and vocational boundaries that tend to demarcate school provision. The advantages attributed to the sixth form college of enabling students to make a fresh start in a more mature and less controlled environment also apply. Students have access to a larger and wider social mix than would be possible at school, or sixth form college, meeting peers from different backgrounds and with different interests and aspirations. Because courses may include both 16–19-year-olds and adults, students are encouraged to mature. The college environment thus prepares young people for adult life. It is also argued that colleges are well attuned to the needs of industry. Their vocational emphasis means that they have staff who are familiar with industrial requirements and over the years they have devised mechanisms for liaising with employers and learning their needs. Parkes (1982) neatly summarizes the strengths attributed to FE. 'FE has its own myths: the myth of the practical man, the myth of the remedy to the mistakes of the schools; responsiveness to industry, commerce and the community; a response to needs otherwise unmet by the education; flexible, adoptive, hard-headed.'

Yet the quotation implies that the advantages claimed for FE may be unreal. Colleges are usually large institutions, dependent upon their full-time students for their community life. Shy and introverted students may encounter problems. Although colleges generally make arrangements to provide students with pastoral care and possibly have supporting arrangements in terms of counsellors and student unions, students have to create new relationships with their teachers. Supporting facilities are more readily available to full than to part-time students, although the latter also require assistance (Cantor and Roberts, 1983). The continuity of knowledge of both individuals and the environment that is maintained by moving up into a school sixth form, is lost in moving to a college. Some students find it difficult to study in a less controlled environment and are unable to excercise responsibility for their own learning. Although some colleges have a matrix structure based on students' courses and teaching subjects, most are organized by departments consisting of groups of related courses. Thus the majority of students are based within a particular department and probably associate most closely with others taking their course or belonging to their department. It is possible for students to take courses that span departments, but it is not always easy. If students or their teachers believe that a student is pursuing the wrong course for his or her needs, the college is likely to have an alternative form of provision available. But change may not be easy in practice. With the majority of courses organized on an annual or biannual basis, a move becomes progressively harder as the year continues. As was mentioned earlier, the FE sector has been criticized by central government for its lack of response to the needs of industry (DE, 1984).

The arrangements for providing post-16 education through collaboration between institutions may well involve colleges in working with schools. Some have been doing this for a number of years in providing link courses, making use of college facilities for teaching school pupils on a part-time basis. Examples occur in providing engineering courses or courses for children with special needs. Such arrangements have not been trouble-free. In some cases they have been marred by demarcation disputes regarding the entry of the pupils involved on school or college rolls and receipt of the associated capitation. They have also been seen as expensive and disruptive, in that they involve travelling. College participation has been seen as motivated by attracting future recruits (King, 1976), although college staff have also complained that they are being used as temporary 'dumping grounds' for the less able or disruptive pupils. New initiatives such as TVEI and CPVE appear to involve the increased practice of pupils and students working in both schools and colleges.

Tertiary Colleges

Problems of choice and linkages are reduced by the tertiary college. This is the major provider for post-16 education and training within a locality and brings academic and vocational provision, for full and part-time students, together as one institution. Tertiary colleges appear to be increasing in popularity. There are currently nearly forty in England and Wales, and many more under active consideration by LEAs.

The advantages claimed for tertiary colleges lie, first, in their efficiency. Because they are the major local providers they have large numbers and can offer a wide range of courses. This enables resources to be used to maximum effect, with viable class sizes and full use of specialist staff and facilities. Ideological advantages are also claimed (Janes, 1981). Tertiary colleges are comprehensive institutions. They can promote egalitarianism and break down traditional educational boundaries. Students can select a programme that matches their needs and can unite academic and vocational elements. Operating under FE Regulations gives tertiary colleges flexibility to offer courses of varying duration and modes of attendance to cater for particular needs, such as those of a particular company or of the unemployed. Because they are the focus for all further education they can become the educational centre for the local community, offering continuing education and recreational courses to meet local needs. Colleges can thus synthesize the best of FE and schools (Dean *et al*, 1979). They can offer the attractions of an adult learning environment with a wide social mix of students, and continue the caring traditions of schools in terms of pastoral support (Holt, 1980). Because they are the major local provider of post-16 education, there is an incentive to set up procedures for working with local secondary schools and handling student recruitment.

The possible disadvantages are partly those of sixth form colleges and FE colleges in general: the break at 16, the large size of colleges, the freer environment, the need for links with secondary schools for curriculum planning and handling the transition from school to college. The curricular choice may be too wide to offer a coherent education and provide the student with a sense of identity. The diversity of provision and types of student may work against the establishment of a strong collegial community. 16–19-year-olds on full-time courses are unlikely to have much in common with adults, or with students from the same age group attending vocational or YTS courses part-time. This separation is particularly likely if the college occupies a split site. Much depends on the ethos and emphasis adopted by particular colleges. This is partly a matter of history; whether their origins were in FE or academic provision. It also depends upon the senior managers and the emphases they develop. Whether, for example, they stress pastoral care arrangements or how they value academic as against vocational or community provision. It is likely that tertiary colleges are better suited to some circumstances than others, working best where they serve a geographically compact community with good public transport and shared educational values.

Pattern of Provision

Does the type of provision matter? It is debatable whether it influences student choices. The research evidence is unclear or conflicting, although the opportunity of a break at 16 and entry to sixth form or tertiary colleges has been claimed to increase the staying-on rate. What does seem clear from this review is a growing convergence between school-based and college-based provision. Both provide academic and vocational elements and are wrestling with ways of dismantling the barriers between the two areas and catering for a wider clientele with new demands.

The type of 16–19 provision is not statutorily defined. Latterly central government has been concerned with *what* is done in post-16 education, not so much with *where* it is done. It may be that the presence of MSC as a national training agency has lessened the need to reform the organization of local education provision. Consequently there is a wide variety. Three-quarters of the LEAs in England responded to our survey of institutional arrangements for the 16–19s. According to these responses, the various possibilities can be ranked in the order in which the arrangements are applied by LEAs (Whitaker, 1985):

(i)   Sixth forms in all secondary schools with FE colleges.

(ii)   Sixth forms in some secondary schools, sixth form colleges and FE colleges.

(iii)   Sixth forms in some secondary schools and FE colleges.

(iv)   Sixth forms in some secondary schools, sixth form colleges, FE colleges and tertiary colleges.

(v)   Sixth forms in some secondary schools, tertiary colleges and FE colleges.

(vi)   Sixth form colleges and FE colleges.

(vii)   Tertiary colleges only.

From this survey it was clear that the majority of LEAs had a mixed pattern of post-16 arrangements, providing different types of opportunity in different parts of their authorities. LEAs explained this by historical factors, having inherited their provision from past local administrations, and by local circumstances which caused one form of education to be appropriate in one part of the authority and another form elsewhere. This matched the conclusions of the Macfarlane Report. Each type of post-16 education had its strengths and its weaknesses and decisions must ultimately be based on local considerations (DES, 1980). But this was not a recipe for inaction. In order to decide what suited local circumstances LEAs were urged to examine their provision from the two standpoints of educational effectiveness and resource management, giving attention to the financial consequences of their chosen pattern.

Although the DES has subsequently invited each LEA to 'review, plan, and take the necessary action to organize their 16–19 provision in order to maximize educational effectiveness and value for money' (DES, 1987) our survey suggested that the message had already struck home. Most LEAs responding were actively engaged in reviewing their arrangements. They saw reviews as necessary because of financial restrictions, falling rolls, patterns of student recruitment and new educational initiatives. Reviews could lead to changes. A third of authorities reported that they were considering closing some secondary schools. But most authorities saw themselves continuing to provide a mixed pattern. First, this was expedient. The degree to which an authority could change its provision was limited by finance, by demography, by public attitudes and the presence or absence of political support. There were many pressures and constraints. Arguments for change were rarely clear cut; economy might pull in one direction, quality in another. LEAs had to balance pressures for change with the constraints. Second, mixed provision made sense educationally. Different local circumstances did call for different institutional arrangements. A variety of institutions developed a range of different educational strengths. This assisted flexibility in an uncertain environment and allowed students and employers a degree of choice. Pluralism remained an important value in education.

Students' ability to take advantage of this pluralism is limited. Local education systems rarely provide the choices of a free market. Choices are conditioned by what students and employers know and thus by the existing patterns of provision. They are also dependent on the arrangements for coordination and provision of post-16 education made by the LEA. Colleges serve a larger catchment area than schools and will normally take any students that satisfy the entrance requirements for their various courses. LEAs have been concerned to avoid duplication and gaps in provision between colleges and between colleges and schools. The convergence between what schools and FE are offering has posed a threat. For some time schools have been concerned that colleges were undercutting their sixth forms by providing academic courses, and colleges have latterly been concerned by the development of work-related education in schools. Thus LEAs may define spheres of interest; for example, retaining academic courses for the 16–19 year olds in schools or sixth form colleges and developing vocational courses within colleges. LEA transport policies commonly define the nearest school as the natural site for post-16 provision and only subsidize transport costs elsewhere for courses that the school does not provide. LEAs also attempt to coordinate provision by scrutinizing proposals for new development and holding regular meetings of representatives from schools and college to discuss provision and agree any changes. They are also required to work with MSC in planning the development of all non-advanced FE in their authorities. College catchment areas may well extend across local government boundaries. On a larger territorial scale LEAs are grouped in Regional Advisory Councils (RACs). These are made up of LEA members and officers, FE college principals and teachers, industrial and trade union representatives, representatives from voluntary bodies, examination boards and the local universities, and officials from the main government departments concerned with FE. RACs are primarily concerned with rationalizing the provision of advanced FE, avoiding duplication and gaps. Although the provision of lower level courses is a matter for the LEAs concerned, RACs provide neighbouring LEAs with a mechanism for examining distribution and cross-boundary flows and arranging recoupment of costs. They are also a means of learning the views of industry and of the providers of higher education (Regan, 1977).

Organization of Provision

Figure 2 shows the way in which the different agencies and institutions discussed in this chapter are linked together within local education systems. It also indicates something of their role regarding 16–19 provision and their relationship to clients in helping them determine their needs for education or training. It highlights a number of points that will be referred to again in later chapters.

First, education is provided through a hierarchical system of government. Schools and colleges, careers services and youth and community services are not free-standing. They are all provided and administered by LEAs, are subject to their authority and dependent upon them for their resources. Patterns of LEA administration vary, reflecting past history, size and geography. Some LEAs administer their institutions directly from their central offices, others group their institutions within area or district offices.

This said, the figure suggests that the control exercised by the LEA over provision is limited. As will be discussed in Chapter 5, authority and power in education are not all 'top down'. Responsibilities are distributed between different bodies. Thus schools and colleges are responsible for the detailed organization of their own provision. Hence the variety that is found between institutions within one LEA.

A second feature emphasized by the diagram and fundamental to the theme of this book, is that, local education systems attempt to assist clients in determining their needs and choosing educational provision. This involves the work of careers services but schools and colleges also inform what they have to offer, what is required for entry, and what continued education might achieve. What the diagram cannot show is the coverage and quality of that assistance and the degree to which clients have to take the initiative if it is to be obtained.

Third, the diagram includes MSC within the local education system; a component that would have been absent a decade ago. Over a short space of time it has significantly reduced the traditional separation between education and training. Although MSC is in no way subject to the authority of the LEA or indeed any local political control, its views of educational needs are influential. The role given to MSC by central government in making provision for the 16–19-year-olds and the resources at its disposal, give it power both as a consumer of education and in working with LEAs to shape the nature of provision.

Finally, the diagram is complex. It brings out the variety of agencies

Figure 2: Local Organization of 16-19 Provision

PROVIDERS

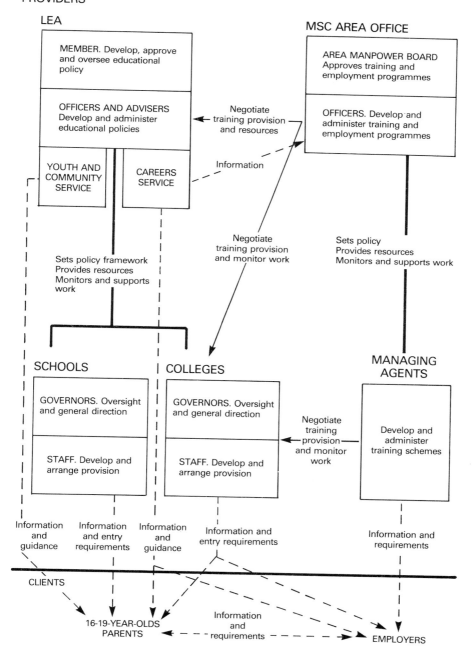

and institutions that have a stake in defining the needs of the post-16 age group and in developing their educational provision. It illustrates the many sources of information that may be directed at potential students, their parents and at employers. This complexity is one of the principal characteristics of the assessment of need in English education and the task of identifying and unravelling the contribution of the various elements is addressed continually throughout the book. Part 2 begins this task by examining the nature of need and discussing some of the explanations that have been advanced for the way in which the education service works.

References

BRIAULT, E. and SMITH, F., (1980) *Falling Rolls in Secondary Schools*, Windsor, NFER.

CANTOR, L. and ROBERTS, I., (1983) *Further Education Today* (3rd edn), London, Routledge and Kegan Paul.

CLARKE, L., (1980) *The Transition from School to Work: A Critical Review of Research in the United Kingdom*, London, HMSO.

DEAN, J., BRADLEY, K., CHOPPIN, B. and VINCENT, D., (1979) *The Sixth Form and its Alternatives*, Windsor, NFER.

DEAN, J. and STEEDS, A., (1982) *17 Plus: The New Sixth Form in Schools and FE*, Windsor, NFER/Nelson.

DE, (1980) *The Careers Service*, London, HMSO.

DE, (1984) *Training for Jobs*, Cmnd 9135, London, HMSO.

DES, (1980) *Education for 16–19 Year Olds* (The Macfarlane Report), London, HMSO.

DES, (1981) *The Relationship Between Size of Sixth Form, Teaching Group Size and 'A' Level Performance in Maintained Schools — Statistical Bulletin 8/81*, London, HMSO.

DES, (1984) *Education for Employees*, London, HMSO.

DES (1985a) *Statistics of Further Education*, London, HMSO.

DES (1985b) *Digest of Statistics: England 1985*, London, HMSO.

DES/DE, (1985) *Education and Training for Young People*, Cmnd 9482, London, HMSO.

DES, (1987) *Providing for Quality: The Pattern of Organization to Age 19*, London, HMSO.

GINZBERG, E. et al, (1951) *Occupational Choice: An Approach to a General Theory*, Columbia University Press.

GORDON, A., (1983) 'The Educational Choices of Young People', in BOYD-BARRETT, O., BUSH, T., GOODEY, J., MCNAY, I. and PREEDY, M. (Eds) *Approaches to Post-School Management*, London, Harper & Row.

HOLT, M., (1980) *The Tertiary Sector*, London, Hodder and Stoughton.

JANES, F., (1981) 'A history of the tertiary college', in COTTERELL, A. and HELEY, E. (Eds) *Tertiary: A Radical Approach to Post-Compulsory Education*, Cheltenham, Stanley Thornes.

KEDNEY, B. and PARKES, D., (Eds), (1985) *Responsibility and Responsiveness: Case Studies in Further Education*, Bristol, Association of Metropolitan Authorities/Further Education Staff College.

KING, M., (1976) *School and College*, London, Routledge & Kegan Paul.

MACDONALD, D., (1980) 'Detached youth work in the late 1960s and the 1970s' in BOOTON, F. and PEARLING, A. (Eds) *The 1980s and Beyond: The Changing Scene of Youth and Community Work*, Leicester, National Youth Bureau.

MACFARLANE, E., (1978) *Sixth Form Colleges*, London, Heinemann.

MAIZELS, J., (1968) *Adolescent Needs and the Transition from School to Work*, London, Athlone Press.

MASON, C., (1984) 'YTS and local authorities: A context', *Local Government Studies*, 10, 1, January.

MSC, (1986) *England and Wales Youth Cohort Study: First Summary Report*, Sheffield, MSC.

NATIONAL ECONOMIC DEVELOPMENT COUNCIL and MANPOWER SERVICES COMMISSION, (1984) *Competence and Competition: Training and Education in the Federal Republic of Germany, the United States and Japan*, London, National Economic Development Office.

Parliamentary Question, 4 March 1987, *Hansard*, Vol. 111, No. 1409, London HMSO.

PARKES, D. (Eds), (1982) *The Changing Face of FE*, London, FEU.

PAUL, L., (1962) *The Transition from School to Work*, London, Industrial Welfare Society.

PECK, D., (1980) 'Local authorities and the Manpower Services Commission: A framework for cooperation in the 1980s', *Local Government Studies*, 6, May/June.

PECK, D., and ROBINSON, F., (1986) 'The contribution of the careers service' in RANSON, S., TAYLOR, B. and BRIGHOUSE, T. (Eds), *The Revolution in Education and Training*, London, Longman.

RANSON, S. and RIBBINS, P., with CHESTERFIELD, L. and SMITH, T., (1986) *The Management of Change in the Careers Service*, Birmingham, University of Birmingham, INLOGOV.

REGAN, D., (1977) *Local Government and Education*, London, Allen & Unwin.

REID, W. and FILBY, J., (1982) *The Sixth: An Essay in Education and Democracy*, Lewes, Falmer Press.

SAWDON, A., PELICAN, J. and YUCKER, S., (1981) *Study of the Transition from School to Working Life, Vol.1*, London, Youthaid.

TAYLOR, B., (1983) *A Parent's Guide to Education*, London, Consumers Association and Hodder and Stoughton.

THEODOSSIN, E., (1986) *In Search of the Responsive College*, Bristol, Further Education Staff College.

Times, 'The Million Who Decided to Train', *The Times*, 26 June 1986.

VENESS, T., (1962) *School Leavers: Their Aspirations and Expectations*, London Methuen.

WALLACE, R., (1985) *Introducing Technical and Vocational Education*, London, Macmillan.

WATKINS, P., (1982) *The Sixth Form College in Practice*, London, Edward Arndd.

WHITAKER, T., (1985) *Educational Planning: LEAs' Assessment of Educational Need for the 16–19 Age Group*, Middlesex, Brunel University.

Part 2
Structural Explanations of Needs Assessment

4   *The Concept of Need*

Chapter 2 documented the way in which education for the 16–19 age group has been subject to various changes to meet what are seen as the new educational needs of these students. But the discussion of the various documents and statements fails to show the underlying bases of what is meant by the term 'needs' nor how they have become defined. Instead it is assumed that need is an objective statement of a condition to which educational provision must respond.

The concept of social need is widely used in the discussion about the aims and objectives of social policies and indeed it has become accepted as the main basis for the distribution of social services. There is now an orthodoxy that these services should primarily be allocated according to the principle of need. But because the term 'need' is used in a prescriptive way and carries with it the connotation that needs must be met, the problem arises that it is frequently used without precision and is open to different interpretations. This chapter probes more deeply into the concept of need. It starts by outlining the philosophical foundation of this term and then goes on to show the development of the term social need and analyzes some of the issues surrounding its use in the field of social policy. Finally the chapter discusses the application of need to the field of education and specifically provision for the 16–19 age group.

The Philosophical Foundations

As a starting point it is important to identify the key elements of the term need. Walton (1969) comments that the following statement — 'X, a person or group of people, is in need' can be divided into three statements:

(i)   X is in state Y;
(ii)   state Y is incompatible with the values held in society;
(iii)   therefore state Y should be changed.

It should be noted that this statement does not say anything about how Y should be changed only that this state is deficient in some way. Therefore the term need as used here refers to a condition or state that is absent or deficient in some way. Walton also shows that this type of statement includes both a factual assessment (that X is in position Y) and a normative assessment of whether this state Y is in fact incompatible with certain values and ought to be rectified. This 'discrepancy' definition of need, whereby need refers to a condition that is lacking is one of the most commonly used definitions found in the discussions of need in education and social policy and will be used throughout this book (Witkin, 1984).

The question arises of whether need, once it has been identified, should automatically be alleviated through providing appropriate services. Barry (1965) argues that need is not by itself a principle which can be used to justify the provision of services. He maintains that the statement, X is necessary to produce Y, does not provide a reason for doing X because it must be shown that Y is a desirable end to pursue. The principle of need must therefore be used in conjunction with a justification of another kind before a service is made available and the purposes for which it is needed must be outlined and be accepted. The other pre-condition that Barry notes is that if a course of action is deemed necessary to meet a need then this course should be demonstrated as the best alternative to pursue.

A further problem with the definition of need is the question of how needs differ from the notion of wants (Plant *et al*, 1980). The conventional distinction in the field of social administration is that wants are satisfied by the mechanisms of the economic market whereas needs are fundamentally different, because the prescribed remedy might not be wanted or desired by the individual concerned. A further assumption is that the state should meet social needs because these would not necessarily be satisfied in the economic market. Miller (1976) notes that needs are different from wants because they consist of some kind of objective statement made about an individual, whereas wanting is a psychological state and reflects the behaviour of the individual. An illustration of this would be an individual who is judged by the professionals to require a course of education or training but may not want it. This carries with it the connotation that needs are best defined by the experts because the individual's assessment is subjective and hence more limited.

The discussion so far has highlighted the role of values in the consideration of needs both in recognizing what might be a deficiency and deciding whether action is necessary or desirable to meet this need. A further point is whether there are needs which might be essential and should be met in social policy. It is usually accepted that physical survival and human autonomy are basic human needs which should be met and which underly other needs. Yet even accepting this, these fundamental needs may still be relative because they may vary from country to country and change over time. For example, values about the distribution and aims of education have changed over time and new definitions of need emerge. This raises the issue whether it is possible to rank different needs in terms of their priority. Taylor-Gooby and Dale (1981) maintain that the discussion of needs can operate at different levels. At the highest level is the discussion of the 'final' needs or the ends of human activity. At a second level they argue that needs can be seen as 'intermediate' or the means towards these ends. Similarly, Maslow (1943) states that a hierarchy of needs exists in society ranging from those needs relating to basic individual survival to more expressive needs. In a different vein the Marxist discussion of needs by writers such as Marcuse (1964) seeks to identify 'true' needs in contrast to 'false' ones which are generated by the nature of the social system.

The preceding discussion, therefore, has outlined and discussed some of the key philosophical issues surrounding the term need and the way the term is used. It shows the complexity of the term and the uncertainty with which it is used. The main lesson is that need is not a value free term but must involve a consideration of the values involved in both identifying the problem and the ends to be pursued.

The Measurement of Need

As mentioned in the introduction to this chapter, the principle of need has assumed importance in the literature on social policy as the main criterion in the allocation of welfare goods and services. Some writers have gone further in asserting that the development of the social services is a reflection of the recognition and meeting of different needs through the provision of services. Indeed Forder (1974) states that the definition of need defines the objectives of the services. This orthodoxy has been reflected in the way in which need has been promoted in different policy areas as the major principle for the planning of social services. For example, the Seebohm Report on Social Services argued that need should be the basis of provision of social services. It noted that the existing structure of social services departments constrained the definition and measurement of need. In both the fields of health and local government services the same trend can be noted for these services to be better able to identify and respond to the needs of their localities (Stewart, 1974; Walker, 1984).

Accompanying these moves for a greater responsiveness to needs have been attempts by social policy analysts and planners to define and measure the incidence of needs for use in planning provision. This has resulted in a large literature particularly in the health and social services fields which provides insights into how to create objective indicators of needs. Several approaches have been developed which employ different methods of measuring needs (Smith, 1980).

One important approach is the use of questionnaires on population samples of those who do and do not receive a service. In education this has been used for example in asking groups of 16-year-olds about their perceptions of the education they want, their views on types of courses or different types of institutions (Dean and Steeds, 1981; Bradley *et al*, 1983). In these cases the potential demand for services is taken as an indicator of need. The main characteristic of this type of approach is that the term need assumes more of a 'subjective' assessment rather than the 'expert' assessment by an outsider.

An extension to this type of approach is the use of indicators of need which would act as surrogates for the measurement of need and be objective and independent measures. Carlisle (1972) defines a social indicator as an '. . . operational definition of any one of the concepts central to the generation of an information system descriptive of the social system'. She differentiates between the various types of indicators. Informative indicators describe what is happening in policy areas and are used to monitor changes. Predictive indicators allow theoretical extrapolations to be made from past or present measurements. Problem oriented indicators measure problem areas in order to produce policies. Finally, programme evaluation indicators allow the progress of policies to be measured.

Different types of indicators have been employed in a number of service sectors. In health they have been used by the Resource Allocation Working Party (RAWP) to allocate resources to areas of greater health need, independent of the supply and demand of health care. This involved developing indicators of the need for health, such as the use of mortality statistics to measure the relative needs for acute hospital services. In the field of education, the setting up of Education Priority Areas was an early attempt of using social indicators to allocate extra resources to schools which scored highly on rates of educational disadvantage. The additional educational needs were measured using factors which were viewed to create educational disadvantage, such as children in receipt of free school meals and parents in semi or unskilled manual occupations. The Inner London Education Authority's index for the designation of educational priority areas was another example of this approach (Little and Mabey, 1972). Another more recent example in the field of education is the DES classification of LEAs by additional educational needs which again uses objective measures of educational deprivation (DES, 1982). This exercise enabled groups of LEAs to be identified which have similar levels of additional needs.

Despite the attempt to create measures of need which are meant to be independent of both the supply and demand of services, there are many criticisms in the use of indicators of need. The main problem with the concept of educational need is how to measure it with precision.

The American Needs Assessment Movement

In the field of education in this country, apart from indicators of educational need, the use of systematic techniques to assess educational needs has been rare. In contrast in the United States a needs assessment movement has developed as a prescriptive method of ensuring that the planning of services meets the needs of the population. This uses systematic techniques in identifying the needs of clients in areas such as education and health. Kaufman, one of the main proponents of this type of approach in the field of education defines needs assessment as, '. . . a formal analysis that shows and documents the gaps between current results and desired results (ideally concerned with gaps in outcomes), arranges the gaps (needs) in priority order, selects the needs to be resolved' (quoted in Witkin, 1984). Here there appear to be two main characteristics: the measurement of a defined population and assessing the resulting information to determine priorities for policies and services. Needs assessment thus becomes a major part of the planning process and is used in all the stages of policy-making and evaluation.

There are various methods used under the rubric of needs assessment and it is not at all clear that there is a consensus about the main approaches (Kaufman and English, 1979; Warheit *et al*, 1977; Siegel *et al*, 1978; Scriven and Roth, 1978; Jordan and Stultz, 1976). As Kimmel (1977) notes in his review of this literature there are a number of broad aims of needs assessment and different views about what it constitutes: 'It appears that needs assessment can be almost anything: a change oriented process, a method for enumeration and description, an analytical procedure, a decision making process, a process for the resolution of many viewpoints etc.'

Kaufman (1972) suggests that there are a number of generic strategies which can be employed by policy makers in assessing educational needs. The first is the *inductive* model and this starts with finding out the goals, expectancies, and outcomes for education from the community to form a programme which is based on these data. This approach then seeks to find out how students are behaving now. These expectancies are compared with the existing goals of education to prepare detailed objectives for bringing about a change in behaviour and from these the educational programmes would be devised and implemented. The second of Kaufman's models is the *deductive* approach which starts from existing goals and 'deduces' an educational programme. The existing goals of education are identified and then the 'change requirements' are determined from the various partners in the education system. The next stage would be to look at the performance data to see whether the criteria were being achieved. If there were discrepancies, then objectives would be set and programmes formulated.

Kaufman's final model is the *classical* type, which he maintains is the way that most educational agencies operate at present. This starts with the general statement of goals and then programmes are developed, implemented and evaluated without any measurement or empirical data on needs or performance.

The techniques employed in needs assessment vary in the ways they find out the needs of the population. Kimmel (1977) lists some of the main methods used in recent American studies. The first set involve gathering opinions and judgments about what needs exist, using key informants, community forums, public hearings and the like. The second method focuses on the collection and analysis of service statistics such as waiting lists and utilization rates. A third type are the epidemiological studies such as those used in the health field. Related to this are the studies on the incidence and prevalence of social problems. Another method used is the development of social indicators to measure the variables associated with need. The next commonly used method is the survey of different groups in the population, to solicit information about need. Finally, there are studies which undertake secondary analysis of existing studies or collected data about need. It should be noted that all these different approaches are alternative ways of gathering data about needs and many of the needs assessment studies prefer to be eclectic in ways of defining need.

It can be seen from the previous review that the term needs assessment is quite wide in its inclusion of different approaches. One problem is that although they focus on ways of assessing and measuring needs for use in planning, there is still a lack of clarity about what is actually meant by the term need. Witkin (1984) outlines some of the different views of need used in these approaches. Need is most commonly used as a noun; to indicate a discrepancy between some accepted or desired state and the actual or perceived state. A second approach is to use need to refer to a set of problems identified by the service providers or those that receive the services. Witkin notes the ambiguity in the use of the term need. She states,

> In education, the term has often been used to describe a problem (such as vandalism or excessive absenteeism from school), a program (such as remedial reading program), a symptom (such as low test scores in mathematics), a resource (such as teacher aides in the classroom or more money for instructional materials), and a solution to a problem (such as stricter disciplinary measures or a new method of teaching a basic skill).

Despite the absence of any unified theoretical approach the American literature on needs assessment is important in our examination because it is designed to be a more systematic way of using the concept of need in the planning and evaluation of services than what commonly occurs in policy-making. In particular, it can be seen to be related to a rational model of policy making which is discussed in Chapter 6.

Bradshaw's Taxonomy of Need

All the different approaches to needs assessment reviewed so far display an ambiguity in the way they treat need. In particular it is unclear whether need is viewed as being diagnostic, to identify a problem, or prescriptive, in terms of the help or services required (Thayer, 1973). There is also an uncertainty about the bases of the different definitions. One useful way of classifying the various methods of needs assessment is to focus upon the different usages of the term 'needs' made by policy makers. Bradshaw's (1972) taxonomy of social need provides a framework which emphasizes that need cannot be treated in isolation from the way it is defined.

Bradshaw differentiates between four ways of defining need. *Normative* need is the most frequently used and is what the expert defines in a given situation. A 'desirable' standard is laid down and this is then compared with the state of an individual or group and if this falls short of the standard then this is classified as a need. Bradshaw accepts that these standards are likely to vary with the value position of the expert in question and these may also change over time as values or knowledge change. *Felt* need is closely related to the notion of want. Using this definition the researcher would ask respondents whether they need a particular service and the answer gives a subjective perception of their needs. As Bradshaw notes, this has an appeal because it is assumed that it is an important right of individuals to provide definitions of their own needs. This type of approach has particularly been used in studies of the elderly and other client groups. *Expressed* need refers to the demand for a service or in other words, is felt need turned into action. The measurement of this would be through the use of the demand, such as waiting lists for treatment or course enrolments. Finally, *comparative* need is obtained through studying the characteristics of a particular population in receipt of a service and those with similar characteristics who do not. This latter group is then defined as in need. In this definition need refers to a gap between services in one area and services in another. This notion of need can be seen to be related to the principle of equality and Davies' concept of territorial justice (Davies, 1977).

The value of Bradshaw's taxonomy is in showing the different definitions and the problems and benefits of using them. He shows, using the example of housing, that it is possible for the policy maker to assess the amount of need under each of these definitions and to combine them to produce twelve different categories of need. The policy maker then decides which category should constitute real need or which category should be given priority. As Bradshaw notes, this approach is helpful, 'to clarify and make explicit what is being done when those concerned with the social services are studying or planning to meet social needs'.

There are particular problems with each of Bradshaw's categories which also apply to much of the empirical research on need. Clayton

(1983) reviewing the taxonomy applied to the field of sheltered housing, states that it is unclear whether the statement of need is descriptive, explanatory, or predictive in what it is saying. Another problem in using this classification is that individuals are classed as being in need or not in need. The Bradshaw model has only two dimensions and there is no measure of the intensity of need. Clayton also notes that the data derived from each definition of need are not necessarily comparable. For example, felt need may be gathered from a small sample whereas expressed need is usually derived from the total eligible population. Moreover the concept of need in Bradshaw is individual specific which rules out other sources of data such as population forecasts. Although Bradshaw treats each definition as separate, it is apparent that there are relationships between the different categories. For example, the expressed need may in part be a product of past definitions of normative need. Similarly comparative need is a sub-set of normative need. Inevitably much of the data collected using these definitions will be reflections of past and current patterns of provision and it may be difficult to estimate future needs.

Furthermore, each of Bradshaw's definitions has its own problems. With felt need it is methodologically difficult to gain respondents' own views of their individual needs without influencing their responses through the line of questioning (Shaw, 1978). Also it can be difficult to rely on the clients' views of their needs as these are likely to be influenced by such factors as their individual circumstances, their knowledge, the characteristics of the particular service and other factors, such as their own views on the level of provision. In education there is even a problem of deciding who is the client. Expressed need or demand is likewise influenced by the problems of the clients' knowledge of existing services and whether they want that kind of service. Demand is also influenced by a whole number of supply and demand factors which are not necessarily made explicit and can vary between the different types of services (Webster, 1982). For example, some services may be based on a principle of uniformity, providing the same level and type of service to all areas. Comparative need suffers from the charge that the receipt of a service in one area does not necessarily mean that those individuals are in need. Once again the actual distribution of services is influenced by a variety of factors and response to need may only be one influence. Finally, with normative need it is difficult to assess the validity of statements or how precise they are in their assumptions. Statements of normative need may have been derived from objective assessment and measurement or in a subjective way using implicit criteria. It also tends to be assumed that professional practitioners are responsive to their clients' needs but this is questionable in practice. Normative need may vary between areas because different criteria are used. A more serious criticism is that there is no apparent consensus about normative needs and there may be conflicts within the professional group whose competing definitions cannot be reconciled. For example, in 16–19 education there is a debate about whether vocational training or more general education should be provided for 'less academic' students. Normative need will also be further influenced by the particular characteristics of the policy area in question such as the level of political interest or the access to technology. Another dimension of normative need is the impact of central government guidelines about need which may become important determinants of local assessments of need, particularly in a period of resource constraints. Finally, there is the question of whether there are 'national' needs which have to be taken into account by policy makers. Bradshaw's approach is intended to be of help to policy makers and therefore the classification is primarily of heuristic value.

Criticisms of the Concept of Need

The traditional concept of need used in the previous research studies has come under criticism from a number of different standpoints. Gilbert Smith (1980) is one writer who is critical of the way that this 'traditional' notion of need has been operationalized. He sees the literature as a desire to develop a universal criterion of need which will be unambiguous and capable of objective definition. Need in this way is viewed as an objective and static phenomenon which is an attribute of the client. This he criticizes on several grounds: there is a lack of definitional clarity, with need which is frequently defined in terms of the way it is measured; there is an overdependence on official administrative and practitioner categories; and an overconcern with the question of measurement rather than on the validity of the research material. In his own research on client reception, intake and allocation in a Scottish social work department, he demonstrates an alternative approach. He argues that need is used in different ways and in different situations. It is not an attribute of the client but arises out of the process of the interaction between welfare provider and client. His research shows that routine administrative procedures, together with the ideologies of need held by the social worker, create categories of need which clients are then fitted into. The value of Smith's analysis is that it directs attention to the values and beliefs of the provider of services and the way that these are related to the creation of need. Similarly Spicker's (1987) discussion of the concept of need used for the allocation of council housing shows that housing departments have their own ideology of need.

A different criticism of the term need comes from economists and is directed against what is viewed as a 'romantic' notion of need which is found in the traditional social administration perspective. This, it is argued, constantly makes the claim for more services to meet growing needs without any consideration of the different ways of meeting these needs (Knapp, 1984). Needs research is therefore too service oriented and sees only a narrow choice of ends and means. This can be seen to be similar to the incremental model of policy-making which uses only a limited number of policy alternatives. This criticism is by no means confined to the economists; Rein (1969) reviewing needs research makes the same argument and notes that 'with unflagging regularity' such studies want more services and this becomes a social aim. Morever, this research tends to reaffirm the existing form and structure of service provision rather than producing radical changes in the services required to meet needs.

The economists' critique goes further than this to question whether government should automatically meet needs without taking into account the costs they represent. Nevitt (1977) states that social need can be seen to be only those demands that society has considered important enough for government intervention. She argues that demand is a more valid concept for policy makers to take into account. Bleddyn Davies (1977) extends this point to formulate a different notion of need which is the quantity of resources judged to be appropriate to allocate to recipients with particular characteristics, taking into account the costs and benefits from all possible uses of these resources and any budget constraints.

Evaluating the Term Need

The preceding review of the many usages of the term need both in research and planning shows some of the difficulties with this concept. One of the problems is the widespread appeal of the term with the result that it is used without precision. Cuyler (1972), in reviewing these problems, came to the view that, 'that the word need should be banished from discussion of public policy'. Our own view is that 'need' has to be used carefully and the underlying basis of the definition made clear when the term is used in planning. This does not mean that the term should be banished from discussion about public policy.

It is useful to summarize some of the main issues in the use of the term need found in the literature. The first issue is what definition of need is used. Here there is no consensus about what constitutes need and in practice the term is used in different ways. One distinction is whether the term is used in an individual or collective sense. A more important issue is what the term refers to; it appears to be used interchangeably between a discrepancy, a recognized problem, the requirement for more services, and the wants of people. A second issue is how the definition is made. There is a distinction in the literature between quantitative and qualitative assessments. The measurement of need can be tackled in different ways with varying degrees of sophistication. Another key characteristic relates to who is responsible for making the assessment and there are a range of possible participants. The main ones are likely to be the professional, politician, and researcher. Each of these will have their own distinct values and interests which may well influence the definitions of need made and statements of what services are required (Klein, 1977). For example, Smith (1980) writes 'need as used by welfare professionals, is not simply a single concept but rather a set of interrelated options and assumptions about what is viewed as the proper object of social work activity. It is helpful to view this body of ideas in terms of a professional ideology about the nature of need'.

The range of participants involved in the assessment of needs will vary and it becomes important to determine their relative influence in this process to see whose definition counts the most. The previous discussion has demonstrated the importance of values in the consideration of needs. There is a tendency in some of the literature to assume that needs are objective facts which only have to be identified and measured for use in planning. Yet, the evidence is that the way in which the definitions are framed is of fundamental importance in determining in ranking the different need definitions. Some definitions will have a greater legitimacy than others, both in their 'political' appeal and the way the definition has been framed. A further issue is therefore how definitions of need become used in policy making and in the determination of service provision. Some of the research literature has sought to examine the relationship between needs and the services delivered but as has been noted, there is a major difficulty in this analysis in reaching an accurate and value free statement of needs. Instead Clayton (1983) argues that there ought to be more studies showing how policy makers actually define needs in practice and how these become used in policy-making. It is by no means a simple automatic relationship but is part of a more complex political process.

Our own study seeks to show and analyze how professionals in local education authorities and institutions actually define the educational needs of the 16–19s and how these assessments figure in planning provision for this age group. The definition of need that we use relies upon the work of Gilbert Smith (1980) and others. Need is a perceived discrepancy or gap between some desired condition and the assessed condition, which has consequences for the type of education provided and its distribution. This can therefore be assessed on different criteria as in the Bradshaw taxonomy. However, we have concentrated on the way that professionals define and use the term need relying on their perceptions and how they operationalize these. By 'needs assessment' we mean the many different methods, both structured and informal, which are used by practitioners to assess student needs.

Needs in 16–19 Education

Much of the previous discussion of need has focused upon studies from different fields of social policy. The task is now to explore the way in which the term need is used in education and specifically with 16–19 education. Chapter 2 showed the numerous pronouncements about the needs of the

16–19 age group and, as noted earlier, it is unclear on what basis these definitions are made and how they were arrived at. Recent curricular initiatives also talk about the learning needs of the students. It is therefore important to show the way that needs are treated in education (Dearden, 1972).

There are various types of educational needs. One classification suggested by Johnson (1980) in secondary education makes a distinction between institution-specific, maturation-specific and future-specific needs. The first category arises because of the institutional format of secondary schooling and includes the need for security, the smooth running of the school, material needs and life support needs. The maturation-specific needs develop because of the pupil's stage in life and can be divided into learning needs, moral development, physical development needs and emotional development needs. Finally, future-specific needs relate to post school life and are divided into knowledge needs and guidance needs.

In education there are likely to be differing views of the nature of these needs and how they should be met. This is because of the values held about education. Kogan (1985) has demonstrated how there have been a number of different aims of education propounded since the 1944 Act which are a product of changing expectations about the role of education in society. These are in some cases conflictual and have to be reconciled. In terms of defining educational needs the role of the professional becomes important to consider, as in other areas of social policy (Donnison, 1975). In education this is all the more important because of the way in which services are provided at the institution level. Kogan (1983) defines schools and colleges as 'prime institutions' because this is the level at which important decisions are made regarding the provision of education. One implication of this is that they can possess a high degree of discretion in their activities and so in Bradshaw's terminology, normative definitions of need will assume importance. Therefore the existing provision made available by the educational institutions will be of paramount importance in framing the way that definitions of need are made. However, there is also the question of the views of students and their parents and also, of increasing importance, those of employers which may have to be taken into account. Finally, education is part of a national system and there are societal needs which become articulated by central government. The impact of national examination board requirements is also likely to be important in framing how definitions of need are made.

A consideration of the needs of students in the 16–19 age group is distinctive for a number of reasons. First, educational provision at this stage is not compulsory and there are a number of different routes which can be taken, including training provided by MSC. Secondly, in some cases post-16 education involves a break in institutional participation which can create a lack of continuity in provision. Third, this stage of education acts as a phase in the transition to further education or employment opportunities and so needs are likely to be viewed in terms of what a student may require in the future. Finally, this stage of education has been subject, as seen earlier, to a number of different influences — new educational thinking, changing pressures from central government and the pressures of youth unemployment.

The next chapter continues our analysis by outlining the various theories that can be employed to understand the way that education is provided.

References

BARRY, B., (1965) *Political Argument*, London, Routledge & Kegan Paul.

BRADLEY, J., *et al*, (1983) *The Transition from School to Adult Life: A Review and Annotated Bibliography*, Windsor, NFER.

BRADSHAW, J., (1972) 'The concept of social need', *New Society*, 30 March.

CARLISLE, E., (1972) 'The conceptual structure of social indicators' in SHONFIELD, A. and SHAW, S., (1972) (Eds) *Social Indicators and Social Policy*, London, Heinemann.

CLAYTON, S., (1983) 'Social need revisited', *Journal of Social Policy*, 12, 2.

CUYLER, A.J., (1972) 'Health indicators', in SHONFIELD, A. and SHAW, S. (Eds) *Social Indicators and Social Policy*, London, Heinemann.

DAVIES, B., (1977) 'Social services studies and the explanation of policy outcomes', *Policy and Politics*, 5, 3, March.

DEAN, J., and STEEDS, A., (1981) *17 Plus: The New Sixth Form in Schools and Further Education*, Windsor, NFER.

DEARDEN, R.F., (1972) 'Needs in education' in DEARDEN, R.F. (Ed.), *Education and the Development of Reason*, London, Routledge and Kegan Paul.

DES, (1982) *Statistical Bulletin 8/82*, London, HMSO.

DONNISON, D., (1975) *Social Policy and Administration Revisited*, London, Allen & Unwin.

FORDER, A., (1974) *Concepts in Social Administration*, London, Routledge & Kegan Paul.

JOHNSON, D. *et al*, (1980) *Secondary Schools and the Welfare Network*, London, Allen & Unwin.

JORDAN, K.F. and STULTZ, J.R., (1976) 'Projecting the educational needs and costs of elementary and secondary education' in ALEXANDER, K. and JORDAN, K.F., *Educational Need in the Public Economy*, Gainesville, FL, University of Florida.

KAUFMAN, R.A., (1972) *Educational System Planning*, Englewood Cliffs, NJ, Prentice Hall.

KAUFMAN, R.A. and ENGLISH, F.W., (1979) *Needs Assessment: Concept and Application*, NJ, Educational Technology Publication.

KIMMEL, W.A., (1977) *Needs Assessment: A Critical Perspective*, US Department of Health, Education and Welfare.

KLEIN, R., (1977) 'The conflict between professionals, consumers and bureaucrats', *Journal of the Irish Colleges of Physicians and Surgeons*, 6, 3, January.

KNAPP, M., (1984) *The Economics of Social Care*, London, Macmillan.

KOGAN, M., (1983) 'The central-local government relationship: A comparison between the education and health services', *Local Government Studies*, 9, 1, January/February.

KOGAN, M., (1985) 'Education policy and values', in MCNAY, I. and OZGA, J. (Eds) *Policy-Making in Education: The Breakdown of Consensus*, Oxford, Pergamon.

LITTLE, A. and MABEY, C., (1972) 'An index for designation of educational priority areas' in SHONFIELD, A. and SHAW, S. (Eds) *Social Indicators and Social Policy*, London, Heinemann.

MARCUSE, H., (1964) *One Dimensional Man*, London, Routledge & Kegan Paul.

MASLOW, H., (1943) 'A theory of human motivation', *Psychological Review*, 50.

MILLER, D., (1976) *Social Justice*, Oxford, Clarendon Press.

NEVITT, D., (1977) 'Demand and need' in HEISLER, H., (Ed), *Foundations of Social Administration*, London, Macmillan.

OLKINUORA, E., (1973) 'On the problems of developing education indicators', *Acta Sociologica*, 16, 4.

PLANT, R. *et al*, (1980) *Political Philosophy and Social Welfare*, London, Routledge & Kegan Paul.

REIN, M., (1969) 'Research design and social policy' in RYAN, M. (Ed), *Distress in the City*, Cleveland, OH, Case Western Reserve University Press.

SCRIVEN, M. and ROTH, J., (1978) 'Needs assessment: Concept and practice', *New Directions for Program Evaluation*, 1, Spring.

SHAW, J., (1978) 'Consumer opinion and social policy' in BULMER, M., (Eds), *Social Policy Research*, London, Macmillan.

SHONFIELD, A. and SHAW, S., (Eds), (1972) *Social Indicators and Social Policy*, London, Heinemann.

SIEGEL, L.M. *et al*, (1978) 'Need identification and program planning in the community context' in ATTKINSON, C.C. *et al* (Eds) *Evaluation of Human Service Programmes*, London, Academic Press.

SINFIELD, A., (1980) 'Meeting client need: An ambiguous and precarious value' in GRUNOW, D. and HEGNER, F., (Eds) *Welfare or Bureaucracy: Problems of Matching Social Services to Clients' Needs — Research on Service Delivery*, Vol. II, Oelgeschlager.

SMITH, G., (1980) *Social Need: Policy, Practice and Research*, London, Routledge & Kegan Paul.

SPICKER, P., (1987) 'Concepts of need in housing allocations', *Policy and Politics*, 15, 1, January.

STEWART, J.D., (1974) *The Responsive Local Authority*, London, Charles Knight.

TAYLOR-GOOBY, P. and DALE, J., (1981) *Social Theory and Social Welfare*, London, Edward Arnold.

THAYER, R, (1973) 'Measuring need in the social services', *Social and Economic Administration*, 7, 2, May.

WALKER, A., (1984) *Social Planning: A Strategy for Socialist Welfare*, Oxford, Basil Blackwell.

WALTON, R., (1969) 'Need: A central concept', *Social Services Quarterly*, 43, 1.

WARHEIT, G.J. *et al*, (1977) *Needs Assessment Approaches: Concepts and Methods*, Maryland, National Institute of Mental Health.

WEBSTER, B., (1982) 'The distributional effects of local government services' in LEACH, S., and STEWART, J., *Approaches to Public Policy*, London, Allen & Unwin.

WITKIN, B., (1984) *Assessing Needs in Educational and Social Programs: Using Information to Make Decisions, Set Priorities and Allocate Resources*, San Francisco, CA, Jossey-Bass.

5   *The Nature of Local Education Systems*

The assessment of educational need occupies an interface between individuals, with their desires and interests, and educational structures designed for collective purposes with characters and interests of their own. The focus of our research study was on the role of local educational organizations in assessing need. Therefore we sought explanations of the nature of the process from theories that purport to explain facets of the operation of social and political structures, drawing on social, and particularly political, science.

Educational Government

At the time of writing the public education service still reflected the arrangements laid down in the 1944 Education Act. One interpretation is that it is a national service, administered locally. Education is one of the responsibilities of the elected national Parliament and is administered on its behalf by the Department of Education and Science (for England and Wales) and the Scottish and Northern Ireland offices, all of which are led by government ministers. Other central government departments also have an important educational role. The Department of Employment, with responsibility for the MSC and careers services, is particularly relevant for 16–19-year-olds. Educational responsibilities are placed upon, and powers delegated to, local authorities (county councils, metropolitan districts, outer London boroughs and the ILEA in England; regional boards in Scotland; education areas in Northern Ireland). These are governed by elected councils (except in Northern Ireland where members of area boards are drawn from elected lower tier authorities) and education is administered on their behalf by education departments whose work is led by education committees, made up of councillors and coopted members. In their turn, local authorities place responsibilities upon, and delegate powers to, agencies and institutions. These responsibilities and powers are normally vested in the senior employee, for example in the headteacher or principal careers officer. Schools and colleges have their own representative institutions in the form of governing bodies, (school councils in Scotland), made up of council appointees and members elected or appointed by other interests, such as parents, teachers or local employers. Governing bodies have responsibility for overseeing the nature of educational provision and conduct of the institution. Although a recent study concluded that their authority had not been matched by the delegation of significant powers (Kogan *et al*, 1984), they have been seen as a means of strengthening parental influence and their role has been somewhat clarified and extended in the 1986 Education Act.

An exploration of the way in which needs are identified and assessed that followed liberal-democratic traditions of government could therefore point to the presence of elected assemblies that allow the expression of the public will. This will is manifested through designated roles linked by lines of authority that are confirmed by law. Further, the arrangement of educational responsibilities and powers recognizes the existence of national, local and community interests and provides mechanisms via Parliament, local councils and governing bodies, for these different perspectives to be expressed.

It has become fashionable to denigrate formal and traditional explanations of government as naive and limited. They fail to take account of the realities of political life such as the effect of party systems on representative government, the power of government employees, be they civil servants or teachers, to formulate and follow their own policy objectives or the ability of particular interests to dominate the political process. Nonetheless the increased emphasis given to vocationally relevant education in recent years described in Chapter 2 demonstrates how perceptions of need held by national politicians can be imposed on the remainder of the education system (Ranson, 1985). Similarly, local authorities have the necessary authority to require institutions to review their education for 16–19-year-olds and consider coordinating their provision with each other (Whitaker, 1985). The traditional hierarchy of authority, depicted in Figure 2 in Chapter 3, remains an important reality in education, not least because hitherto it has represented the chief route for the disposal of resources. Central government can affect the teaching that is provided in the local sixth form. It can do so directly, by means of the courses of study that are approved and, indirectly, through the money that is allocated to education. The local education committee can similarly determine the range of local opportunities through its policies and resources. Headteachers and principals can decide the educational emphasis and the work routines in what are still widely regarded as 'their' schools or colleges. The evidence of our research demonstrates that the positions of authority in the hierarchy remain important points in assessing what is, or is not, a need and the priority that it should carry.

Top-down hierarchical explanations of government are criticized from a number of perspectives. First, they do not allow for the considerable numbers of interests that are involved in systems of public provision. These interests depend upon each other and combine to form policy communities. Rhodes suggests that education represents an example of a highly integrated policy community (Rhodes, 1986a). In isolation no single interest would be able to provide the service. Yet each has its own aims and objectives and access to its own sources of power which provides some immunity from the formal hierarchy of authority. Local government, with its own legitimization by the electorate, is an obvious example. A similar case could be made for educational unions and associations, legitimized by their membership, and for educational institutions, legitimized by parental support. Interests can be delineated vertically in the education service — as between central and local government or between local departments and institutions, or horizontally — as between different departments in an institution and different agencies — and in terms of broader groupings that cut across organizational and government boundaries — provider, management or political interests. Educational government is thus seen as political rather than hierarchical, and prone to conflict. Because of the power possessed by these different interests and the interdependency between them, policy-making has to be pluralistic and depends upon the outcome of political bargaining. Even if those interests occupying formal positions of authority in the hierarchy succeed in imposing their will, the resultant conflict is likely to be vexed and require the expenditure of a great deal of energy, as the recent history of central and local government relationships demonstrates, and it may be dysfunctional in destroying necessary cooperation and trust (Bulpitt, 1983).

A second, related, strand of criticism is that the formal structure of authority provides no guide to the way in which policy is actually made or implemented. If issues are to be taken up in policy, Solesbury (1976) has suggested they have to, first, command attention and gain political visibility. Second, they must claim legitimacy and, third, invoke action. Youth unemployment provides an example of an issue that has: gained considerable public attention; is seen as something that government, both local and national, can help alleviate; and, has experienced a number of initiatives. But policies may be symbolic, demonstrating a concern without any meaningful commitment to action (Edelman; 1971, Ham, 1982). Neither do policies necessarily originate at the top of an organization but may well develop from the practice of those who deliver or manage services locally. The assertion that schools and colleges are better able to identify and respond to local educational needs than the more remote LEA is a powerful argument for institutional freedom. Further, it is likely that policies become modified and altered as they are applied by different parts of service systems. So, for example, the intentions of the LEA regarding the demarcation of courses between institutions may be ignored by schools or colleges that see an opportunity to increase their student numbers or extend their range of provision. This argument applies well to education, where the service providers — the teachers, lecturers, careers officers — have to respond to situations and needs that cannot necessarily be predicted in advance, and are physically and functionally far removed from the higher reaches of the hierarchy. In discussing Figure 2 in Chapter 3 it was remarked how LEAs' hierarchical authority was limited and that even without delegated financial independence or the possibility of 'opting out' of LEA control, schools and colleges retained considerable authority to shape the detail of their own provision. The fact that both LEAs and their institutions have a development role can be argued as a source of strength. It keeps education dynamic and responsive to new needs. But it is also a source of tension, for institutional and LEAs' ideas of development will not necessarily agree. Institutional freedom can become a stumbling block and a source of conflict when schools and colleges have to collaborate or develop coherent working arrangements with other agencies.

Writers in this area also stress the pluralism of government, with its multiplicity of interests. Explanations for the nature of policy outcomes are similarly sought in terms of identifying and explaining the operation of policy networks, analyzing relative power and in negotiating and bargaining behaviour (Strauss, 1978; Barrett and Fudge, 1981; Barrett and Hill, 1985; Rhodes, 1986b).

On this interpretation of government, the education service would be particularly prone to fragmentation of power because the delivery of services is in the hands of occupations that can claim to be regarded as professional. Examples would obviously include teachers and lecturers, but also LEA officers and advisers and careers officers. The characteristics of the education service match the criteria set out by Ham and Hill (1984) for the extensive employment of professionals. High expertise is required from the lower ranks of the organization, the tasks to be performed are complex, it is difficult to develop effective patterns of supervision and educationalists are required to work flexibly and to be open to change. It is an attribute of professions that their members are, given a fair degree of freedom in the way in which they work. Indeed, strong professionalism is more readily associated with collegial than with hierarchical patterns of management. Decisions rest with the professional collective as a whole and authority is applied by general consent according to expertise and the needs of the situation (Bush, 1986). Members share a common culture, which stresses the importance of the service provided to clients and this culture is influential within the organizations where professionals are employed. The shared professional ideals provide common ground between staff employed in different parts and at different levels of organization. These criteria would appear true of the British educational system. Certainly one of its characteristic features is the expectation that managers at both the local and institutional levels — headteachers, principals, local government officials — will have gained some prior experience as teachers. Professional communities, made up of the leading members, participate in policy discussions with government (Laffin, 1985). Dunleavy (1981) provides a functional explanation for professional power. With increasingly technical and specialized work to perform, governments have no choice but to allow professionals considerable discretion. The extent of professional influence goes some way towards providing an elitist rather than a pluralist explanation of government. In that it is claimed that collegial organization stimulates commitment of members and encourages change and development, it has attractions in the present inconstant educational environment.

Professional power is criticized as motivated by self-interest (Robinson, 1978; Wilding, 1982) and there have been demands in education, as in other service areas, for greater public accountability. Kogan (1986) has pointed out how collegial institutions may become absorbed in self-defined missions and unresponsive to external demands. The way in which authority to determine the nature of education has been traditionally decentralized to institutions has both enhanced the power of the professionals and made it more visible to the public.

Claims of professional omnipotence in education, as it currently operates, can be overrated. First, they do not accord with the realities of power. Teachers, the largest professional grouping in terms of numbers, have been categorized as a mediated profession (Johnson, 1972). They, and all the other educational professions, are employed by government and it is government, be it national or local, that determines their terms of entry and conditions of work. The professionals do work in hierarchical organizations and are accordingly subject to the authority of superiors. Although they have national societies and associations, they have no professional councils to provide collective representation in negotiations with government which could give them the means of regulating their own conduct. On the contrary, their interests are most obviously represented by trade unions, which speak with divided voices.

Second, other interests would appear to be just as, if not more, powerful as those of professionals. In his study of governing bodies in Sheffield, Bacon (1978) suggested that the educational establishment — the politicians and managers of the system — represented the dominant elite. Tighter controls over public expenditure with its attendant emphasis on efficiency and rationalization of provision, has worked to strengthen managerial interests in public services. The present belief in the necessity for strong management current in government and political circles has been partly attributed to past failures and profligacy when professionals were at the helm (Klein, 1983). Laffin (1986) distinguished 'public service' from 'technobureaucratic' professions. This distinction bisects local education services. The former are represented by practitioners providing teaching and guidance; the latter by senior staff in institutions and agencies, and by officers and advisers within the LEA,

concerned with management and administration. The managerial impera-
tives of the latter category may well clash with the service-oriented ethics of
the practitioners.

Both pluralist and elitist descriptions of government suggest, then, that
assessments of need are going to be made at different points across
educational systems more than might be indicated by the formal hierarchical description of authority. And because of their professional status, the
views of educationalists are likely to be particularly influential. This means
that assessments of need are unlikely to represent objective truths, but
should be regarded with caution as conditioned by the particular interests
of those by whom they are made. The emergence of assessments and the
possibility of their being translated into provision will involve political
bargaining and negotiation. This leads into a consideration of how such
bargaining may be determined. One set of explanations focuses attention
on the power of the participants. Lukes has argued that this should be
studied in three dimensions (Lukes, 1974). First, the ability of an interest to
get its own way; who wins, who loses? This, however, says nothing about
those issues which never become the subject of contention. Thus the second
dimension involves knowing which interests are able to determine the
content of bargaining. Who sets the agenda? Lukes' third dimension of
power is the ability of an interest to so determine public consciousness that
its concerns are unchallenged. Who determines what is, or what is not,
negotiable?

This line of analysis is fundamental in attempting to explain how
educational needs are assessed. It is clearly important to know which
assessments are debated, by whom and whose definitions are taken up and
effected. But this is not enough. It is also necessary to know whether some
definitions never reach the point of debate and why this is the case. And
finally, is it possible that there are views of need that are never seriously
considered because they do not fit with dominant social conceptions of
educational purpose? In the field of health it has been suggested that the
dominant values regarding the way in which society views, and reacts to,
sickness favour the interests of the medical professions (Ham, 1982). The
current uncertainties in 16–19 education suggest the absence of a single
dominant ideology. Interpretations of the purpose of education conflict as
between individual fulfilment and economic ends.

An associated approach to understanding the nature of political
bargaining comes from the application of exchange theory. This assumes
that government is achieved through the interrelationships and interaction
of different interests which develop mutual dependencies. The power of
any one interest depends upon the resources that it controls and the degree
to which other interacting interests depend upon these resources. Resources may be financial or legal, including formal authority, but they also
include less prescribable elements such as information and expertise. The
terms by which resources are exchanged are dynamic; the rules alter, and

so the power of different interests waxes and wanes. Exchange theory has been applied to explain the operation of local government (Rhodes, 1979) and the provision of education (Ranson, 1980; Archer, 1981).

According to exchange theory, then, the extent to which any interest succeeds in getting its assessment of needs accepted will depend upon the resources it controls and how these are valued by other interests. Falling rolls, it might be suggested, have caused sixth forms and colleges to look more sympathetically at assessments of need of the less academic 16-year-old. Similarly students' assessments of their own needs might carry greater weight where they were in a position to exercise choice between educational institutions, rather than having to accept what the local college offered or do without post-16 education. Their ability to exercise this choice, and use the resource represented by their attendance, could be rapidly changed if the LEA altered the rules governing subsidized transport. But assessments of need are complicated because they also represent a resource in the exchange process, and constitute a source of information or a demand for money, authority or work. This means that they will figure as important bargaining counters across educational systems. Thus assessments of need might be used by a college to argue the case for additional staffing or by an LEA to justify a rationalization of provision between its institutions. It is wise, therefore, not to take assessments of need on their face value but to consider who gains.

Education as a System

Throughout this book the various components that make up LEA provision are treated as part of a system. That is schools, colleges, LEA agencies and the LEA itself have been seen as interrelated in their work and as sharing a common environment of social, economic and political influences that conditions their activities. Systems theory applies insights drawn from biological science to explain political activity. It was developed by Easton (Easton, 1965) and suggests that, like biological systems, political systems must seek to maintain a balance with their environment. They do so through a process of converting inputs — demands and resources — into outputs — decisions and policies. The system is dynamic, for these outputs determine the outcomes — how the operation of the system is publicly perceived — which affect its relationship with the environment and determines the nature of future inputs. The boundaries of systems can be drawn to suit the purposes of analysis. If the focus is on an individual school or college, this can be treated as a system, or perhaps sub-system, in its own right. At a different level of analysis, the national provision of education may be regarded as a system or as a sub-system of government. Here the concern is with the educational services and provision encompassed by LEAs. Systems theory has been specifically applied to education by Wirt and Kirst (1975) and Howell and Brown (1983).

The approach has a number of merits. It emphasizes the importance of processes in explaining service provision. The demands made on institutions and agencies are separated from the work processes they actually adopt and the outputs they achieve. Assessments of need must obviously represent demands, although they are by no means the only demands and may not be clearly expressed. Earlier discussion in Chapter 4 also suggested that much of the activity associated with assessment of need concerned evaluating work processes and outputs to see if they were meeting identified needs.

Second, the systems approach stresses the permanent but shifting relationship that exists between different components of a system and between the system and its wider environment. Assessments of need are conditioned by economic circumstances, such as the state of the local employment market for school leavers, and by the way in which local educational systems are responding to national political views of the nature of education and how it should be provided. But social systems do not merely respond to changes in the environment. It is advantageous if they can predict change and prepare themselves for different inputs. The incentive to monitor the environment provides a rationale for undertaking assessment of need and the current uncertainties surrounding education have made the incentive stronger. The period of our study has also witnessed quite radical changes in the role of LEAs, sixth forms, colleges and careers services, and in the way in which different institutions and agencies relate one to another. This cannot help but affect how needs are assessed.

The approach does not lack its critics. One of the lines of criticism relevant to needs assessment is that systems theory ignores the realities of power. Demands may be conditioned less by the impact of outputs and their relationship with the environment and more by the interests of service providers. This relates back to the second and third dimensions of power discussed earlier, and focuses attention on 'gate-keeper' roles. Which roles in the system have the power to determine what represents, or does not represent, a need? Students' and employers' perceptions of their needs are conditioned by what they know, and educationalists appear to be prominent participants in most of the activities that are currently applied to needs assessment.

The Decision Making Process

Theories of government and systems theory provide explanations of who is involved in deciding assessments of needs and factors that are likely to condition their approach and influence. They provide insights into why decisions are made but are of less value when it comes to considering how.

Yet if assessments of need are to influence educational provision they have to be incorporated in policies and be converted into work. Two sets of theories help with explanations that characterize decision-making. First, Allinson (1971), using the Cuban missile crisis as an example, suggested the distinction between: the rational decision making model, where decisions are informed and processed by clear and consistent goals and objectives; the organizational model, where decisions are determined by organization goals and routines; and, the bureaucratic political model where decisions result from negotiation and bargaining between different interests. Hierarchical, top-down explanations of decision-making would be relevant to the first and second models, whereas in the third decisions would be better understood through pluralism and exchange theory. All three models can be applied to explaining what happens to assessments of need in education. The second, which focuses attention on work processes and routines, is particularly useful given the extent to which need is inferred through processes that serve administrative purposes. And given the wide range of interests in 16–19 education, the third model is clearly relevant.

The second approach considers decision-making along a continuum between rationality and incrementalism. Rational decision-making is characterized by the existence of clear goals and the conscious selection of a particular strategy that is calculated to be the most effective for their achievement (Burch and Wood, 1983). Decision-making is informed, purposeful and predictive. Ends are clearly defined and means selected accordingly. Incremental decision-making is characterized by an acceptance of human limitations in arriving at clear-cut goals and in knowing enough to predict whether one strategy is likely to be any better than another. It focuses upon problems. A limited examination is given to alternative courses of action that offer some hope of making things better (Braybrooke and Lindblom, 1963). The means of getting things done are all important, and must secure the agreement of the interests involved. The ends that are being served can be altered as strategies are amended.

Incremental models of decision-making are held to approximate to the real world with all its constraints. Rational models are more prescriptive and utopian. Not surprisingly, a number of writers have advocated selective approaches to decision-making that fall between these poles, countering the conservatism attributed to incrementalism and the omnipotence seemingly required by rationality. Dror, for example, seeks to combine realism and idealism by advocating the application of creative thought to policy-making and policy issues while reserving detailed examination for the more promising goals and strategies (Dror, 1964). In his mixed scanning model, Etzioni (1967) suggests that policy areas require to be broadly reviewed in order to indicate the fundamental long term issues. Once identified these will suggest those immediate problems that justify more detailed examination and those of lesser importance which can be treated incrementally.

These ideas provide metaphors for describing how policy is made and for comparing different practices. The call for greater rationality in decision-making is a consistent theme in public administration and one that has been influential in government over the last thirty years (Ham and Hill, 1984). It has extended to local authorities as part of the corporate approach to management and planning that accompanied the onset of recession and challenged professional dominance (Stewart, 1983). Latterly there are signs that it has had some effect on financial management in schools and colleges (Simkins, 1986), although the turbulent, rapidly changing and confused environment currently experienced by education hardly facilitates rational decision-making (Bush, 1986).

A rational perspective of educational decision-making would see assessments of need as fundamental. They would be routinely applied to indicate educational goals and measure their satisfaction. An incremental perspective would see assessments emerging as a reaction to problems and characterized by marginal adjustments to the status quo.

Brought together, the above explanations provide a confusing and conflicting view of educational organizations. They combine elements of hierarchy, elitism, pluralism and collegial working. Decision making is rational and incremental, or somewhere in between. This is because their government and organization is dynamic. It is particularly so at the present time with central government engaged in reshaping the educational environment. The triangle of relationships between central government, service-providing agencies and consumers is being recast. As the powers of the first and last mentioned become defined and strengthened, so service providers, such as LEAs and their institutions, exhibit change and uncertainty in their modes of operation.

The necessity to be eclectic in interpreting the nature of local education systems reflected our findings. No single explanation of government or organizational behaviour convincingly encompassed the different mechanisms that were applied to needs assessment. Instead, different ideas, offering different perspectives, proved to be useful in illuminating different aspects of the subject.

References

ALLINSON, G.T., (1971) *Essence of Decision*, Boston, MA, Little, Brown.

ARCHER, M., (1981) 'Educational politics: A model for their analysis' in BROADFOOT, P., BROCK, C. and TULASIEWICZ, W., (Eds) *Politics and Educational Change*, London, Croom Helm.

BACON, A., (1978) *Public Accountability and the Schooling System*, London, Harper and Row.

BARRETT, S. and FUDGE, C. (Eds) (1981) *Policy and Action*, London, Methuen.

BARRETT, S. and HILL, M., (1985) 'Policy, bargaining and structure in implementation theory' in GOLDSMITH, M., (Ed), *New Research in Central-Local Relations*, Aldershot, Gower.

BRAYBROOKE, D. and LINDBLOM, C.E., (1963) *A Strategy of Decision*, New York Free Press.

BULPITT, J., (1983) *Territory and Power in the United Kingdom*, Manchester, Manchester University Press.

BURCH, M. and WOOD, B., (1983) *Public Policy in Britain*, Oxford, Martin Robertson.

BUSH, T., (1986) *Theories of Educational Management*, London, Harper and Row.

DES (1986) *Education (No. 2) Act*, London, HMSO.

DROR, Y. (1964) 'Muddling through: "Science" or inertia', *Public Administration Review*, 24.

DUNLEAVY, P. (1981) *The Politics of Mass Housing in Britain*, Oxford, Clarendon Press.

EASTON, D., (1965) *A Systems Analysis of Political Life*, New York, Wiley.

EDELMAN, M., (1971) *Politics as Symbolic Action*, Wisconsin University Institute for Research on Poverty.

ETZIONI, A., (1967) Mixed-scanning: 'A "third" approach to decision-making', *Public Administration Review*, 27.

HAM, C., (1982) *Health Policy in Britain*, London, Macmillan.

HAM, C. and HILL, M., (1984) *The Policy Process in the Modern Capitalist State*, Brighton, Wheatsheaf.

HOWELL, D.A. and BROWN, R., (1983) *Educational Policy-Making: An Analysis*, London, Heinemann.

JOHNSON, T., (1972) *Professions and Power*, London, Macmillan.

KLEIN, R., (1983) *The Politics of the National Health Service*, London, Longman.

KOGAN, M., (1986) *Education Accountability*, London, Hutchinson.

KOGAN, M., *et al* (1984) *School Governing Bodies*, London, Heinemann.

LAFFIN, M., (1985) 'Professional communities and policy communities' in GOLDSMITH, M. (Ed) *New Research in Central-Local Relations*, Aldershot, Gower.

LAFFIN, M., (1986) *Professionalism and Policy: The Role of Professions in Central Local Government Relationships*, Aldershot, Gower.

LUKES, S., (1974) *Power: A Radical View*, London, Macmillan.

RANSON, S., (1980) 'Changing relations between centre and locality in education', *Local Government Studies*, 6, 6.

RANSON, S., (1985) 'Contradictions in the government of educational change', *Political Studies*, 33, 1.

RHODES, R., (1979) *Research into Central-Local Relations in Britain: A Framework for Analysis*, London, SSRC.

RHODES, R., (1986a) *The Natural World of Local Government*, London, Allen & Unwin.

RHODES, R., (1986b) 'Corporate bias in central-local relations: A case study of the Consultative Council on Local Government Finance', *Policy and Politics*, 14, 2, April.

ROBINSON, T., (1978) *In Worlds Apart*, London, Athlone.

SIMKINS, T., (1986) 'Patronage, markets and collegiality: Reflections on the allocation of finance in secondary schools', *Educational Management and Administration*, 14, 1.

SOLESBURY, W., (1976) 'The environmental agenda', *Public Administration*, 54, Winter.

STEWART, J., (1983) *Local Government: The Conditions of Choice*, London, Allen & Unwin.

STRAUSS, A., (1978) *Negotiations*, San Francisco, CA, Jossey-Bass.

WHITAKER, T., (1985) *Educational Planning: LEAs' Assessment of Educational Need for the 16–19 Age Group*, Middlesex, Brunel University.

WILDING, P., (1982) *Professional Power and Social Welfare*, London, Routledge & Kegan Paul.

WIRT, F.M., and KIRST, M., (1975) *Political and Social Foundations of Education*, Berkeley, CA, McCutchan.

Part 3

The Process of Needs Assessment

6   *A Framework for Needs Assessment*

The four preceding chapters pose problems that have to be accommodated in explaining how educational needs of the 16–19-year-olds are identified and assessed. Chapter 2 explained some of the ambivalences and conflicts that surround the context of 16–19 education. In particular, it pointed out that educational systems are not just expected to respond to needs presented by students but must also have an eye to those of employers and the MSC which acts on behalf of central government. Chapter 3 showed the complexity and variation of educational arrangements, both within authorities and between them across the country. Chapter 4 suggested that the concept of need is slippery and capable of diverse interpretations according to where and by whom it is made. Chapter 5 presented a number of different and partially conflicting explanations of the way in which the education system works and services are provided. There is yet a further difficulty. Needs assessment is about gathering and interpreting inform-ation. Leaving aside specially commissioned surveys, which are rare in this country, it is usually accommodated within the day to day work processes of educational organizations. Our research revealed the variety of activities that contribute to needs assessment, so it was necessary to categorize the different means of assessment in a way that located them in local education systems and told something about their characteristics and use. Once identified, the various mechanisms could receive more detailed scrutiny and analysis. Categorization enabled comparisons to be made and gave an understanding of educational needs assessment as currently practised. This chapter describes and illustrates the analytic framework that was devised. In this framework the various mechanisms commonly used to assess needs are classified according to:

(i)   their location in local education systems;
(ii)   their focus on individual or collective needs;
(iii)   the purpose of making an assessment;
(iv)   their form;

(v)   the type of information they generate;

(vi)   their participants;

(vii) the type of definition in terms of Bradshaw's categorization (Bradshaw, 1972).

The framework assumes two sources of educational needs; students and employers. Others might have been included, such as those of higher education institutions, but students' and employers' needs were given priority because they are potentially significant for the whole range of 16–19 education. Further, the ability of education to receive and respond to employers' needs is a current policy issue and was one of the main areas of enquiry in the research. Since it was readily apparent that students' needs were largely identified and assessed through different processes from those of employers, inclusion of the two categories significantly broadened the scope of the research. The framework could readily accommodate further sources but by so doing would inevitably be more difficult to understand and use for analysis.

The Framework

Location of Assessment

Needs assessment is carried out by institutions, such as schools and colleges, by agencies such as the careers or youth and community services, and by the LEA itself. Thus the means used for assessment can be classified according to where within local education systems they are undertaken. Because students and employers' educational needs are frequently assessed in different ways, it is useful to separate the means of assessment accordingly. Table 2 below begins our analysis by listing the various means used to assess the educational needs of *students* and of *employers* according to the *part of the education system involved* — institutions, careers services and LEAs. Some means overlap locations. Thus careers guidance given by a careers officer within a school is categorized as institutional needs assessment, insofar as it is part of a schools' careers guidance programme. Since it also forms part of the careers service's general guidance to all schools, so schools careers guidance is also attributed to careers services.

At this initial point the diversity of means is striking. Some are discrete activities; others are continuous processes. Some involve interaction between the clients and educationalists; others require the scrutiny of information. Further categorization is required to draw out the important distinctions for needs assessment, although the distinction between the location of assessments and concern with students' or employers' needs will be retained throughout to aid analysis.

TABLE 2: LOCATION OF NEEDS ASSESSMENT

	Student Needs Assessed By:	Employer Needs Assessed By:

Institutions	Recruitment process
	Pastoral care
	Student progress
	Careers guidance
	Demand
	Examination results
	Student destinations
	Course drop-out
	  rate/attendance
	Course evaluation
	Student surveys
	Knowledge of other initiatives
		Industrial liaison
		Demand
		Schools/college industrial
		  liaison committees
		Advisory committees
		Conferences/consultations
		Employers' surveys
		Career Service information
		Knowledge of other initiatives

Careers Services	Careers guidance
	Teacher opinions
	Careers meetings and
	  conventions
	Student destinations
		Employers' visits
		Schools/college industrial
		  liaison committees
		Advisory committees
		Conferences
		Employers' surveys
		Recruitment patterns

Local Education
  Authority
	Complaints about access to
	  course
	Demand
	Examination results
	Course provision
	Student destinations
	Forecasts of demand
	Population forecasts and social
	  trends
	Application for grants and
	  awards
	Monitoring of provision
	Knowledge of other initiatives
	In-service training
	Student surveys
		L.E.A./employers' committees
		Employment trends
		Personal contacts

Individual or Collective Needs

Needs assessment is concerned both with the individual student or employer and with the needs of students or employers en masse. The need for education is an individual phenomenon. Consequently many of the means for identifying and assessing educational needs are directed at individuals. Recruitment procedures, careers guidance, tutorial systems all deal with individuals. However, educational management and planning have to work in terms of larger groupings. 16–19-year-olds then become treated in terms of categories. Examples of such categories include whether they are: receiving education; in a YTS programme; employed or unemployed; attending a particular course or institution; full-time or part-time students; taking academic, vocational or pre-vocational courses; resident in a particular area. Employers' needs are likewise commonly treated in terms of industrial sectors, such as: manufacturing or service industries; engineering or construction; hairdressing or catering. Thus activities that contribute to needs assessment can be distinguished according to whether they are focused on individuals and their specific situation and requirements, or deal with the needs of some collection of 16–19-year-olds. Table 3 maintains the distinction between the location of means of assessment in the education system and whether the focus is on students' or employers' needs, but adds a further dimension by categorizing the various means of needs assessment according to whether they are used for assessing *individual* or *collective* needs.

In practice, the means of assessment cannot be categorized as discretely as Table 3 suggests. Examination results, for example, are located as a means of assessing collective needs. Yet they are also likely to be used to assess individual needs as part of the recruitment process or monitoring student progress.

As might be expected, the majority of the means used to assess individual needs are located within institutions, where educational services are delivered. LEAs, concerned with the provision of education across a territory, have to think in terms of larger groupings.

It might be thought that the means for assessing individual and collective needs would be identical. Individual assessments would be aggregated to provide collective assessments which could be broken down to provide individual assessments. Undoubtedly this does occur. Staff perceptions of the needs of individual students contribute to their views of the needs of students en masse. The review of examination results achieved by a course may draw attention to an individual case. But the conclusion from Table 3 is that individual and collective assessments are generally arrived at by different and separate means.

Purpose of Assessment

As was emphasized in the preceding chapter, needs assessment can serve a number of purposes. Our research suggested four. Needs have to be identified, considered in planning, matched with provision and the extent of their satisfaction evaluated. To clarify the purposes of needs assessments, activities were accordingly classified according to the following headings.

Discovery — learning what needs are, as might be the case from surveying the opinions of a group of employers.

TABLE 3: FOCUS OF NEEDS ASSESSMENT

		Means of Assessment	
		Individual Needs	*Collective Need*

Institutions	— Students	Recruitment process
		Pastoral care
		Student progress
		Career guidance
			Demand
			Examination results
			Student destinations
			Course drop-out
			    rate/attendance
			Course evaluation
			Student surveys
			Knowledge of other
			    initiatives

	— Employers	Industrial liaison	Demand
			Schools/college industrial
			    liaison committees
			Advisory committees
			Conferences/consultations
			Employers' surveys
			Careers Service
			    information
			Knowledge of other
			    initiatives

Careers Services	— Students	Careers guidance Teacher opinions	Careers meetings and conventions Student destinations
	— Employers	Employers' visits	Schools/college industrial liaison committees Advisory committees Conferences Employers' surveys Recruitment patterns

LEAs	— Students	Complaints about
		    access to courses
			Demand
			Examination results
			Course provision
			Student destinations
			Forecasts of demand
			Population forecasts and
			    social trends
			Applications for grants and
			    awards
			Monitoring of provision
			Knowledge of other
			    initiatives
			In-service training
			Student surveys

	— Employers	Personal contacts	LEA/Employers' committees Employment trends

Testing — finding out whether needs will be better satisfied by a proposed change, as might be the case where college staff seek the opinions of the careers service regarding a new course or call a special conference of employers to discuss a new proposal.

Diagnosis — deciding how needs can best be met from existing provision, as might be the purpose of a careers interview or a tutorial meeting with a student.

Evaluation — considering how far existing provision is, in fact, satisfying needs, as might be indicated by recruitment figures, by examination results or from surveying the opinions of students, staff and employers.

Table 4 indicates the *purpose* or *purposes* of needs assessment for the various means we have identified.

Again, purposes of assessment are not as clear cut in reality as depicted in Table 4. Information gained diagnostically, say in helping a student to make better use of his or her time in studying a particular subject, may feed into staff evaluation of current provision and perhaps be used as a test case in arguing for a change in the curriculum. Purposes of needs assessment can be associated in sequence, from discovery to evaluation, but this is exceptional. They are usually discrete. It is rare, and perhaps impossible, for any assessments of educational need to start from a blank sheet. Even if it is unstated, assessments are conditioned by what is seen as education's role, by what has been provided or accomplished in the past and by what opportunities are thought realistic for the future.

However Table 4 (overleaf) does draw attention to some important features of needs assessment. First, it appears that as applied to students the concern is predominantly diagnostic, how to make the best use of the existing provision, or evaluative, whether the provision is succeeding in meeting needs. There is less concern with discovering what needs might be or with testing whether particular needs exist. This is not the case for employers, where more of the available means of assessment enable needs to be discovered. Second, the widest range of purposes appears to be served by formal mechanisms that bring clients and educationalists together, such as school and college industrial liaison committees, or college advisory committees. Professional knowledge of developments elsewhere, of the intentions contained within new policies or of the nature of existing provision, also provides an important stimulus for considering local needs.

Form of Assessment

Direct or indirect

Means of assessment may be designed to inform about needs or they may provide information indirectly, as a by-product of serving some other function. Examples of the former would include a survey of employers, discussion with an applicant during a college recruitment interview or a careers officer's discussion with a school leaver during a careers interview. But assessments of educational need are also made from activities that serve some other purpose or are inferred from information that is not directly concerned with needs. Demand, for example, is commonly used as a proxy for needs. If demand is high, it can be assumed that a course or institution is satisfying need. If demands is low, needs may have been misjudged or have altered. Examination results provide a similar example. If these are good then here is evidence that needs are being met. Poor results may be taken as indicating a failure to meet needs. Thus, means of assessment can be distinguished according to whether they are direct or indirect.

Discrete or continuous

A further distinction can be made according to whether the activity through which needs are assessed is discrete or part of a larger, continuing process. For example, an LEA or college might undertake a student survey as a one-off investigation to learn the opinions of a sample of students. Equally a survey might form part of a tutorial relationship, initiated by the tutor at regular intervals as part of the process of monitoring students' progress.

Mandatory or discretionary

Some activities contributing to needs assessment are mandatory while others are discretionary. Educationalists rightly place considerable store upon the relationship forged between teacher and pupil as a means of identifying and assessing needs, but this depends upon how each sees his or her role and upon the quality of personal relationships that develop. Student contact is mandatory but whereas some teachers and tutors feel able to provide students with careers guidance, others refer them to the careers teacher. Similar claims are made that through their contacts with industry, college staff in vocational departments are well able to learn employers' needs. Contacts may be mandatory but their content depends upon how employers and lecturers use the opportunity. Industrial visits may be devoted to arranging work experience placements or the problems encountered by individual students, rather than considering employers' needs.

Table 5 categorizes the means used for assessment according to whether they are *direct* or *indirect* and whether they are essentially *mandatory* (M) or *discretionary* (D).

Again the categorization of the different means of assessment in Table 5 is a simplification. We have defined them as mandatory or discretionary according to common practice but are aware that there may be variations

TABLE 4: *PURPOSE OF NEEDS ASSESSMENT*

		Means of Assessment	*Purpose of Assessment*
Institutions	— Students	Recruitment process	Diagnosis
		Pastoral care	Diagnosis — Evaluation
		Student progress	Diagnosis — Evaluation
		Careers guidance	Discovery — Diagnosis
		Demand	Evaluation
		Examination results	Evaluation
		Student destinations	Evaluation
		Course drop-out rate/attendance	Evaluation
		Course evaluation	Evaluation
		Student surveys	Discovery — Testing
		Knowledge of other initiatives	Diagnosis — Testing — Diagnosis
	— Employers	Industrial liaison	Diagnosis — Testing
		Demand	Evaluation
		Schools/college industrial liaison committees	Discovery — Testing — Diagnosis — Evaluation
		Advisory committees	Discovery — Testing — Diagnosis — Evaluation
		Conferences/consultations	Discovery — Testing
		Employers' surveys	Discovery — Testing
		Careers Service information	Discovery — Testing — Evaluation
		Knowledge of other initatives	Discovery — Testing — Diagnosis
Careers Services	— Students	Careers guidance	Discovery — Diagnosis
		Teacher opinions	Diagnosis
		Careers meetings and conventions	Discovery — Diagnosis
		Student destination	Evaluation
	— Employers	Employers' visits	Discovery — Diagnosis
		School/college industrial liaison committees	Discovery — Testing — Diagnosis — Evaluation
		Advisory committees	Discovery — Testing — Diagnosis — Evaluation
		Conferences	Discovery — Testing — Diagnosis
		Employers' surveys	Discovery — Testing
		Recruitment patterns	Discovery — Evaluation
LEAs	— Students	Complaints about access to courses	Diagnosis
		Demand	Evaluation
		Examination results	Evaluation
		Course provision	Testing — Diagnosis — Evaluation

	Student destinations	Evaluation
	Forecasts of demand	Testing — Diagnosis — Evaluation
	Population forecasts and social trends	Diagnosis — Evaluation
	Applications for grants and awards	Discovery — Evaluation
	Monitoring of provision	Testing — Diagnosis — Evaluation
	Knowledge of other initiatives	Discovery — Testing — Diagnosis
	In-service training	Discovery — Testing — Diagnosis — Evaluation
	Student surveys	Discovery — Testing
— Employers	LEA/Employers committees	Discovery — Testing — Diagnosis — Evaluation
	Employment trends	Discovery — Evaluation
	Personal contacts	Discovery — Evaluation

both between and within authorities and as experienced by different types of student. And although a particular means is categorized as mandatory, the way in which it is performed and applied to needs assessment may well be discretionary. It appears to be mandatory for institutions to monitor their students' progress but the way in which they do this, and make use of teachers' judgments, test results and reports, varies greatly. Those means categorized as direct assessments do enable an explicit focus on needs but they, too, may serve other purposes. Pastoral care, for example, may be primarily concerned with maintaining discipline (Johnson *et al*, 1980). Recruitment processes may be dominated by the need to gain numbers. LEA monitoring of provision is categorized as both a direct and indirect means of assessing needs. On occasion monitoring may be explicitly concerned with needs, as when an adviser evaluates a particular course or the provision made for a certain category of student. In other situations monitoring has some other purpose and if needs are learned it is as a by-product. An officer's discussion of the progress of a college building programme with a principal may give an insight into the needs perceived by the college.

The table indicates some important characteristics of needs assessment. Many assessments are indirect, inferred from processes that serve other purposes. Thus assessments of need may be secondary or distorted. As might be expected since they work directly with students and employers, institutions and careers services make greater use of direct assessments of need. LEAs have, perforce, to rely more on indirect assessments. A considerable number of the means that serve needs assessment are discretionary, particularly those that directly assess needs. This accounts for the wide variation in the way in which needs assessment is practised between and within authorities.

TABLE 5: FORMS OF NEEDS ASSESSMENT

| | | Means of Assessment | |
		Direct Assessment	Indirect Assessment
Institution	— Students	Recruitment process D	Students' progress M (some elements)
		Pastoral care D	Demand M
		Careers guidance M (content discretionary)	
		Course evaluation D	Examination results M
		Student surveys D	Student destinations D
			Course drop-out rate/attendance M
			Knowledge of other initiatives D
	— Employers	Industrial liaison D	Demand D
		Schools/college industrial liaison committees D	Careers Service information D
		Advisory committees M	Knowledge of other initiatives D
		Conferences/consultations D	
		Employers' surveys D	
Careers Services	— Students	Careers guidance M	Teachers' opinions M
			Careers meetings and conventions D
			Student destinations M (at 16)
	— Employers	Employers' visits M	Recruitment patterns D
		Schools/college industrial liaison committees D	
		Advisory committees D	
		Conferences D	
		Employers' surveys D	
LEAs	— Students	Complaints about access to courses M	Demand M
		Monitoring of provision M	Examination results M
			Course provision M
		Student surveys D	Student destinations M (at 16)
			Forecasts of demand M
			Population forecasts and social trends D
			Applications for grants and awards M
			Monitoring of provision M
			Knowledge of other

		initiatives D
		In-service training M
— Employers	LEA/Employers' committees D	Employment trends D
	Personal contacts D	

Information Generated

Recorded or unrecorded

Is the information formally recorded or does it remain unrecorded, reliant on the participant's memory? Examples of recorded information include records of careers officers' interviews with pupils and students, tutors' records and minutes of college advisory committee meetings. Undoubtedly much other valid information is unrecorded and surfaces, possibly far removed from the activity where it originated, in discussions and in opinions and attitudes. Practices vary between and within educational establishments regarding what is required to be recorded and, of course, between individuals in the way in which they keep records. Different departments of a college, for example, may follow different procedures regarding the information that tutors are required to record. One department may require its tutors to evaluate whether students believe that their needs are being satisfied. Another may leave the content of the tutorial entirely to the tutor's discretion. And tutors, themselves, will vary in how they see their role. Some regard it as an important component of their professional work, others as an unwelcome administrative chore. Such feelings must affect the way in which they approach record-keeping.

Qualitative or quantitative

A second, and related, distinction is whether the available information is quantitative or qualitative. Quantitative information is expressed numerically, facilitating measurement and comparison. Examples of quantitative information include: data on demand for courses or institutions; attendance and drop-out rates; examination results; and, pupil or student destinations. We found that the quantitative information that was available was regarded as important for management and planning. Despite the ease with which statistics can be distorted, it was seen as possessing some objectivity and less open to special pleading and interpretation than was qualitative information. Quantitative information appeared to be transmitted widely across local education systems. This was not true of qualitative information, which appeared more restricted in its use to the organization, or part of the organization, where it originated. Qualitative information records an individual or group perspective of a situation and is likely to require oral and/or written explanation. Because of its subjectivity, it was treated with some reservation in management and planning.

Qualitative perspectives require interpretation if they are to be used comparatively, and there are problems in circulating material, particularly material that may be of a personal and sensitive nature, to settings where an interpreter may not be available. Thus the transmission of qualitative information was greatest where there were mechanisms that brought staff from the different parts of the educational system together. Examples included governing bodies, meetings between institutional representatives and the LEA, consortia, or where roles had been deliberately designed to move between different parts of the system, as was the case with inspectors and advisers.

Qualitative information was available for all the different purposes of assessment of need categorized previously in Table 4. Advisers or careers officers are likely to have views as to whether there are needs that are not being met. Employers or school staff can make a judgment whether a proposed course, such as the CPVE, is likely to meet the needs of their recruits or pupils. Teachers and lecturers will have ideas as to how existing arrangements might be altered to meet needs better and students and teachers will have some idea, although there is always the problem of premature judgment, whether existing provision does succeed in meeting needs.

Although qualitative information appears to be more haphazard than quantitative in its contribution to needs assessment, depending on circumstances, patterns of organizational decision-making and personal relationships, it is no less influential.

Concern with education

A further distinction can be made according to the aspect of education with which the information is concerned. It may be concerned with: inputs, as in the case of information on demand for courses; process, as for information on student progress collected by tutors; or, outputs, as for information on examination results, staff opinion of courses or student destinations. It is striking how most of the quantitative information that was available appeared to be concerned with inputs or outputs. There was little quantitative information available to relate assessment of needs to the educational process.

Table 6 categorizes the means used for needs assessment according to whether they provide *quantitative* or *qualitative* data. Some means of needs assessment have been placed in both the quantitative and qualitative columns since they commonly yield both types of information. Information on students' progress, for example, may be expressed quantitatively in terms of test results but teachers and tutors will also continually make qualitative judgments. Similarly employers' visits may provide careers services with quantitative information on a company's size and recruitment but careers officers will also make qualitative judgments on the educational needs of its recruits. It is equally hard to be definitive as to whether

TABLE 6: *TYPE OF INFORMATION GENERATED IN NEEDS ASSESSMENT*

		Quantitative	*Qualitative*
Institutions	— Students	Students' progress Demand Examination results Student destinations Course drop-out rate/attendance Student surveys	Recruitment procedures Pastoral care Students' progress Careers guidance Course evaluations Knowledge of other initiatives
	—Employers	Employers' surveys	Industrial liaison Demand Schools/college industrial liaison committees Advisory committees Conferences and consultations Careers Service information Knowledge of other initiatives
Careers Services	— Students	Student destinations	Careers guidance Teachers' opinions Careers meetings and conventions
	— Employers	Employers' visits Employers' surveys Recruitment patterns	Employers' visits Schools/college industrial liaison committees Advisory committees Conferences
LEAs	— Students	Demand Examination results Student destinations Course provision Forecasts of demand Population forecast and social trends Applications for grants and awards Student surveys	Complaints about access to courses Course provision Population forecasts and social trends Monitoring of provision Knowledge of other initiatives In-service training
	— Employers	Employment trends	LEA/employers' committees Personal contacts

information was or was not recorded. It was often the case that some material relating to needs assessment would be recorded, whereas other perceptions would remain in the participants' heads or be transmitted orally. This happened when a tutor and students evaluated a course, or when advisers and officers monitored provision.

Table 6 does indicate that a fair number of the means used to assess need generate quantitative information which, it was suggested above, is more readily used across local education systems than is qualitative information. But it will be noted that the quantitative information concerns a narrow range of means with similar information being aggregated or disaggregated at different parts of the system. Further, much of the quantitative information is primarily concerned with the management and control of resources. Its use for assessment of need, if it occurs, is indirect.

Participants Involved in Assessment

It is instructive to note who is involved in the different activities that contribute to assessing need. An obvious distinction can be made between service providers and clients but both can usefully be delineated further. Service providers can be categorized according to the organization to which they belong — careers officers, college lecturers, LEA advisers — and by their chief role within the organization — manager, provider or politician. College principals do not participate in the same range of needs assessment activities as do lecturers or councillors serving on the education committee.

Clients

Pupils/students are clearly the clients of education as, perhaps, are their parents. Until the age of 16 parents are regarded as proxies for their children's interests and have legal responsibilities to ensure that they receive education. Once the period of compulsory schooling is past, the situation is less clear cut. Full-time students require parental support and will probably do better if their parents know what is intended and agree that it meets the needs of their offspring. Our research has shown that many schools and colleges go to considerable lengths to involve parents of full-time students, both at the time of initial recruitment and in monitoring students' progress throughout their courses. But these factors do not apply with the same force to students on part-time courses and there is, in any case, some feeling that by the age of 16 students should be beginning to take responsibility for their own destinations.

16–19 education is also intended to meet the needs of employers. Colleges of FE have a tradition of recognizing employers as clients and have developed a number of mechanisms for maintaining contacts. The requirement represents more of an innovation for schools, but is one that, as mentioned in Chapter 3, is receiving emphasis form central government.

Central government has also created a third important client for education — the MSC. Despite reservations about the precise nature of its role, it must now be accepted as a major participant in education. As the MSC has gained experience and as its organizational arrangements have become settled, so it has become more assertive in its own assessments of what young people need from education.

Interaction between participants

It is not sufficient merely to know who is participating in assessments of need; it is also important to know if there is any interaction. Given the different interests involved in the provision of education, are there opportunities for different assessments to be tested against each other? Can a student assert his, or her, own view of needs against the view of his teachers? Can staff within a college department discuss their assessments of the value of their courses or what they might be providing with the college principal and other senior managers? Can staff from an institution debate the future of its provision with LEA officers in the light of Authority thinking? As Hegner (1980) states, 'interaction processes not only induce redefinitions of administratively predefined interests or demands, they also may affect the expectations and felt needs that clients bring to the situation'.

Interaction can be encouraged by appropriate organizational design but it is not completely amenable to legislation. Interaction is also dependent upon individuals and their knowledge and abilities, the power they can exert, their preferred styles of working and relating to others, and upon their willingness to express their personalities and respect the personalities of others.

Table 7 indicates the main participants in the various means of needs assessment according to their location in local education systems and concern with students' or employers' needs. It distinguishes between the *clients* for post-16 education and the *providers*. The latter are distinguished by role. (The category 'senior institutional managers' includes principals, headteachers, deputies, senior masters and mistresses and heads of school.) The table generalizes the pattern of participation in needs assessment found in the research and cannot show its degree. However, it does suggest the heavy involvement of service providers, particularly those in management roles. It also suggests some differentiation. Junior or specialist staff are involved in direct assessments of need that require interaction with clients, whereas senior staff are involved in indirect assessments that require the interpretation and evaluation of information. Overall, assessment of educational need appears to be a professional activity with little political involvement, although political assessments may be made in other settings that make use of different mechanisms.

Definitions of Need

It is useful to apply the categorization made by Bradshaw (1972) that was discussed in Chapter 4 to distinguish the nature of the various definitions of need. Bradshaw suggested the use of four separate definitions of need:

(i)   normative need, defined by experts on the basis of their

TABLE 7: PARTICIPANTS IN NEEDS ASSESSMENT

		Means of Assessment	Clients	Providers
Institutions	— Students	Recruitment process	Students, parents	Heads of Dept., course leaders, teachers
		Pastoral care	Students, parents	Tutors, counsellors, teachers
		Student progress	Students, parents	Teachers, tutors
		Careers guidance	Students, parents	Teachers, tutors, careers teachers, careers officers
		Demand		Heads of Dept., course leaders, senior leaders, senior institutional managers, governors
		Examination results		Heads of Dept., course leaders, senior institutional managers, governors
		Student destinations		Heads of Dept., Course leaders, senior institutional managers, careers teachers, careers officers, governors
		Course drop-out rate/attendance		Heads of Dept., course leaders
		Course evaluation	Students	Tutors, teachers, course leaders, Heads of Dept.
		Student surveys	Students	Heads of Dept., course leaders, senior institutional managers
		Knowledge of other initiatives		Teachers, institutional managers, advisers, HMIs
— Employers		Industrial liaison	Employers	Teachers, liaison officers
		Demand	Employers	Heads of Dept., course leaders, senior institutional managers
		Schools/college industrial liaison committees		Senior institutional managers, local careers office managers, LEA officers

	Means of Assessment	Clients	Providers
	Advisory committees	Employers, feeder schools	Senior institutional managers, Heads of Dept., careers officers, LEA officers, governors
	Conferences/consultations	Employers	Senior institutional managers, Heads of Dept., course leaders
	Employers' surveys	Employers	Liaison officers, Heads of Dept., senior institutional managers
	Careers Service information		Careers officers, careers teachers, Heads of Dept., senior institutional managers
	Knowledge of other initiatives		Teachers, institutional managers, advisers
Careers Services — Students	Careers guidance	Students, parents	Careers officers, teachers
	Teacher opinions		Careers officers, careers teachers, teachers, tutors
	Careers meetings and conventions	Students, parents	Careers officers, careers teachers, Heads of Dept., course leaders, senior institutional managers
	Student destinations		Careers officers, local careers office managers, careers teachers, tutors
— Employers	Employers' visits	Employers	Careers officers
	Schools/college industrial liaison committees	Employers	Local careers office managers, senior institutional managers, LEA officers
	Advisory committees	Employers	Careers officers, local careers office managers, senior institutional managers, Heads of Dept., LEA officers, governors

TABLE 7: CONTINUED

	Means of Assessment	Clients	Providers
	Conferences	Employers, students	Careers officers, local careers office managers, senior careers service managers
	Employers' surveys	Employers	Careers officers, local careers office managers, senior careers service managers
	Recruitment patterns	Employers	Careers officers, local careers office managers, senior careers service managers.
LEAs — Students	Complaints about access to courses	Students, parents	LEA officers, counsellors
	Demand		LEA officers and advisers
	Examination results		LEA officers and advisers
	Course provision		LEA officers and advisers, senior institutional managers
	Student destinations		LEA officers and advisers, senior careers service managers
	Forecasts of demand		LEA officers and advisers, senior institutional managers, councillors
	Population forecasts and social trends		LEA officers and advisers, planners
	Applications for grants and awards	Students, parents	LEA officers
	Monitoring of provision		LEA officers and advisers, senior institutional managers, Heads of Dept., course leaders.

Means of Assessment	Clients	Providers
Knowledge of other initiatives	Students	LEA officers and advisers, HMIs
In-service training		LEA advisers, teachers
Student surveys		LEA officers
— Employers		
LEA/Employers' committees	Employers	LEA officers, senior officers from other depts., councillors
Employment trends	Employers	LEA officers, senior careers service managers, MSC officers
Personal contacts		LEA officers and advisers, councillors

TABLE 8: *DEFINITIONS OF NEED*

		Means of Assessment	*Definitions of Need*
Institutions	— Students	Recruitment process	Expressed, felt,
		Pastoral care	normative
		Student progress	Felt, normative
		Careers guidance	Normative
		Demand	Felt, normative
		Examination results	Expressed
		Student destinations	Comparative
		Course drop-out rate/	Expressed
		attendance	Expressed
		Course evaluation	
		Student surveys	Felt
		Knowledge of other	Felt
		initiatives	Normative, comparative
	— Employers	Industrial liaison	Felt, normative
		Demand	Expressed
		Schools/college industrial	Felt, normative
		liaison committees	
		Advisory committees	Felt, normative
		Conferences/consultations	Felt
		Employers' surveys	Felt
		Careers Service	Normative, comparative
		information	
		Knowledge of other	Normative, comparative
		initiatives	
Careers Services	— Students	Careers guidance	Felt, normative
		Teacher opinions	Normative
		Careers meetings and	Felt, normative
		conventions	
		Student destinations	Expressed
	— Employers	Employers' visits	Felt
		Schools/college industrial	Felt, normative
		liaison committees	
		Advisory committees	Felt, normative
		Conferences	Felt
		Employers' surveys	Felt
		Recruitment patterns	Expressed
LEAs	— Students	Complaints about access	Felt, expressed,
		to courses	normative
		Demand	Expressed, comparative
		Examination results	Comparative
		Course provision	Normative, comparative
		Student destinations	Expressed
		Forecasts of demand	Expressed, normative,
			comparative

	Population forecasts and social trends	Comparative
	Applications for grants and awards	Expressed
	Monitoring of provision	Normative, comparative
	Knowledge of other initiatives	Normative, comparative
	In-service training	Normative
	Student surveys	Felt
— Employers	LEA Employers' committees	Felt, normative
	Employment trends	Expressed, comparative
	Personal contacts	Felt

            specialist knowledge, for example an assessment of a student's needs made by a teacher;

(ii)   felt need, defined by clients on the basis of what they believe they want, for example a survey of employers' opinions;

(iii)   expressed need, defined by observing what services clients actually use, for example studying the demand for courses or recruitment patterns;

(iv)   comparative need, defined by comparing the characteristics of those who receive a service with those who do not.

All four of *Bradshaw's categories* can be applied to the means by which local education systems assess need and this is done in Table 8.

In practice the distinction between Bradshaw's definitions becomes blurred. It is difficult to say with certainty, for example, how far a careers interview between a pupil and a careers officer contributes towards normative or felt need. The answer depends upon the nature of the interaction between the two participants in the interview. Recruitment to an institution involves a pupil in presenting expressed needs through the act of application. If an interview is provided this may enable the pupil to present his, or her, felt needs and the member of staff to make a normative definition of the pupils' needs. Further, one definition of need may be subsequently interpreted by the use of another definition. Demand represents a statement of expressed need but its application in management and planning is likely to be modified by normative interpretations from educationalists explaining why demand exhibits particular characteristics. Nonetheless, Bradshaw's definitions are valuable in drawing attention to the different status of definitions of need and alert us to the different interests and commitments they contain. Table 8 suggests that there are potentially opportunities for clients to express their own opinions of their needs, particularly in those parts of education systems concerned with service delivery. It also indicates the importance of normative definitions, the views and standards of the educationalists, throughout local systems.

This framework enables the identification of the many disparate activities that currently constitute needs assessment. It locates them within educational systems and illustrates some of their significant characteristics. In the following three chapters we examine their application in three key areas — providing information, contributing to planning and the nature of relationships between different parts of local educational systems. Then, in Chapter 10, we draw the analysis together to summarize the current practice of needs assessment in education. But throughout, our examination of the process of needs assessment is informed by the material presented earlier: by an understanding of the changing context of post-16 education, discussed in Part 1, and by the application of ideas regarding the nature of needs and the operation of education, that were covered in Part 2.

References

BRADSHAW, J., (1972) 'The concept of social need', *New Society*, 30 March.

HEGNER, F., (1980) 'Can microinteraction work as a social mechanism to bridge the gap between service organizations and the public served?' in GRUNOW, D. and HEGNER, F., (Eds) *Welfare or Bureaucracy: Problems of Matching Social Services to Clients' Needs — Research on Social Delivery*, Vol. II, Oelgeschlager.

JOHNSON, D. *et al*, (1980) *Secondary Schools and the Welfare Network*, London, Allen & Unwin.

7   *Information About Needs and its Uses*

The supply and analysis of appropriate information is fundamental to needs assessment. It is noticeable how the collection and analysis of information occupies a central position in the American literature on needs assessment strategies (Witkin, 1984; Stufflebeam *et al*, 1985) discussed in Chapter 4. Indeed, in any rational model of decision-making, needs assessment is impossible without information. This is, first, because informing is part and parcel of the act of assessment. Any meaningful assessment of individual requirements must be based upon some knowledge of aspirations, requirements, achievements and of the available courses of action. Assessments of collective need likewise require knowledge of the characteristics displayed by larger groupings and of the provision available to them. This is particularly the case for education where provision is designed around what pupils and students have achieved in the past and what they are hoping to achieve in the future. Educational provision is complex. Needs assessment involves the collection, transmission and exchange of information by, and between, individuals, institutions and agencies. If local educational provision is regarded as a system, 'information inputs are signals that enter the system and indicate to the components how and when they are to interact' (Silver, 1983).

This chapter, then, begins with a discussion of the information about needs that is available within local educational systems. It examines the characteristics of the information and the way in which it is used in schools and colleges, careers services and LEAs. The chapter concludes by drawing attention to significant issues regarding the way that information for needs assessment is obtained and applied.

Information on Needs

Institutions

The teacher/student relationship

Staff in the schools and colleges claimed to be well informed about the needs of those students who were receiving education. This information was gained directly through teaching, pastoral care and careers guidance. It was qualitative in character, much of it went unrecorded and it contributed informally to staff assessments of students' individual needs and to their views of the adequacy of educational provision. For full-time students the information gained by staff through relationships with students was supplemented by records passed on from former schools or by details recorded during the recruitment process. However neither of these sources of information necessarily told much about needs and they were not regularly drawn upon by teachers and tutors.

Students' progress

Teachers' views of students' needs were also based upon evaluations of their progress. These included their performance in class, examination and test results, work placement reports, behaviour and attitudes, and their attendance and destinations on leaving. Some of these sources of information were recorded; for example, examination and test results, attendance and work placement reports. Recorded information provided a focus of attention, and indicated departures from the norm. Some items, such as examination results, attendance figures and student destinations, could be expressed quantitatively and aggregated to provide information related to groups of students. But not all evaluations of student progress were formally recorded. Many were qualitative. Their collection and transmission depended upon the personalities and expectations of the staff. What represented poor behaviour for one teacher was creative working for another.

Information relating to students' progress was concerned with existing students; 16–19-year-olds who had already expressed their needs in choosing courses. Generally it contributed to both individual and collective assessments of needs in a haphazard fashion. It was applied if there was a problem, such as a student performing badly or questioning whether he, or she, was doing the right thing. Staff experience of students' progress might or might not contribute to course planning. The production and use of information concerned with students' progress could be fostered through the work processes laid down by senior staff. Examples of such processes encountered in the case studies were of :

    (i)   attendance being regularly monitored by heads of sixth form or

       course leaders and being used as a vehicle for evaluating
       students' satisfaction with, and needs from, their education;

(ii)   staff concerned with a course being formally required to evalu-
       ate its success in meeting students' needs in terms of examin-
       ation results and destinations achieved;

(iii)   at the conclusion of a course, tutors' undertaking a formal
       evaluation of students' satisfaction and the extent to which it had
       satisfied their needs;

(iv)   tutors' undertaking a formal evaluation of students' satisfaction
       with their course and the extent to which it was satisfying their
       needs, at regular stages as the course proceeded. The results
       were used to aid the process of tutorial guidance and support.

Demand

Demand was treated as the chief indicator of whether or not institutions
were meeting collective needs through their provision. It was taken very
seriously by all institutions, and was recorded for constituent courses as
well as for schools or colleges as a whole. Using demand as an indicator of
needs meant assuming that students arrived at their own assessments of
need. It provided a quantitative representation of expressed needs, indicating the popularity of existing provision. The verdict might be conditioned by
external factors, such as the nature of the local employment market, and
would certainly reflect the range of educational opportunities that were
locally available. Demand was also used to make inferences of students' felt
needs. Here it was a negative indicator, capable of suggesting that
institutions might not be meeting felt needs but not of indicating their
nature. If demand was low and external influences could be discounted,
some thought had to be given to providing courses that were more popular.
If demand was high it could be assumed that institutions were meeting
needs, although this was not automatically the case. Where new courses
were being developed it was necessary to attempt to establish that they
would succeed in attracting demand.

Professional knowledge

Institutional provision was not shaped solely by information gained on
students' expressed needs. Institutional staff saw that they had to respond
to educational and political definitions of need. The majority of these were
imposed upon them in the form of national examination courses. These
reflected central government views on the needs that education should be
meeting, together with the assessments of examination boards on what was
likely to prove viable. The rationale for these courses included information
on the needs that they were intended to meet, although this was in general
rather than local or individual terms. The introduction of the CPVE and

GCSE provide current examples. Headteachers, principals and heads of department had to look to government information, to professional debate, to the educational press, to members of HMI and LEA advisers and to in-service training for information on the needs that would be met by new policies. Senior staff in institutions saw it as a general part of their role to gather information about different ways of meeting needs and consider if these could be applied to their own school or college. Again this was haphazard. It might result from professional contacts, or be directed by a particular interest or awareness of a particular problem. It might be fostered by making a particular appointment, such as a member of staff responsible for courses for those with special needs or for pre-vocational courses.

Here, then, the assessment of needs is based primarily on normative information. Provision is determined by what educationalists and/or politicians think is needed.

Links with employers

The employers involved in our case studies expressed themselves as satisfied with the extent of their contacts with educational institutions. For their part, college staff, particularly those concerned with vocational courses, claimed to be well informed of employers' educational needs in general terms. In part this referred to those employers who made use of existing provision or were prepared to give time to working with education. Much of the available information was gained through teaching, particularly through contacts with employers in arranging and monitoring students' work placements. But staff concerned with vocational teaching commonly had prior experience of industrial employment and it was claimed that this gave them a wider understanding of industry's needs. More generally staff formed judgments of industry's needs on the basis of their own experience as educationalists or from professional literature and debate. All this information contributed haphazardly and ad hoc to staff perceptions of need and their evaluation of current provision.

However, colleges, and on a lesser scale schools, exhibited two approaches to gaining information on employers' felt needs that were not widely applied to students or potential students.

First there were a number of formal mechanisms that brought employers and senior staff together in a context where they could consider needs. These mechanisms, many of which are longstanding, have, as discussed in Chapter 3, been recently encouraged by central government as part of its policy to make education more related to industry. They provided a forum which enabled the headteachers, principals and heads of department concerned with institutional management and planning to learn how employers valued their provision. Further, they could learn if employers had needs that were not being met and whether new developments would be attractive. Examples include college advisory committees, school/industry liaison committees and Science and Technology Regional Organizations (SATROs). Perceptions of the value of these bodies varied and informing about needs was only one of their purposes. It might take second place to marketing school or college provision, to making employers familiar with education or to arranging industrial support in terms of work placement or assistance for teaching projects. In his study of what practices might be used by a college that is responsive to the needs of industry, Theodossin (1986) was sceptical of the ability of these formal mechanisms to identify needs. He concluded that whatever other purposes they serve, advisory committees do not and cannot work as a market research tool. Yet we concluded that these mechanisms did have a strength in presenting information on employers' needs directly to those with the authority and power to influence the nature of educational provision. It was clear, however, that the latter enjoyed considerable discretion in deciding whether, and how, to use what they heard.

Second, institutions appeared to be willing to invest time and effort in learning how employers perceived their own needs. Unlike the case of students, it was not held that provision was necessarily dictated by what was currently available to by what employers were already using. Thus institutions, particularly colleges, created liaison roles, part of whose function was to learn employers' needs. Theodossin found that specific contacts for specific purposes were seen as the most useful way of identifying employers' needs. Colleges also appeared willing to expend resources on surveying employers' needs by questionnaires or arranging conferences that enabled staff to hear what employers felt they needed or to gauge their reaction to possible changes in provision.

Supply of information

Since students and employers were felt to decide whether or not to make use of educational provision on the basis of their own assessment of their needs, it was necessary for institutions to provide them with some assistance. At a minimum this meant telling them what was available. Following the 1981 Education Act, schools are required to provide written information about their provision and booklets setting out the various options for post-16 education are provided and distributed by LEAs and/or their careers services. At the maximum it meant helping them to decide whether what was available would meet their needs. Practice appeared to vary considerably between different schools and colleges, reflecting such factors as the extent to which senior managers were publicity conscious, the amount of local competition between institutions, whether or not 16–19 education involved a change of institution and the degree to which staff were prepared to act as counsellors. Institutions were also dependent on the arrangements for careers guidance that were adopted in pre-16 schools and on the catchment areas for institutions defined by LEAs. Schools that took pupils through from 11–19 provided written details of their sixth form provision. This would be supplemented by information provided in the course of the careers education programme and during subject teaching. Subject departments generally had a keen eye to attract suitable candidates and maintain their sixth form work. Schools with a sixth form were understandably protective of its interests.

Arrangements appeared to encourage choice where pre-16 schools were not themselves seeking a sixth form and where there were a number of institutions seeking a 16–19 intake (CPRS, 1980). This meant that the school was not afraid of its potential sixth formers being 'poached' and sixth form colleges or FE colleges had an incentive to make contact with the school and display their wares. Information was also made available where arrangements for the majority of 16–19-year-olds meant transferring to one local tertiary or sixth form college. The certainty of the arrangements and their general application meant that it was worth staff in the school and college setting up procedures for providing information. An example of the former situation was provided by an 11–16 school whose leavers were able to attend three tertiary or FE colleges in the neighbourhood. Each year each college was allocated a separate fifth year parents' evening to describe their provision. An example of the latter situation was provided by a tertiary college which provided the main source of 16–19 education for all the schools in its locality. The provision of information followed an annual pattern, as shown in Table 9 below.

Schools and colleges did not restrict their information on provision to the final year of compulsory schooling, since choices were likely to be conditioned by courses selected earlier. There were examples of colleges participating in third and fourth year school parents' evenings and in school career programmes. However, here colleges were more dependent upon careers teachers and careers officers being aware of their provision and providing information to pupils. The fairness, or lack of it, in providing information on available choices was a common theme.

We found that schools and colleges were giving greater attention to getting information to potential students. This expressed itself in efforts to keep headteachers and careers teachers aware of what was provided and of new developments. In some cases this was structured through annual meetings; in rather more it depended upon personal contacts. It appeared a common practice for colleges to make particular members of staff responsible for liaison with schools. This could be done by nominating one member of staff to associate with one pre-16 school or by making one or two members of staff responsible for liaison with all. Schools, too, nominated members of staff to liaise with colleges, although this was less common. Liaison was more frequently seen as an implicit part of the role of the fifth year tutor or of the careers teacher. The existence of liaison officers

*TABLE 9: RECRUITMENT PROCESS FOR SCHOOL LEAVERS
BY A TERTIARY COLLEGE*

October	— College holds three open evenings for parents of fifth year pupils to describe provision.
October/November	— Schools liaison officer visits local schools to describe provision to fifth years.
November/December	— College departments visit the schools to describe their provision to fifth year pupils at an afternoon meeting, and to fifth year pupils and parents at an evening meeting.
November onwards	— College departments hold school nights or open days which pupils and parents can attend.
February	— College sample week. Prospective applicants can attend the college to experience the facilities and experience the courses in which they are interested.
March onwards	— Applications are processed by the college. If career intentions are given these are vetted by college careers staff to ensure that proposed courses are appropriate. Applicants are interviewed by college staff. Parents are encouraged to attend these interviews which are seen as important in clarifying needs.
August	— Applicants offered places attend the college with their results. A further interview is provided if applicants wish, or have been forced, to change their plans.
September	— College opens with an induction week.

provided a point of contact for the exchange of information.

But colleges, in particular, did not solely rely on links with schools for transmitting information. This would not attract students who were in employment or unemployed, neither would it attract employers. Here again careers officer were seen to have an important role in making employers and young people aware of the available provision. Colleges also relied upon their own efforts in industrial liaison and in publicizing their provision by prospectuses, through newspaper advertisements, through provision of information in public places and to community organizations, and through the creation of information that was directed at the needs of a particular clientèle, such as an ethnic group or the unemployed. The attention and importance attached to publicity varied considerably between institutions. It reflected the degree to which college managers perceived that their traditional clientèle was uncertain and the priority they attached to marketing provision.

Providing information did not necessarily mean that attention was given to assessing needs, but there was an association. The activities involved in publicizing provision brought staff from schools and colleges into contact with potential students and their parents. This made the staff aware of needs. Further, staff felt that they were able to give more attention to individual needs if demand was high and they were not constrained by having to recruit sufficient numbers to keep courses running.

Characteristics of information used by institutions

The most important sources of information appeared to be demand and the knowledge or beliefs of senior managers: headteachers, principals, deputies, heads of department, heads of year or course leaders. But the way in which institutions used information for needs assessment varied considerably. This was true both of the information used, and of the way in which it was used. This said, there were three common characteristics.

First, the available information was diffused across institutions. Much was held by individual departments or course teams; more was lodged in the minds of individual staff members. Particular procedures, such as constructing a report on a student or determining the next year's courses, brought together different sources of information, although the extent of their application still depended upon staff judgment and participation. In the larger institutions it was difficult for those responsible for total institutional planning to gain a comprehensive view of the needs of existing students, let alone those of potential clients. Processes that yielded information on needs, such as pastoral care, recruitment, careers guidance and liaison with employers, were undertaken differently within, as well as between, institutions. We noted that a few institutions were attempting to standardize these processes; for example, developing a central record of all contacts with employers, ensuring that the tutorial process included particular activities or that departments followed a common recruitment process. This would help provide a common information base. However, our study predated the joint planning of non-advanced FE by LEAs and the MSC. It was suggested that the requirements of this process would lead LEAs to develop standardized information processes in their institutions. The MSC, too, has recently funded experimental institutional projects concerned with generating key management information on students in non-advanced FE which could be recommended nationally.

Second, most of the available information was qualitative, based upon individual observations and interpretations. It was thus open to argument. Assessments of need required explanation by those who made them. Many were circumstantial, triggered by a teacher's perception of a problem and not necessarily applied in settings concerned with evaluating or planning provision. The quantitative information that was available avoided this relativity. So, too, did information that institutions were obliged to accept because it was connected with provision imposed upon them by central government or LEA policies.

Finally, there was little information available, especially with respect to students, that focused explicitly on needs. Needs were generally inferred from information that was collected for other purposes, such as monitoring students' progress, marketing provision or recording demand. Undoubtedly inferences on need *could* be drawn from a student's attendance, from reactions of parents at a school open evening or from the numbers applying for a course but, again, they depended upon *how* the information was interpreted.

Careers Services

Information on felt needs

Careers services were information brokers. First, they gained information on the felt needs of individual pupils and students. In the careers services studied all 16-year-olds provided information on their aspirations and interests as part of the careers guidance process. Some careers services, however, operated selective guidance processes at 16 concentrating on those who appeared in need of assistance. As a result their knowledge of school leavers' felt needs was partial. This was the case generally for the post-16-year-olds, where information could only be obtained for those who made use of the service. Although information on aspirations had limited predictive value it indicated priorities for guidance and contributed to its subsequent context. Careers services appeared to make increasing use of computer based programmes to record aspirations and help pupils and students with their formulation. Examples included the Job Ideas and Information Generator — Computer Assisted Learning (JIIG CAL) and the Careers Advisory Service Computer Aid (CASCAID).

Careers services were able to gain information on the felt needs of employers, both in terms of filling specific vacancies and their recruitment requirements in general. This information was obtained by careers officers systematically visiting employers. Following a visit basic information about the company was recorded on the employers' register while a fuller and more impressionistic report of the visit was made available for reference. Again some careers services had computerized their employers' register, which broadened its coverage and increased the scope for matching pupils'/students' and employers' needs. Information gained from direct contacts was on occasion supplemented by surveys and conferences. Contacts with employers also gave careers officers insights into what employers wanted from education, although this information was not generally recorded.

Careers services also had to be aware of the requirements and provision of educational institutions. These were known through careers officers working in schools and colleges, by maintaining general contact with institutions and collecting brochures and prospectuses.

Information for career choice

These various perceptions of felt needs and available provision were brought together in the guidance process. Here the careers officer would help pupils or students to assess their needs in the light of the school or college assessment of their capabilities and the officer's knowledge of the available opportunities. The careers officer's advice could thus represent a mix of normative definition of needs, the officer's assessment of what should be done, and the clarification of the client's felt needs. This was recorded for each individual interviewed and a copy provided to the pupil or student and his, or her, tutors. It would therefore be available as an aid to any subsequent guidance, although it was a subject for complaint that individual files did not always follow students if they moved to a different authority or even to a different careers district. Some careers services computerized individual records. It was claimed that this aided the process of matching job seekers with available vacancies, and enabled particular features of the labour market to be analyzed, such as the effects of location or ethnic origin.

Following the interview, careers officers might supply pupils or students with information relating to careers or educational courses. They also supplied such information on other occasions, participating in school careers programmes or attending parents' evenings. The ability of officers to provide an information service partly reflected the available support from their central services. A centralized information service could circulate local offices with details of vacancies and changes in entry requirements. This helped officers keep up to date. It was particularly useful in the summer for advising pupils or students who had been forced to make a quick change of plan because of poor examination results.

Careers services also produced general information to guide pupils and students in the mechanics of careers choice, explaining the different options available and the process of careers guidance. This was distributed to fourth or fifth year pupils at school.

Information to employers

Although careers officers did not feel that employers were their principal clients, they were increasingly being called upon to provide employers with information. For example, to inform about the abilities and aptitudes of young people, the requirements of the YTS and developments within education.

Information to education

Although careers services acted as information brokers in assessing individual need, their contribution to assessments of collective educational need appeared more limited. If their knowledge of pupils' and students' felt needs contributed to educational planning, it was largely informal and on a personal basis. Information on felt needs was not aggregated and analyzed, although we encountered examples of careers officers undertaking research in this area. Careers officers did not generally participate in school or college planning and evaluative mechanisms. However, there were signs that institutions were more ready to seek advice from careers officers on the felt needs of employers. This was particularly the case when officers participated in institutional mechanisms that brought educationalists and employers together, such as advisory or industrial liaison committees.

Careers service knowledge of felt needs did contribute to LEA planning. This, too, was largely on a personal basis: through senior careers officers serving on award panels, taking part in working parties, participating in liaison arrangements with institutions or being consulted by officers or advisers. The extent to which the careers service was used in this way varied between authorities and appeared to reflect the local standing of the service and its senior officers. It also reflected the way that careers services were still seen by other parts of local education systems as 'employment services'. Their participation was described as more likely if the issue involved employment rather than being defined as purely educational.

Careers services had a clearer role in providing information on expressed needs; the choices made by pupils and students and the recruitment patterns of employers. They commonly recorded the destinations of 16-year-old school leavers, analyzing the information according to whether they remained in education, gained employment, joined a YTS programme, were unemployed or had moved away. This analysis was prepared by local offices. It was broken down to show the pattern for each school and collated to show the figures for the authority as a whole. Some careers services undertook a similar exercise for 17 and 18-year-old leavers, although this was not universal practice and the information was less likely to be complete. But, as is discussed in the following chapter, information on destinations was felt to be too general to be much help in planning.

Information on destinations was, however, seen as valuable for planning YTS programmes. All unemployed 16-year-olds were eligible for a YTS place and the MSC needed some estimate of numbers to plan their provision. Given that available opportunities remained similar, the pattern of the previous year's destinations could be used as an indication of likely demand and the careers service could update the figures for MSC as they learned the likely choices of school leavers through their guidance programme.

Careers services commonly provided LEAs with information on the pattern of recruitment of young people into employment. This was analyzed by occupational categories and provided evidence as to which areas of industry were expanding or contracting. It therefore carried implications for educational provision which might be taken up by officers and advisers. Careers services also undertook special studies of recruitment and likely future recruitment patterns for particular industrial sectors. Some careers services were undertaking exercises to compare individual job placements with initial aspirations and intentions as agreed with careers officers after guidance. As well as being supplied to the LEA, information on recruitment patterns would be circulated within careers services and might be distributed to schools and colleges. It was seen as valuable to the former in improving guidance; giving careers officers an indication as to which areas of employment were most promising for career choice. Careers officers passed on their assessments of the local job market to MSC officers to guide the provision of YTS programmes.

Characteristics of information used by careers services

Giving careers guidance to individuals required careers services to obtain and integrate a number of different perceptions of need: pupils' and students' views of their own needs; teachers' views of their pupils' and students' needs; and, employers' views of their own needs. In addition they had to be aware of the needs met by educational institutions. Careers services seemed able to obtain this information and to obtain it in an objective form that did not totally rely upon a careers officer's interpretation. This is partly a result of the extent to which LEAs have made use of developments in information technology. Careers services had been using computers to assist in information collection for a number of years. Computerization improved their capacity to use the information and match-up different perceptions of need, although the application of information technology reflected local priorities and characteristics and had gone further in some services than others (Ballantine, 1980). The advent of YTS had meant that local priorities required integrating to provide a common perspective. In 1983/84 the Department of Employment initiated a scheme to provide half the cost of computerizing the recording of clients' characteristics and available opportunities. Two-thirds of the LEAs in England took advantage of the scheme and the Department of Employment subsequently extended its scope.

Yet it was apparent that the information applied to help individuals assess their needs was not applied to the same extent in making collective assessments of needs that could aid educational planning. Here the careers service's main contribution was to supply a quantitative record of the outcome of their work in the form of destinations and recruitment patterns. Educational needs could be inferred from demand but the process was circular in that the choices individuals had made were limited by the provision made available. Information on destinations and recruitment could not show whether these represented the choices that individual pupils or employers wished, or were advised, to make. Careers services had some of this information but, in our judgment, it was neglected. Its application was haphazard, depending upon personal relationships between careers officers and teachers, or between senior careers officers and LEA officers and advisers.

The absence of this input may be attributed to the way in which the service was viewed as concerned with employment rather than education. While there were signs that schools and colleges saw that the careers service could supply information that would enable them to become more attractive to employers, there was little recognition that the careers service could do the same thing with reference to pupils and students. Educationalists believed that they had better opportunities to learn the needs of their pupils and students than could careers officers through their brief and intermittent contacts. Institutions also have a strong self-interest in controlling the information relating to pupils' and students' needs because of its affect on future provision and resources. Although careers services are not involved in institutional promotion, lack of bias or the application of wide perceptions in advice may appear as a lack of support from the institution's viewpoint. So the full potential of the career service's role as an information broker between students, employers and institutions was not realized.

LEAs

General planning data

Some of LEAs' information comes from their own sources or makes use of data collected by other local authority departments. Our national survey found that most LEAs made use of population forecasts of the numbers of 16–19-year-olds, perhaps projecting separately for the likely school and FE population. Population forecasts were seen as providing a predictive indicator of the needs that the system might have to face. They were difficult to use with any precision because of the variables involved. Forecasts varied from ten to thirty years ahead and some authorities tried to cover different eventualities by producing high and low projections based on different assumptions of the staying-on rates.

LEAs made less use of information on social trends. Although policy documents testified to LEAs' general knowledge of social characteristics, their impact on education was not examined in any detail. Youth and community services might provide information on such problems as drug abuse, homelessness or youth unemployment. Indeed youth unemployment had attracted more attention. A few LEAs had mounted action research projects associated with outreach courses for the unemployed. These provided information about social characteristics and the attitudes of the unemployed to education. Some of the information on social trends came from other local government departments. Housing departments supplied details of new developments and migration rates. One council's Policy

Services Unit had carried out surveys of the young unemployed, ethnic minority pupils at school and college attendance by unemployed adults. Much of the information from other departments and agencies came informally, as a result of officers' and advisers' ad hoc contacts.

Award and grant applications

A number of authorities mentioned using the annual round of grant and award application as a source of information about needs. Requests for grants to study courses in other LEAs might indicate deficiencies in the local pattern of provision. Although this information was of limited use in identifying needs, its analysis had a financial incentive. With automatic recoupment of fees, cross boundary flows could represent a considerable expense and another uncertainty in LEA planning. This information could be expressed quantitatively but it had to be interpreted with care, taking account of local circumstances and traditions and applicants' motivation and knowledge.

Professional knowledge

Officers' and advisers' own knowledge of the local system was seen as a most, possibly *the* most, important source of information. As part of their management and planning role, LEA staff had to monitor, evaluate and coordinate provision. This gave them insights into its ability to meet needs and into new demands and approaches. In some contacts with other parts of the service the concern with needs would be explicit and direct. For example, a college principal would be asked to explain the rationale for a new proposal, an adviser might evaluate the provision for a particular student category, such as those with special needs, or an officer might discuss provision of a new one-year sixth course with a headteacher. Discussion of other subjects could also illuminate needs. A discussion of a college's estimates could lead to a consideration of the reasons for requiring additional staff or of areas of provision that were over or under-used. Officers and advisers pointed out how the interaction with teachers and lecturers during in-service training gave advisers insights into needs and their satisfaction. Similarly the work of clerking governing bodies provided officers with insights into the needs perceived and being met by schools and colleges. This local knowledge helped shape professional understanding and attitudes. So, too, did information gained from wider professional discussions, from knowledge of what was being done in other authorities, from keeping up with the professional press and literature and from the detail that accompanied new policy initiatives. If councillors and officers were to make informed judgments about their own performance, they required information that allowed them to compare their own authority with others. Senior officers and advisers saw it as part of their role to keep abreast with educational developments and debate.

There was evidence that the processes for obtaining and exchanging professional knowledge of needs were attracting more attention. LEAs appeared to be making increasing use of formal mechanisms to coordinate provision between institutions. At one extreme these might involve consortia and coordinating committees; on a lesser scale regular meetings of headteachers and principals with officers and advisers, and their participation in working parties. These mechanisms, which are discussed more fully in Chapter 9, did produce information about existing provision and about proposals for change and their implications. Thus although they represented a means for LEA management, coordinating mechanisms also provided a regular source of information on needs. Needs and their satisfaction were reported as figuring more explicitly within in-service training, and in conferences to discuss the future shape of education organized by LEA officers and advisers with senior institutional staff.

Student surveys

Most LEAs, then, relied heavily upon their officers, advisers and politicians to interpret what pupils, students and employers wanted from education. A few authorities had, themselves, surveyed the opinions of students in the 16–19 range. Most of these surveys were small scale, applied to pupils in the fifth year at school or to students undertaking college courses, seeking information on motivations, career choice and satisfaction with current provision. Where it was collected, this information was not seen as particularly useful. It largely confirmed professional judgments rather than indicated new directions and it did not provide criteria that could readily be used in planning.

Information from employers

Most LEAs had their own direct links with employers, although they represented a recent innovation for some. Education-industry consultative committees were common. In some cases they focused upon educational provision; in others education was an aspect of a concern with employment or economic development. Industrial representation was commonly provided through the CBI; educational representation included the senior officers and advisers. Where LEAs made use of area coordinating committees, employers were frequently included as members and this brought them into contact with officers and advisers. Participation in Science and Technology Regional Organizations proved another means of contact as also did participation in the newly-formed TVEI steering groups. These arrangements gave officers and advisers an opportunity of learning how employers perceived their educational needs and their satisfaction with existing provision. They also provided a means of familiarizing employers with educational developments and changes. Officers also came into contact with employers when servicing governing bodies. Many members of education committees were themselves in employment, and they had contact with employers who served as councillors or who lived, or worked, in their wards. The knowledge of needs gained from these contacts with employers appeared to contribute indirectly to management and planning. They influenced political and professional perceptions of the value of provision and the desirability of change. In a few cases they had resulted in particular initiatives. A Metropolitan District LEA reported participating in a CBI sponsored study investigating the local employment and training needs of those who had been on YTS programmes.

Information from the MSC

The majority of LEAs we surveyed reported regular contact with the MSC. The information gained was described as largely concerning the scope and character of the MSC, and particularly YTS, provision. But the joint planning of non-advanced FE would require information from both the LEA and the MSC regarding the range of existing provision and the emerging needs of local employers and students.

The sources of information discussed above were collected by LEAs to help them evaluate and manage their provision. However, LEAs also assessed needs in the course of interpreting information that was routinely sent to them from other parts of local education systems.

Demand

Schools and colleges are obliged to furnish LEAs with details of their recruitment. All LEAs knew the number of students attending different institutions and most had figures for the numbers attending different types of course. This information was required for resource management but it was also seen as providing an indication as to whether individual institutions were succeeding in meeting needs and whether the LEA's provision was adequate. The Age Participation Rate could be analyzed historically, or compared between different localities in the Authority, with other authorities and with the national rate. Such analyses could indicate changes and discrepancies. This might point to the existence of need which could then be taken up in planning. Although information on recruitment was objective, it might take a number of years for trends to become apparent. Information on what the figures revealed or implied relied upon professional interpretation.

Examination results

The same could be said for much of the other quantitative information passed to LEAs. Schools were obliged to furnish LEAs with details of their examination results. Some colleges did the same; in other cases LEA officers learned the results via governing bodies. Examination results were analyzed in different ways: by subject, by school, by examination board. They were seen as one means of evaluating whether institutions were meeting the needs of pupils and students but, again, they were not easy to interpret. Interpretation required some knowledge of the institution; of its results in previous years and the nature of its intake. It appeared common practice for results to be scrutinized by advisers, who could take up discrepancies with the institutions concerned as part of their monitoring role.

Course provision

The majority of LEAs monitored the range of courses provided by institutions, although the collection of detailed information represented a recent development for most. Efforts to secure the efficient use of resources and remove small, uneconomic classes had led a number of authorities to undertake detailed analyses of provision. The purpose was not solely economy. Information about the courses available and their utilization also told something about the needs provided for and their popularity. It gave officers and advisers an indication of gaps or unused provision. This could be taken up with the institutions concerned and in considering new developments within the authority. Monitoring of courses provided would form part of the review of 16–19 provision that LEAs have been invited to undertake in the recent circular from the DES (DES, 1987).

Institutional forecasts

Schools had to supply LEAs with estimates of their future attendance as part of the annual budgetary process. Colleges, similarly, had to provide estimated budgets based on attendance forecasts. LEAs would not automatically accept institutional estimates but would compare them with other sources of information at their disposal, such as current recruitment or population forecasts, and revise them where necessary. Estimates were used as predictive indicators, representing needs that institutions and, through the education budget, the LEA were proposing to meet. There was less evidence that LEAs used estimates to review the nature, as opposed to the scale, of provision. This was partly because much of educational provision was committed. If students attended for education, national and local policies mean that provision had to be made available. It was also the case that the chief and immediate concern with estimates was financial;

with the size of the budget rather than what it represented in terms of needs met or foregone. And formal presentation represented the closing stage in the preparation of estimates. Presentation may have been preceded by discussion and negotiations between officers and advisers and institutional staff that considered the nature of provision, institutional performance and, inter alia, its capacity to meet needs.

Student destinations

Most LEAs, as mentioned earlier, gained information from their careers services on past patterns of pupil and student destinations. This, along with estimates, recruitment figures and population forecasts, contributed to the picture of the demands facing the service.

Employment

Just under half the LEAs in our survey reported making use of statistics on the local labour market. Careers services provided LEAs with data on recruitment patterns and some LEAs made use of statistics produced by the MSC's regional manpower intelligence units. It was felt that this information gave LEAs a general indication of whether the education they made available met employers' needs. Further, it might alert officers and advisers to areas of industrial expansion or decline that would affect educational demand and should be reflected in educational opportunities. But it was considered risky to read any direct implication for educational provision into past recruitment patterns. Experience through the recession had shown the uncertainty of predicting industrial futures, and a number of respondents to the survey stated their reluctance to attempt to forecast changes in employment.

Supply of information by LEAs

LEAs also supplied information to help pupils and students assess their own needs. The recent circular from the DES on the pattern of organization to 19 emphasizes the importance of LEAs providing adequate information and guidance to students who wish to continue in education (DES, 1987).

Just over half the LEAs responding to our survey produced a brochure that set out all the courses available in the authority. Others, predominantly county authorities, produced brochures describing the opportunities available within separate education divisions or districts. Where area coordinating committees or consortia existed, these might be given the responsibility of producing the information for the provision they collectively encompassed. In a minority of cases providing information was left to the institutions concerned, although the careers service, as mentioned previously, would be likely to circulate a pamphlet to fifth year pupils reminding them of the need to make informed choices of a career, and of the mechanisms available for guidance and some of the major options for continuing with education.

The format and content of brochures varied widely. At a minimum they listed the courses that were available at different institutions. Others were more attractive in their presentation and more detailed. Details of courses were supplemented with particulars about financing, MSC programmes and (the hallmark of the 1980s) the support available for the unemployed. Brochures appeared to be normally distributed by the schools, although in some cases distribution was through the careers service. They were also made available through public libraries and youth and community centres. Officers expressed some scepticism as to how far LEA information about available courses influenced student choices compared with that gained from schools, careers services, parents and the peer group. However, it did present a wide and perhaps more objective view of the possibilities.

LEA officers and advisers were also a source of information for other parts of local education systems regarding new approaches and educational developments. They could thus stimulate new assessments of need. Officers believed that institutional uncertainties in respect of many of the new initiatives in 16–19 education had caused a more receptive climate for LEA information and guidance.

Characteristics of information use by LEAs

The most influential sources of information appeared to be information on, and forecasts of, demand and the knowledge and beliefs of senior officers, advisers and politicians. From our survey and case studies, LEAs appeared to have access to a considerable amount of information that could be used to assess needs and there were signs that they were improving their capacity to collect and analyze data. Much of the information was quantitative. This facilitated analysis. Historical and territorial comparisons could be made and trends and discrepancies from the norm were highlighted.

Yet in its raw state the available information was not seen as readily applicable to assessing needs. It was disparate, collected for aiding the management of the authority and particularly for the control of resources. It was not, for the most part, directly concerned with needs. Nonetheless it was possible to read inferences and indications of needs from data on demand, examination results, course provision, future estimates, destinations and recruitment patterns.

These inferences and indications relied upon professional identification and interpretation. This was subjective and conditioned by personal interests and values. Indications of needs contained within the information collected by LEAs were tested against professional experience. Information sources were frequently described as confirming what officers and advisers already knew from their own experience. Confirmation was useful and it added weight to professional arguments. Indications of needs from different sources would accumulate and this increased their currency in policy-making. They would also trigger further explicit enquiry. But the research indicated that professional contributions were haphazard and incremental. They depended upon who had access to information, how they interpreted it and the extent to which they were able to convince others that it contained implications for need. The call on professional definitions of need also depended upon the situation facing LEAs' services at any given time and how this was interpreted. Thought about needs was stimulated where there was a perception of a problem or if change was in the offing. It was less in evidence where services were established and running smoothly. The way in which information was processed by LEAs added to this incrementalism. Education departments encountered formidable problems in aggregating the information they received; some went to one section, some was the concern of another. Information on 16–19 recruitment in schools would be collected by the schools division, while recruitment in colleges went to the FE division. The officers analyzing recruitment patterns would not necessarily be the same as those handling applications for grants and awards. Thus views of needs were partial, dependent upon the information to which officers and advisers had access. Only senior officers‚were in a position to have an overview of the information, and they had many calls upon their time.

It is an important part of any LEA's function to monitor the efficiency and effectiveness of its educational provision. Thus, much of the information that was routinely and formally collected by LEAs concerned existing provision and performance. This provided some indication as to whether provision was meeting needs that had already been recognized. It could not indicate whether recognized needs were a reality, or whether unrecognized needs existed. LEAs gained some insight into this through their formal contacts with employers and from the political process. Fresh insights depended heavily upon the professional contacts of officers and advisers and their familiarity with educational developments and new policies.

Issues in the Use of Information

Reviewing the information used for needs assessment in local education systems, and the ways in which it was applied, prompts a number of general observations.

First there is a considerable variation in the type of information collected. Different bodies collect different forms of data: some relating to students, some relating to employers; some relating to the existing use of provision, some to possible future uses; some in quantitative form, some qualitative; some focused on an individual or an institution, some with a wider and less specific focus. The information is selective but this is because schools and colleges, careers services and LEAs use what is available or what they decide they can gather rather than the consequence of rational choice. Studying the responsiveness of colleges to employers' needs, Theodossin (1986) found a broad commitment across his sample to 'data collection based on subjective evaluation, intuitive judgment, hunch and "feel" '. In part this variation reflects the general usage of the term need. Although needs may be seen as a relevant issue in respect of a specific problem, the design of a course or the case for resources, the information that is applicable in each case will be different.

As a result, information is not readily aggregated and comparable and it contains different messages regarding needs. This is a common problem with information inputs. Organizations find that the information at their disposal is not in a form that suits all their purposes. Generalizing with reference to the definitions of social indicators of need made by Carlisle that were presented in Chapter 4 (Carlisle, 1972), our review suggests the existence of informative indicators, such as the Age Participation Rate and recruitment figures, and predictive indicators, such as population forecasts and estimates of recruitment. Information providing problem orientated indicators was primarily qualitative and there was little information that could be classed as programme evaluation indicators, although student destinations and examination results clearly contribute and the MSC is in the process of developing evaluation measures.

Because the available information cannot be readily applied to needs assessment it has to be translated and interpreted. In educational organizations it is the professional staff who provide most of the interpretation. Consequently their subjective and, in Bradshaw's definitions of need, normative views, are enormously influential. However, as was discussed with reference to LEAs, this presents problems in that qualitative professional opinions are particularly difficult to aggregate and compare.

Clearly not all information can be immediately applied to decision making. Organizations have to devise means of storage and recall if information is to contribute to best effect. This is difficult if information is reliant upon the powers of recall of individuals based in different locations and is applied through 'second or third hand' interpretations (Wilson, 1966). So although professional interpretations of need were important, they were haphazard in their contribution.

Statistical information avoided these problems; it was transmitted more readily and was less dependent upon interpretation. Statistical information was available regarding student demand and achievement: recruitment, attendance, future forecasts, course provision, examination results, pupil and student destinations. Consequently the statistical feedback from the operation of the existing system represented a major source of information about needs. However, to inform about needs the statistics still required professional interpretation. The assessment of needs was indirect and measures of performance did not provide particularly sensitive indications. Also, as Harnqvist (1978) points out, the different statistical measures tend to be repeated separately for different parts of education systems and for different phases of the educational process. They have to be aggregated and related to each other to be useful for planing.

As a result of the disparate nature of the available information on needs and its reliance on professional interpretation, there was no comprehensive overview. Professionals and politicians gained partial insights according to their experience and the information that came their way. Senior LEA officers and leading educational politicians, and senior managers in institutions and agencies, had access to the most information. It was the information that was readily to hand that was used. Generally there was neither time, nor perhaps the incentive, to analyze information in depth for what it told about needs, or to mount specific enquiries. We found no examples of institutions or LEAs undertaking exercises to aggregate the available information in order to assess its implication for needs.

Second, referring back to the categorization developed by Kimmel discussed in Chapter 4 (Kimmel, 1977), much of the harder information used for needs assessment is based on the collection and analysis of service statistics. Information from clients as to their needs or studies of the incidence and causes of need within local populations contribute less. As a result the information is weighted towards what already exists. It can therefore provide some indication as to how needs that have already been recognized are being met, but does not indicate whether these have been assessed correctly. Neither does it inform of the existence of felt needs. This emphasis in the information that is available to assess needs means that it is biased towards those who are already in the system. It can tell little about the needs of the non-participants, such as the small firms or the unemployed young people who have left school.

This, again, is a common problem with information collection. There is a tendency to keep information inputs to the minimum required to operate a system and keep its components interacting. Inputs beyond the minimum are required to enable systems to meet their purposes and to develop (Silver, 1983). Our study suggests that LEAs, their agencies and their institutions, are increasingly disposed to try and learn what employers believe they need and are developing formal mechanisms for that purpose. Institutions have industrial liaison officers and advisory committees; they participate in education-industry liaison arrangements and arrange conferences for employers. Careers services have devoted more time to making and maintaining contacts with employers. LEAs participate in authority-wide liaison arrangements with employers. The existence of similar mechanisms to gain the opinions of students or potential students is less common. Perhaps this is because the contacts are already seen to exist, as part of the teacher/student relationship. Perhaps it is because provision for students is seen as conditioned by what they have accomplished in their past school careers and by the demands of the various examination courses to which the system is committed. Few authorities or institutions surveyed the opinions of students or groups of 16–19-year-olds. And where this was done, doubts were expressed as to whether it provided fresh insights or insights that it was possible to act upon.

Finally, local education systems collected considerable information regarding individual needs. This was done through the work of teachers and lecturers in schools and colleges, and by careers officers. However, Table 3 in the framework developed in the preceding chapter suggested that the mechanisms used to assess individual needs made little direct contribution to collective assessments. Education did not appear to work from the particular to the general, building up collective assessments from knowledge of individual cases. Rather, collective assessments were based upon information concerned with global aspects of performance, such as demand and course provision. The preceding analysis suggests two reasons. First, individual assessments were made by professionals for professional rather than system usage. In the case of institutions the information gained was not necessarily recorded, although this was not so for the assessments made by careers officers. In neither case was the information aggregated in a quantified form that made for easy transmission. Second, individual assessments were largely the province of junior or specialist support staff, whereas collective assessments were made by senior staff as part of their management and planning roles. Because of this separation in function, and because the information generated was not easily transmitted, knowledge of individual needs made little contribution to collective assessments

Direct Assessments of Need

Education has been criticized for its limited use of information (Psacharopoulos, 1980). Our observations suggest that education systems are becoming more information conscious. Manual methods of collecting data have been unable to cope with the volume of work (Banghart, 1969) and computer and information technology has been applied to collect, store and analyze the available material. However the stimulus appears to be improved resource control not better identification of needs. The latter presents a problem for information collection. If, as Korner advocated with reference to the health service (DHSS, 1984), the data collected for statistical purposes should be gathered as a by-product of operational procedures, it is likely to be restricted in informing about needs. Our study suggests that management procedures can have effect in improving the collection of information. Communication channels require to be structured (Poster, 1976). But, more important, the assessment of needs merits attention in its own right, not as a by-product of operating the system. Our general impression is that currently the available information is only of haphazard relevance and use in needs assessment. Making better use of information entails both regularly scanning across the range of existing information for indications of need and undertaking some direct investigations where information is lacking or unclear. Thus if demand for courses appeared to bear no relationship to student destinations, a LEA might make further inquiry regarding student aspirations and course provision. If sectors of local employment were seen to make little use of college provision, they might be approached to learn why. This point is taken up again in Chapter 11.

References

BALLANTINE, M., (1980) *The Application of Computers in the Careers Service*, London, DE.

BANGHART, F., (1969) *Educational Systems Analysis*, London, Macmillan.

BRADSHAW, J., (1972) 'The concept of social need', *New Society*, 30 March.

CARLISLE, E., (1972) 'The conceptual structure of social indicators' in SHONFIELD, A., and SHAW, S. (Eds) *Social Indicators and Social Policy*, London, Heinemann.

CENTRAL POLICY REVIEW STAFF, (1980) *Education, Training and Industrial Performance*, London, HMSO.

DES, (1987) *Providing for Quality: The Pattern of Organization to Age 19*, London, HMSO.

DHSS, (1984) *Health Services Information: Second Report to the Secretary of State* (The Körner Report) London, HMSO.

HARNQVIST, K., (1978) *Individual Demand for Education: Analytical Report*, Paris, OECD.

KIMMEL, W.A., (1977) *Needs Assessment: A Critical Perspective*, US Department of Health, Education and Welfare.

POSTER, C., (1976) *School Decision-Making*, London, Heinemann.

PSACHAROPOULOS, G., (Ed) (1980) *Information: An Essential Factor in Educational Planning and Policy*, Paris, UNESCO.

SILVER, P., (1983) *Educational Administration*, London, Harper & Row.

STUFFLEBEAM, D., McCORMICK, C., BRINKERHOFF, R. and NELSON, C., (1985) *Conducting Educational Needs Assessment*, Norwell, Kluwer Nijhoff.

THEODOSSIN, E., (1986) *In Search of the Responsive College*, Bristol, Further Education Staff College.

WILSON, R., (1966) *Educational Administration*, London, Merril.

WITKIN, B., (1984) *Assessing Needs in Educational and Social Programs: Using Information to Make Decisions, Set Priorities and Allocate Resources*. San Francisco, CA, Jossey-Bass.

8   *Planning 16–19 Provision*

The last chapter showed the range and type of information collected by LEAs and their institutions which was used to indicate and identify the educational needs of the 16–19 age group. This chapter turns now to examine how the planning of educational provision is carried out within the local educational system — the processes involved, the dominant characteristics and the main influences upon it. In particular it seeks to answer the question of how far planning takes the assessments of identified needs into account in determining provision.

The last fifteen years have seen a greater impetus for more planning to be carried out at all levels of the educational system. As was shown in Chapter 2 this has been partly prompted by resource constraints and the desire for more cost effective delivery of provision. Yet there is also a concern that the complexity of influences on provision requires some order and control. At its simplest planning is commonly regarded as prescriptive; as a way of attempting to influence change to meet aims (Midgley, 1984). It is clearly more than the sum of individual decisions that might be taken in response to discrete problems. However, there is still a question of what is meant by 'planning' as practised and whether it adequately explains how changes in educational provision are made. This question will be discussed in this chapter using the evidence from the survey of LEAs and our six case study authorities.

In order to analyze the way that planning is carried out it is necessary to outline the main dimensions which will be taken up in this chapter. The first is the focus of concern in planning. There is a distinction between a focus on *substantive* issues, such as the aims of the curriculum or the priority attached to different client groups, and *procedural* concerns such as the allocation of finance to meet aims. Related to this is the difference between *strategic* and *operational* decisions arising from planning as well as the whole question of how decisions are implemented (Barrett and Fudge, 1981). A second important dimension is the structure of the planning process and the range of participants that contribute. Thirdly, there is the

process of planning used; the sequence of producing actions, the information utilized, and techniques employed. Finally, there is the question of
how policies are evaluated; who is involved, what criteria are used and the
impact of these evaluations (Kogan, 1986). In all these dimensions the
contribution of needs assessment will be examined.

Local Education Authority Planning of 16–19 Provision

The Impetus for Planning

The formal role of the LEA in determining educational provision is laid
down in the 1944 Education Act which gives it the responsibility for
securing that efficient education is provided so as to be able to meet the
needs of its area. This is set within the Secretary of State's promotion of
national educational policy. Thus education has conventionally been
regarded as a partnership between central and local government but this
partnership has altered with the growing concern of central government to
see national policy more effectively implemented. LEAs now face a number
of new constraints in how they carry out the planning of provision
particularly with regard to 16–19 education; not least the emergence of the
MSC as an agent for the implementation of central government policies.

The Macfarlane Report (DES 1980), produced by the DES and the
local authority associations, urged LEAs to review the institutional basis of
their 16–19 provision with regard to its efficient delivery. More recently
DES Circular 3/87 emphasized that LEAs have a role in reviewing all 16–19
provision in their areas (DES, 1987). All our case study LEAs recognized the
importance of the increased planning 16–19 provision and this was
prompted by a number of common factors.

First, there was a broadly held view amongst politicians, officers, and
advisers that post-16 provision should be extended. This required a change
in the traditional patterns of working in order to transcend the separation of
academic and vocational education and the separation of institutions. Some
saw the LEA as the natural initiators of change which meant exercising
greater leadership across the system (Hainsworth, 1986). The introduction
of three-year development plans for work-related NAFE has also had an
effect in stimulating LEAs to plan their provision in that part of 16–19
provision.

Secondly, the effects of tightening financial control led officers and
politicians to argue for more cost effective provision. Resources had to be
used to the best effect across the authority as a whole. This was the more
necessary because of falling rolls which in many authorities were beginning
to affect the 16–19 age cohort. Increasingly schools and colleges would be
competing for a smaller age group and institutions would compete to the
detriment of equity and economy. Schools with small sixth forms were

experiencing problems as a result of declining numbers made more difficult by the growing need to provide broader, work-related courses for the less academic. These influences were common to all our case study LEAs but a number of other factors were relevant to the circumstances of particular LEAs such as the constraints of geography or the legacy of past patterns of institutional arrangements within the authority. For example, the county authorities studied were affected by their large size and their mixed system of institutional arrangements that had evolved over time. This meant that they tended to deal with problems on an area basis.

All these factors meant that LEAs were being pushed to play a stronger planning role which would change relationships within the local education systems. Yet, despite this, it was still recognized that the traditional pattern of institutional autonomy remained important in terms of views about how provision should be determined. One county authority explicitly saw themselves as having a 'laissez faire' policy on provision with the LEA providing support to institutions. With the need for more central direction from the LEA this raised the question of how this would be operated. Thus it was accepted in all our LEAs that change would be difficult to achieve. Underlying these views can be seen to be a number of fundamental value questions about how provision should be determined in local education systems; questions relating to direction, autonomy, competition, economy, inequality and equity. These were important both in understanding how planning was conducted and how needs were perceived and taken up in planning and policy making.

Strategic Planning

The stimulus for LEAs to be more directive in planning 16–19 provision was accompanied by the need to act on giving a lead to the local education system (Ranson and Travers, 1986). The main indication of this was for authorities to produce a policy on 16–19 provision. In many authorities policies took the form of statements about the form and nature of 16–19 provision. Our survey of LEAs showed that 45 per cent had a current policy for this sector. These· were represented by guidelines set by the LEA and endorsed by elected members. For example, in one of the case study county LEAs a consultative document had been produced in 1982 following consideration by a working group of members. This set a number of policy objectives dealing with various aspects of 16–19 education which were couched in general terms. It was intended by officers to be advisory and stimulate institutions to develop their own provision. Other authorities followed a similar line in setting objectives in the form of policy documents. These were generally concerned with three main types of issue: identifying desirable forms of education for particular categories of students particularly those not on academic or vocational courses; coordinating provision across the system, in some cases demarcating the responsibilities of different categories of institutions; and, in developing new centres of provision. In the case study LEAs these statements of policy had usually been initially framed by officers and then endorsed by politicians. This officer initiation is similar to the findings of other studies of the way that education policy making is carried out in LEAs (Jennings, 1977; David, 1977). It was felt in a number of our case study LEAs that councillors did not actively promote their own conceptions of need but responded to the views presented by others. In some cases proposals for policies came from a working party representing a range of interests in the education system — headteachers and principals, and the careers service.

These statements in policy documents reflected the views of the professionals and normative definitions of need. The educational values of officers, advisers and elected members were therefore important in determining the scope of the initiatives in 16–19 education. Also of importance was the effect of national initiatives in policy and the extent to which these were implemented at a local level. The actions of central government were important for LEAs both in identifying the needs of particular groups of students and in determining what curricula ought to be provided. This was the case, for example, with students following one-year courses in response to the introduction of CPVE across local education authorities.

Policy objectives were often couched in general terms based on the services that should be provided. Their function was frequently symbolic in showing that the authority recognized the existence of problems and that it was responding. Some officers in our authorities doubted whether such statements were precise enough or indeed were ever capable of being implemented. Moreover, the objectives were not necessarily placed in an order of priority which created a concern by those in institutions who saw this as a lack of clear direction from the LEA. An alternative view expressed by officers was that it was valuable to provide a public statement of the priorities to show that the LEA was meeting the challenges. Yet policy statements were important because they indicated the broad scope, orientation and distribution of 16–19 provision.

Operational Planning in LEAs

The case study LEAs followed similar processes for undertaking the operational planning of 16–19 provision which were similar to the findings of our survey of LEAs.

Institutional forecasts

LEA planning commenced with the information gained from the institutional forecasts of students following post-16 courses. These were collected by the education department, although frequently separately by the schools and FE sections. As was seen in the previous chapter these forecasts were expected to indicate needs although it was assumed that institutions had the ability to recognize and respond to them. In practice forecasts were largely seen to reflect the demand for existing provision rather than scope for new initiatives. Forecasts of age participation rates in the schools sector were calculated on the basis of the percentage of fifth form students transferring to the sixth form, but this was more difficult in the FE sector and in those LEAs with sixth form colleges because of the inter-institutional flow of students. Officers stated that it was difficult to estimate future age participation rates because of the uncertainty of the employment market and the choices of students regarding YTS. Staying on rates also fluctuated because of factors such as institutional popularity and changing trends in the choice of courses. This information was used for physical planning and in the budget exercise. Although it provided 'hard' information which might be used in planning, it still had to be interpreted on the basis of officers' and inspectors' or advisers' judgments about the availability of resources and the implications for the wider local educational system. Moreover, forecasts had to be assessed against other available information on future demand.

Monitoring provision

As was noted in the last chapter, LEAs monitored the quality and range of what was provided in their institutions and this was carried out in different ways. The normal method was to use the advisory staff or inspectorate to provide information on the capacity of the service to meet needs. Examples of these monitoring activities included day to day contacts with the institutions, knowledge gained through running in-service training courses, and knowledge of new initiatives. The way in which monitoring activities applied to the 16–19 age group varied. LEAs did not always have an adviser with specific responsibility for 16–19 provision and in general there tended to be separate advisers for secondary and further education. LEAs varied in how systematically they collected information. In one of our case study LEAs officers felt that the authority did not have enough information about provision and was unable to analyze trends. In this authority the task of information collection had been given to the coordinator of 16–19 provision who had undertaken a manual exercise to document the courses available in schools and the examination boards used, and to analyze teaching group sizes. In contrast, the development of computerized information systems in some LEAs appeared to make the task of monitoring easier. In one county authority a computerized curriculum monitoring exercise had been introduced which provided annual data on students, teaching staff, and the range of courses provided in the schools and sixth form college sector. Its main purpose was to allow the authority to monitor provision in more detail than hitherto and to determine trends in provision for both the whole authority and for its constituent parts. This scheme was in its early stages and only beginning to be used in planning. The collection of information about existing provision was more difficult in those authorities where responsibilities within the education department were split between a schools and a further education section. In these cases the FE section would then undertake its own collection of statistics on student numbers, staffing and contact hours for its colleges.

Although LEAs collected this type of information on an annual cycle, specific evaluations were undertaken by the advisers for particular developments such as CGLI foundation courses. Other administrative mechanisms linking the LEA to its institutions also provided information about provision. Examples included governing bodies, officers' own contacts with institutions and the different coordinating mechanisms.

Financial planning

The construction of the education budget could provide a broad indication of LEA priorities as reflected through the views of officers and politicians about what should be provided or indeed protected in the allocation of finance. In most cases the resources available to LEAs had been reduced which affected the way that LEAs were able to plan their budgets. In some LEAs this resulted in what Hewton has termed the 'crisis culture' which was marked by the development of particular defensive strategies and responses by those working in LEAs (Hewton, 1986). Common to this context was the control of contraction and coping with uncertainty.

The construction of the budget followed an annual cycle in all the case study LEAs. The starting base was the continuation of existing provision with account taken of demographic trends and policy decisions made by the LEA. As has been noted by other commentators, this base was frequently left unchallenged because of the difficulties of reviewing all provision made and the acceptance of the previous year's provision (Danziger, 1976; Dennison, 1984). Changes therefore tended to be made at the margins of the budget. The usual practice was to receive bids from the various parts of the LEA which were then negotiated. The final decisions were made by the senior education officers in conjunction with councillors serving on the particular sub-committees. Moreover, the LEA had to compete with other services provided by the local authority and this meant involvement by the Policy and Resources Committee and central departments. These decisions were further influenced at various stages by national financial considerations which affected the guidelines set for the overall budget of the local authority and its priorities.

The creation of the education budget was therefore acknowledged by all those officers interviewed in our case study LEAs, as being incremental in character and concerned with making changes at the margins of provision whilst keeping the base intact. Although this was the practice of most of the LEAs studied, one case study authority was moving in a different direction and earmarking growth money in the budget to distribute to institutions to meet agreed measures and developing the means of allocating expenditure against performance indicators. Some of the officers concerned with the budgetary process in the LEAs studied considered that forward financial planning was made difficult because of the uncertainties surrounding local government finance. The budget allowed only limited scope for growth as new developments were increasingly dependent upon earmarked monies from central government; as with MSC, specific Educational Support Grants and from the EEC.

All the LEAs studied allocated finance to the institutions in a similar way. In the FE sector colleges constructed their own budgets in consultation with their governors. This could indicate the needs that they were proposing to meet although the more obvious use of budgets was for financial management. The allocation of finance to schools in the case study LEAs was based upon the pupil teacher ratio with a per capita allowance for books, stationery and equipment. In some of the authorities additional finance was made available to schools on the basis of additional educational needs according to the authority's social priority index using selected indicators of need. In other authorities more staff could be made available where it was felt necessary by advisers.

Officers felt that it was difficult to use finance to stimulate changes in provision. Financial allocations reflected student numbers and institutions were judged to possess a considerable amount of autonomy when it came to deciding how they would deploy resources. Indeed in some authorities it was difficult to monitor how resources were being used even though officers saw the value of this type of exercise. Nevertheless one of the LEAs studied was experimenting with local financial management which was designed to give institutions greater freedom and flexibility in allocating the finance they were given. Generally institutions, and particularly the schools, were able to determine what provision they made subject to the condition that they kept within existing financial allocations. In some of the LEAs the development of new courses was discussed with the advisers or the area education officers but there was no formal requirement that this should be done. In LEAs with consortia systems, then these bodies were frequently expected to provide a forum for the review and development of new types of provision.

Planning FE provision

In the FE sector controls over provision were different from those in the schools sector. The LEAs expected a minimum group size before a course could run and there were mechanisms for the approval of new courses which required evidence that a course would attract demand and satisfy local employment needs and was not in competition with other colleges. Colleges also might be required to submit vocational courses to the RACs for approval. Yet although these mechanisms enabled LEA officers to give a view on provision and sometimes to stimulate developments, their contribution to FE planning tended to be reactive to the initiatives from the colleges.

Planning YTS provision

The planning of YTS provision was carried out separately by the local officers of the MSC using information provided by the careers service. There were mechanisms of contact between the LEA and MSC such as regular officer level contact and contacts through the Area Manpower Board (Challis *et al*, 1984). These mechanisms appeared to concentrate on coordinating YTS arrangements more than relating YTS to educational provision. Some education officers wanted to see a greater influence by the LEA in the planning of YTS so as to ensure connection with other forms of post-16 provision. This separation between LEAs and MSC may lessen as they collaborate in constructing annual plans forecasting the development of non-advanced FE over the coming three years (MSC/LAA, 1985).

The planning of 16–19 provision by the LEA was therefore limited in its scope. The LEA was at the apex of the local education system and had to reconcile a number of different demands. Authorities varied in the nature and type of their strategic policies and the extent to which they were seeking to be directive in determining provision. The planning of provision thus served a number of purposes: to provide institutions with the resources in order for them to satisfy needs; to advance the policies made by the Education Committee; and, of increasing importance, to ensure that provision was cost effective in its delivery. Within all of this the assessment of needs by the LEA was largely secondhand, relying in the main on the institutions' own views of needs. Planning was therefore only loosely linked to the identification of needs.

Evaluating provision

Part and parcel of planning was the evaluation of provision. In the LEAs studied this was carried out in a continuous way and not as a discrete exercise at the end of the planning process. Several types of criteria were commonly used according to the concerns and policies of the particular authority although there tended to be a uniformity in what criteria were used. This commonly included the range of provision; the cost effectiveness of existing provision; the extent to which provision met the perceived 'needs' of the area; its quality; and the way in which these needs were defined. There was also the issue of the response to central government initiatives and the extent to which these were implemented at a local level. In all

LEAs studied officers generally felt that they were having to give more attention to the initiatives made by central government.

Information   It was noted in Chapter 7 that LEAs relied on different types of information as indicators to judge the effectiveness of existing provision. The information related to different parts of the education process being concerned with inputs to the system, such as student demand, the processes such as courses, and the outputs from the system such as exam results or destinations.

As was seen earlier, most LEAs carried out some form of monitoring of their existing provision and this was used to identify areas where provision was lacking. The results from monitoring might be used as an indicator of the comparative needs of the authority but there was also concern that provision should be equitable in its distribution. Another source of information about distribution came from the statistics on mandatory and discretionary awards which provided an indication of the pattern of student choice and individual demands. In a similar way the information on the numbers of post-16 students attending courses in institutions outside the authority boundaries was an important indicator of whether the same courses should be provided in the authority. Attempts to change the distribution of provision depended on the relationship between the LEA and its institutions and the extent to which it sought to be more directive in its planning and coordination.

Financial effectiveness   Apart from evaluating the quality and distribution of provision LEAs were concerned with its financial effectiveness. This was reflected in the increased amount of information collected by LEAs about the cost effectiveness of provision. However, authorities varied in the extent and detail of the information they possessed. There was also a problem in measuring cost effectiveness of 16–19 provision as this information was usually separately collected by the school or further education sections of the education department.

Outputs   In terms of outputs of the education system, the main information collected was on examination results and student destinations. The collection and analysis of information on results was undertaken by the LEA and then presented to the Education Committee before being published. This was used in planning as both an indicator of the general quality of provision across the authority as well as being used to compare institutional performance.

Student destinations   Chapter 7 showed how information on student destinations was collected by the careers service and supplied to officers and members. This was regarded as one indicator of the quality of the outputs of provision and might be analyzed historically to indicate trends in provision in relation to the employment market. But views varied on how far it could provide a basis for service planning. One view was that this type of information gave a general indication of trends that could be used in more detail if necessary. It was certainly used in the planning of courses in FE colleges but less so in the schools sector. A contrasting view was that this information did not influence planning because it was marginal in its application and was difficult to link with specific action. More specific studies of recruitment were undertaken by careers services at the request of officers who might want to review particular types of courses.

Information from outside education   As was seen in the last chapter, information was also used from outside the education world. The needs of employers were defined from several different sources — the careers service, from the feedback of institutions, and from direct contact with employer representatives. The aggregation of these different types of information was carried out by officers and was seen to provide a general indication of employment trends which might be followed up with specific exercises to find out in more detail. Information was also available from other local authority services and agencies, as for example the youth and community service. Other local authority departments collected inform-ation related to their own concerns which was supplied to the education department. All these types of information were ingredients in the planning process but tended to be used in an ad hoc manner, depending on the concerns at the particular time. For example, the introduction of CPVE in one of our case study LEAs had involved a working party being set up which included representation from the careers service and discussion with employer representatives.

Involvement in evaluation   The evaluation of provision was mainly under-taken by officers and the advisory staff. It was they who controlled what information would be collected and used and this was related to their views of the criteria by which provision should be judged. The effect of evaluations from elected members varied between authorities depending on the extent of member involvement in the detail of policy and provision. Other participants such as the careers service or employers were not regularly used in evaluation apart from particular exercises and so played a more reactive role in relation to the evaluation process. This can be explained by their lack of influence in the local education system.

Evaluation and planning   The relationship between evaluation and plann-ing was not automatic; the results of evaluation were interpreted by those who determined educational provision. Evaluations carried a number of different consequences. They might influence inputs to the system such as justifying extra staffing or resources. They might explicitly influence planning which could result in the introduction of new courses. Examples from the research included the development of courses for those with special needs and vocationally oriented provision. A distinction can be made between evaluations that were formative, actively influencing the planning process as it was carried out, or summative where evaluation was carried out at the end of the process. But evaluations did not necessarily contain indications of the needs that existed. These might be submerged within, for example, institutional forecasts of demands and not made explicit.

Characteristics of LEA Planning

In our case study LEAs all planned 16–19 provision in a similar way even though they experienced different problems. This was marked by several distinctive characteristics. The first was the external constraints that affected the scope of planning. Planning was carried out in a period of uncertainty which caused difficulties because of changing contextual factors. These included the changing requirements of central government with regard to the post-16 curriculum, and of particular importance, the effect of financial restraints which reduced the capacity to respond to develop new forms of provision. This was compounded by falling rolls which forced LEAs to rationalize existing provision. The second characteristic comprised factors internal to the LEA and the way that planning was carried out. Planning had to start with the existing buildings, resources, staffing and expertise that LEAs possessed and this constrained freedom of action in changing or developing new provision. The LEA itself had to act within the framework of resources set by the local authority. LEA planning relied heavily on institutional forecasts of demand and what institutions felt they should be providing. This was the traditional manner of planning which implicitly accepted the principle of local autonomy and local responsiveness in meeting definitions of need. This was still largely accepted as the way that planning should take place, although increasingly challenged by the need to produce priorities for the system as a whole. However, LEAs faced difficulties both in setting and implementing priorities and in implementing them. Chapter 7 demonstrated that their information was limited mainly to that collected by the institutions themselves, supplemented by knowledge of comparative developments. LEAs lacked the capacity to develop their own information based on local needs and therefore had to rely on the institutional definitions. Moreover, different sets of information were collected by the various parts of the LEA — officers, advisers, and careers service — and these were difficult to aggregate. As was shown earlier, student demand figured as important in planning because of its common currency across the system and heavy reliance was placed on it as the main indicator of needs. This meant that definitions of need were not necessarily the main element of planning.

They tended to be submerged in the information that was collected and were not made explicit in developing priorities.

Institutional Planning

The planning of provision by institutions is discussed here under the patterns exhibited by schools and the colleges.

School Planning

Identifying demand

Planning started with an assessment of the demand for the existing courses provided in the schools and this gave senior staff basic information about what they could make available for the following year. The level of demand was solicited through the process of careers and educational guidance which generally started in the fourth year onwards. The range of sixth form provision was made known to students through talks and brochures. Occasionally schools used a questionnaire to discover student choice of courses. The resulting pattern of student choices was seen to reflect the available provision and the option blocs in the school, although particular combination of courses appropriate to individual students could be arranged. Some of the schools in our case study authorities ran 'sampler' courses in the summer term to give students an idea of the type of courses on offer.

The identified demand for existing courses was therefore the basis for planning what provision would be made. Demand was seen to be one indicator of need which senior staff believed the schools must seek to satisfy. Yet some doubts were expressed by staff interviewed about how far demand was adequate as an indicator of need which would be reliable enough to be used in planning. Demand was seen to be problematic because it was influenced by a number of factors which might cause distortion in what staff thought might be students' 'real' choice. Amongst these factors were: the students' subjective views about courses and the staff that taught them; parental expectations and preferences; and, students' own assessments of their aptitudes and the value of post-16 education. Another factor was the advice given by subject teachers which might be heavily weighted in favour of their own subjects; with falling rolls and institutional competition it was increasingly difficult for heads of department to maintain their 'A' level work. However, demand for 'A' levels was judged as more clear cut than for the one-year vocational courses which shifted over a short period of time. But the main problem with demand lay in the fact that it was inevitably conditioned by available provision made by schools. This provision reflected the schools' view of what was thought to be desirable provision which could be made available within existing resources. Planning also increasingly had to take into account the effect of provision from other sources, including YTS, which would influence student demand.

Determining provision

Having identified the potential demand for courses, the schools had to decide which courses should be provided for the following year.

Budget decisions   Budget decisions at the start of the financial year determined the resources that schools had at their disposal. Within the allocation of financial and staffing resources the schools had a high degree of freedom to develop the provision they saw fit, although senior staff emphasized the resource constraints that existed and the problem of subsidizing the sixth form from the other school resources. This was particularly seen as a problem for the small schools, where the lack of resources was a constant constraint in meeting new needs. Indeed staff interviewed in some small schools felt that they could no longer provide a broad range of courses but rather had to concentrate on particular courses. So in one school in an urban authority only the basic 'A' level subjects were provided where there was staff expertise and minority subjects would have to be taken at the local FE college. In contrast schools operating TVEI schemes had been able to develop new courses because of the additional resources received.

Views on provision   Inevitably the determination of exactly what provision should be made was a complex process, influenced in all the schools studied by the views of senior staff and the characteristics of the school decision-making process. The assessment of need occurred within a context of education tradition and policy that had defined a particular pattern of courses as appropriate for an institution to provide. The values of senior staff regarding the scope of provision affected what courses were provided. Some of our case study schools saw themselves as perpetuating what they saw as an ex-grammar school ethos with an emphasis on academically oriented courses and high achievement. Even schools within the same area of an authority had differing views about what provision should be made. For example, in one school staff were sceptical about the importance of developing vocational courses instead preferring to continue to provide what they saw as a broad general education. This was based on the view that in an area of high unemployment, vocational courses would not result in increased employment opportunities because they would be too narrow. Instead, students should possess more flexible skills to help them with the changing job market. In contrast a neighbouring school had made the decision to increase its provision of vocational courses because it saw these as better preparing students for employment and also enhancing their choice of subjects. This included the development of new 'A' level courses in design and technology and in law. Schools also saw themselves as having particular strengths which had developed through the skills of staff and which should be maximized.

Changes in provision Changes in the pattern were seen to depend on staff diagnoses of what provision would be more appropriate for their clientele. To some extent staff were constantly involved in reviewing their provision. Decisions about these were made through the normal channels of policy making involving senior staff, as well by interested individuals, informal groupings or special teams outside the hierarchical structure. Relevant factors in developing provision included senior managers' perceptions of staff capabilities, available resources and the perceptions of the needs of the students, as well as the dominant views about the orientation of provision. Planning did not necessarily follow a rational sequence of events starting with a consideration of need. Schools are made up of different groupings with their own interests and this may militate against clear institutional goals being developed (Weick, 1976; Cohen *et al*, 1972; Bush, 1986). Instead the formulation of provision followed the processes of negotiation between various participants — subject departments, senior management and groups of staff — relying on their exercise of power (Hoyle, 1982; Shaw, 1975). Initiatives were made from different parts of the school in a 'bottom up' fashion as well as being determined by senior managers. The problem for senior management was how to coordinate and aggregate these initiatives. Changes introduced by senior management had to be implemented within the school and resources had to be allocated to meet these changes (Simkins, 1986). This could provide a barrier to change when the existing staff attitudes did not correspond to expectations of new ways of working. The case study institutions showed a number of examples of where senior staff felt that they were not meeting particular needs of students because the necessary skills were not available.

Changing provision: The example of one-year courses in the sixth form Changes in the orientation of provision, such as the development of new courses, reveal the combination of the above factors and their interrelationships. This process was vividly shown in the research in the way that provision for those students wanting one year courses was introduced in many of the schools in our case study LEAs. This client group had become more visible in all institutions in recent years due to central government initiatives in the curriculum and the rise in youth unemployment, which meant that many students were returning to education. In some of the schools the stimulus for change came from the dissatisfaction expressed by staff that existing provision did not meet the needs of these students. They were seen to have a number of different needs, some wanted to gain further qualifications or wanted to increase their grades, some wanted an extra year at school to protect them from the world of work and to gain greater maturity, and some wanted to gain a job but saw school as preferable to a YTS scheme.

The schools varied in how far they wanted to mount courses for this group but, more importantly, the response to their recognized 'needs' was different according to the values of staff. This shows that the normative definition of need has different professional interpretations. In some cases the staff favoured a continuation of the academic tradition in the form of CEE courses and thought that vocationally oriented courses were inappropriate provision for schools. In most cases staff wanted a more vocationally oriented curriculum which would enhance opportunities for employment. One problem identified was the limited demand for these types of courses despite schools trying to market them. In one LEA schools in a particular area had developed the concept of the 'springboard sixth' to cater for students who were being excluded from education because of inappropriate courses and who were not on YTS schemes. This provided a more flexible form of provision with a variety of non-examinable courses available at any time of the year.

Another factor that had to be considered was the views of parents, both to gain support for the institution and to explain new initiatives. In one case the failure of a CGLI pre-vocational course to attract students was attributed to parental opposition. In another school support was gained from parents by sending out a questionnaire to the parents of students on a pre-vocational course regarding how they perceived their children's needs. Similarly support had to be gained from teaching staff in order to ease the introduction of change. Specific exercises to assess demand provided an indication of where a school might develop its provision and in one school this had shown the demand for more vocational 'A' levels.

This brief examination of the creation of one-year courses shows how this client group had become more visible both as a result of central government activities and schools' experience of their students. Yet the schools' views about needs varied because of such factors as the values of staff, school policies and resources.

Evaluating provision

As with LEAs, evaluation in schools was a continuous activity carried out as part of the process of determining provision. It was the professionals who selected the criteria used in evaluation and this reflected the values they had concerning the scope and orientation of 16–19 provision.

Individual students Evaluation of the individual needs of students was derived from contact between teacher and student as well as from more formal feedback on courses, such as through the report system. The role of the sixth form tutor was particularly important in receiving and aggregating views of the value of courses. Student satisfaction was assessed through information on attendance patterns and the staff views of the general ethos of the student body. However, the information was difficult to use in the planning of provision. It was seen to be subjective, and occasionally unrealistic, and in any case was influenced by a whole number of factors, such as the views of students regarding particular members of staff, different motivations held for undertaking a course and difficulties in adjusting to life in the sixth form. Differences were noted in the views of students taking 'A' levels in comparison with their counterparts following one-year courses. The former were seen as having more instrumental aims particularly those aiming for higher education whereas the motives of students on one-year courses were more varied and they were sometimes less clear about the value of courses undertaken.

Student destinations and examination results   As we have seen in Chapter 7, information on student destinations and examination results was used to evaluate the outputs of the educational process. Examination results were used to review performance in respect of the degree of success in gaining entry to further and higher education. As they were widely used for evaluation throughout the education system, examination results were taken into account by schools. However, it was not common for the results of students other than those on 'A' level courses to be published. Data on student destinations were collected by the careers service as well as by the institution itself. Again this was used as a general indication of the success of provision and some staff believed that it should be used more particularly with vocationally oriented courses.

Views of employers   Another aspect of evaluation was in assessing how far provision met employers' needs. This type of information was received in different ways. Although the careers service was mainly used to provide students with careers guidance, it also relayed the views of employers and provided assessments on the desirability of the introduction of new courses. However, the contribution of the careers service to school planning varied. In some schools studied the local careers officer was automatically consulted on the introduction of new types of courses but in others there was less contact. The views of employers were received in different ways — employer visits, careers advice, work experience, projects undertaken and in some cases employer representation on governing bodies. In the case of schools operating TVEI or participating in SCIP then these contacts were of a more extensive and formal nature. Yet some schools did not have strong contacts with employers, finding it difficult to attract employer interest. Concern was also expressed by staff about the lack of employer knowledge and the lack of clarity of their needs definitions which often resulted in conflicting messages. For these reasons it was uncommon for employers to be automatically included in the planning of new courses although there were instances of employer views sought on, for example, the introduction of CPVE in some schools.

The evaluation process in the schools sector used all these various sources of information at different stages in the planning process. Their use depended on the type of course being evaluated and staff views about the criteria that should be used in evaluation.

College Planning

Institutional planning in the college sector followed a similar pattern although the distinctive characteristics of this type of institution were important. The sixth form colleges operating under school regulations catered for the 16–19 age group whereas the FE and tertiary colleges provided for a broader client group, including those who were on vocational courses above the age of 18. Common to all these types of college was the fact that students had to change institution at the age of 16.

Identifying demand

In estimating the demand for courses the colleges had to publicize their provision and then wait to determine what courses they would mount. This was more of a problem for the FE colleges than it was for the sixth form or tertiary colleges, which tended to have more structured relationships with schools. Recruitment patterns together with past trends, allowed the colleges to determine likely demand for their courses. The colleges used different methods of liaison with schools, such as open days, to publicize their provision and create demand. However, the exact demand was only known when students enrolled in the autumn term. Identification of demand was even more important in the FE colleges where courses had to have a minimum number of students before they were permitted to run by their LEA. This shows the reliance on the 'expressed' needs of students.

Budget preparation

The act of drawing up their budget estimates for the coming year meant that colleges had to set out a broad indication of the needs they were proposing to meet. For the most part the colleges planned on the basis of continuation of existing provision and made their final decision about course provision at the beginning of the academic year. As with schools a view was expressed that there was a measure of departmental self interest in maintaining student numbers.

Determining provision

Decisions about what provision would be made available was dependent on what the colleges saw as their overall scope of provision. As was discussed earlier with schools, colleges possessed views regarding appropriate provision. In the main the colleges studied saw themselves as operating in a local market of students. For some colleges they were the main single provider for post-16 provision in their locality and so it was important for them to have a broad range of provisions including in some cases a wide variety of minority 'A' level courses. For some of the sixth form colleges they were in competition with the larger FE colleges for vocational courses. In one sixth form college staff had identified the need from local employers for basic electronic courses but were prevented from running such a course by their authority because a similar course was already being run at the local FE college. With the tertiary colleges some staff felt that their provision should cater for the needs of a broad group of post-16-year-old students as well as for adult learners and the needs of the community. Yet this presented difficulties in what priority should be given to these different groups of students in college planning.

Decisions about new courses took place within the framework of the college policy-making process. As with schools, new initiatives came from a variety of sources though mainly from senior management. Senior management was concerned with ensuring that the broad scope of the college was able to respond to external demands. The departments of the college were responsible for reviewing new courses and had direct contact with students and so could make an assessment of their needs. Changes at this level tended to be made at the margins of provision such as altering the content of a course for example, in line with new examination requirements. In some colleges studied staff felt that the departmental structure restricted the identification of needs because of the problems of communication across the college. Views about needs were not necessarily shared across departmental boundaries. Once the various initiatives were taken, they entered the formal policy making system involving heads of departments, senior staff and the Academic Board. As with schools, priorities tended to follow a process of negotiation within the college rather than a rational plan for course development. The coordination of college provision was secured through a number of mechanisms such as the heads of department meetings and the Academic Board. In most cases the governing body was not felt to represent a strong source of development or a mechanism for identifying needs, but rather its role was to monitor provision and provide support.

In some colleges course development followed a more centralized pattern, with established procedures for gaining approval and implementation. This was introduced partly to provide more central coordination and to reduce the autonomy of the departments. In one FE college there was a process of eleven stages between the submission of an idea about provision to its formal approval. Departments were sometimes characterized as unwilling to relinquish any freedoms, particularly if it meant that other departments might gain scarce resources. This was indicative of the restraint on resources since the expansion in one area meant a reduction in another. In colleges with a broad range of provision the problem for planning was how to aggregate the initiatives and determine priorities. For example, one tertiary college studied in our research had a number of different markets to service — the first priority given to 16–19 academic provision, then part-time vocational provision for the 16–19s and then the more adult and vocational provision. Yet the problem experienced by staff was that procedures for more centralized planning were felt to be restrictive and an additional source of work. College proposals for new courses had also to be submitted to the LEA and if the courses were of an advanced level, the Regional Advisory Council. These submissions had to demonstrate evidence of demand, the numbers likely to be achieved and the avoidance of duplicating provision with other colleges.

Evaluating provision

Information used   Institutional evaluation in the FE sector followed a similar form to that of the schools sector, with college staff relying on similar types of information, although there were some differences. For example, the drop-out rate from courses other than gaining employment was viewed by college staff to provide an indicator of whether needs were being met. Reports and profiles were kept on students and these were partly used as a way of gauging student satisfaction. In a few cases students completed a questionnaire about the level of their satisfaction with their courses. Student destinations were seen as important means of describing whether or not provision was satisfying needs. Information on student destinations was collected by course tutors with help from the careers service, but it was difficult to gain information on all the students. This was generally analyzed by the college and sent to the governing body for its consideration. This was seen as important because of the vocational nature of many of the courses and it affected the reputation of the institution in the local community. Examination results were also used as an indicator of the quality of provision and these were collected for all courses and could be used for comparative purposes between courses and over time. Student demand was of particular importance in the college sector, because in most cases courses had to have a minimum number of students before they could run. If a course was inappropriate then students could always 'vote with their feet'. Once again this illustrates the emphasis on 'expressed' need in planning.

Views of employers   The views of employers figured as important to the FE colleges as they attempted to relate their provision to employment needs. Contacts with employers followed both formal and informal channels and their extent and nature varied between departments. A formal mechanism was the system of advisory committees for college departments which included representation from local employers. In our case study institutions the main functions of such bodies were to disseminate information about courses and to receive feedback, and they might also act as a sounding board for new developments in provision. However, criticisms were made about their operation. First it was felt that they were mainly reactive to what the college was doing and did not independently promote views of provision needed. Secondly, in some cases doubt was expressed whether the committees had detailed knowledge of the local employment market and members might just represent sectional views. For these reasons some staff expressed caution in acting on the views of advisory committees. The same criticisms were made of the role of college governing bodies which also included employer representatives.

Departmental staff had their own contacts with employers through work experience schemes and the YTS. Some departments arranged specific meetings with groups of employers to publicize provision and discuss specific initiatives. A few of the case study colleges had undertaken surveys of employers to find out their views but the response rate varied and the information was not always able to be used and might not be accurate. For example, in one college department employers had indicated the need for a package of vocational 'A' level subjects in the business studies area but when such a package was mounted this failed to attract demand from students. The careers service also figured as a way of contact with employers, although it was felt in some cases that departmental staff had better contacts. As with schools, the careers service varied in its contact with colleges over curriculum development. College staff commented that despite all these varied contacts, it was still difficult to define employer needs with the necessary precision for planning and that the views received were often conflicting. This meant that staff had to test employers' views against other sources of available information.

Staff views on provision All of these varied sources of information were interpreted by college staff in order to evaluate provision. Their opinion of existing provision was therefore of particular importance (Bennett, 1986). Staff views of the scope and orientation of provision influenced what they felt to be necessary and how it would be evaluated. These views might differ between senior and junior staff and between different areas of the college. In addition there were pressures to implement initiatives from central government. Staff knew about developments elsewhere from professional networks and the educational press. These sources could be used to focus attention on new needs or developments in provision. Yet the use of this knowledge had to be aggregated by senior management and balanced against such factors as the pressures for change and resource availability within the institution.

Conclusion — Planning and Needs Assessment

The American models of needs assessment considered in Chapter 4 provide a method whereby needs can be taken up and used in educational planning. The different models within the needs assessment movement all display a common characteristic in the prescriptive way that the identification of needs is supposed to influence what provision will be made. As the following diagram shows, these models employ a sequence of stages which moves from identifying needs to developing what provision best meets these needs and then evaluating the success of this provision. They are similar to the methods of policy making based on the principle of rationality (Dror, 1968; Carley, 1980). The rational process is characterized by reflective activity and seeks to relate policy means to defined ends which are themselves under constant review. These ends are viewed as distinct from the means available in terms of existing services. The rational policy maker has access to a full range of information with which to evaluate the options. The identification of needs would be a major element of the rational model of policy making and viewed separately from what provision already existed.

How far do the rational needs assessment models approximate to the way that the planning of 16–19 provision is carried out in local education systems? The evidence from the research shows that planning both at LEA level and within institutions displayed a number of key features.

It did not take place in a vacuum, or start from a blank sheet. Of particular importance was the legacy of past patterns of provision which conditioned how needs were defined and priorities produced. This was particularly true of institutions. These patterns might reflect past definitions of need or providers' views about what courses should be made available, without any new explicit consideration of what needs were seen to exist or how existing needs had changed. This highlighted the importance of expressed need or demand for existing courses in the planning process together with the normative views of staff. Unlike the rational model of needs assessment, there was not always a clear separation of the identification and provision for needs. Instead provision tended to condition how needs were perceived. This is similar to Kaufman's third 'classical' model of needs assessment outlined in Chapter 4 where general statements of goals are made and then programmes are developed, implemented and evaluated without much measurement or empirical data on needs or performance.

A second feature relates to the way in which planning was conducted.

Figure 3: The Rational Model of Needs Assessment and Planning

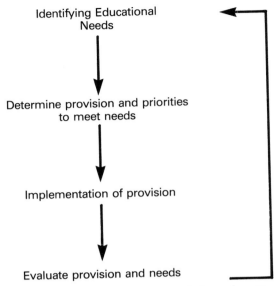

Initiatives for change came from different parts of the education system and there was no automatic consensus on the aims of provision nor the definitions of educational needs. Decisions result from negotiation between various participants, depending on the power and resources that each possessed. Traditionally the hallmark of educational decision making has been the autonomy enjoyed by institutions in defining needs and determining what provision should be made. However, in recent years the distribution of power within the education system has altered; one major change is the increase in the power of central government in their prescriptions of new needs and the nature of provision. Similarly the role of the LEA has changed with growing resource constraints and attempts to rationalize provision. The process of negotiation is also apparent in the way that planning is conducted within institutions. The different groups have their own interests and views about provision which may make it difficult for senior managers to develop priorities (Weick, 1976).

The uncertainty surrounding the planning of provision inhibited the management of change. This uncertainty can be divided into internal and external constraints. The former includes such factors as the structure of the decision making process, the values and interests of LEA decision makers and the staff providing courses, and the need to gain resources to develop new provision. External constraints refer to the environmental contingencies that have to be taken into account by policy makers. One important constraint was the changing nature of the education market which made it difficult to predict changes. Policy makers did not have full access to the information on the needs that existed and were unable to use this in planning. Planning also had to take into account the difficulty of changing curricula initiatives within a short time scale. This might rule out an extensive consideration of what needs existed. Thus planning did not necessarily follow the same sequence of events as suggested in the rational models.

Planning 16–19 provision, therefore, was a complex process made up of different decisions and the effect of a combination of different influences. It tended to correspond with the incremental model of decision making (Lindblom, 1959). The ends were frequently unclear and there was a reliance on the available means. The process was remedial in scope and policies were formulated as and when a problem arose, rather than resulting from a large scale review of needs. Finally, there were different participants in the process with various interests, which meant the lack of a unitary policy making body with a consensus about aims. The main problem with this mode of planning which was raised in Chapter 5 is that whilst it might be more accurate as a description of how planning is conducted it is not radical in the ability to make large scale changes in response to needs.

References

Barrett, S. and Fudge, C. (Eds) (1981), *Policy and Action*, London Methuen.

Bennett, Y., (1986) *A Fragmented View? Professional Accountability and the Maintenance of Standards in Vocational Curricula*, London, FEU.

Bush, T., (1986) *Theories of Educational Management*, London, Harper & Row.

Carley, M., (1980) *Rational Techniques in Policy Analysis*, London, Heinemann.

Challis, R., Mason, C. and Parkes. D. (1984) *The Local Authority and YTS*, Interim Report, Sheffield, MSC.

Cohen, M.D. *et al*, (1972) 'A garbage can model of organizational choice', *Administrative Science Quarterly*, 17, 1, March.

Danziger, J.N., (1976) 'Assessing incrementalism in British municipal budgeting', *British Journal of Political Science*, 6, 3, July.

David, M.E., (1977) *Reform, Reaction and Resources: The 3 Rs of Educational Planning*, Windsor, NFER.

Dennison, W.F., (1984) *Educational Finances and Resources*, London, Croom Helm.

DES, (1980) *Education for 16–19 Year Olds*, (The Macfarlane Report), London, HMSO.

DES, (1987) *Providing for Quality: The Pattern of Organisation to Age 19*, London, HMSO.

Dror, Y., (1968) *Public Policy Making Re-examined*, Chicago, IL, Chandler.

Grunow, D., (1980) 'Constraints on organizational and personal responsiveness towards clients' needs as a consequence of interorganizational service networks' in Grunow, D., and Hegner, F., (Eds), *Welfare or Bureacracy: Problems of Matching Social Services to Clients' Needs — Research on Service Delivery, Vol. II* Oelgeschlager.

Hainsworth, G., (1986) 'Planning the education system in Manchester', in Ranson, S., and Travers, T., (Eds) *The Revolution in Education and Training*, London, Longmans.

Hewton, E., (1986) *Education in Recession: Crisis in County Hall and Classroom*, London, Allen & Unwin.

HOYLE, E., (1982) 'Micropolitics of educational organizations', *Educational Management and Administration*, 10, 2.

KOGAN, M., (1986) *Education Accountability*, London, Hutchinson.

JENNINGS, R.E., (1977) *Education and Politics: Policy Making in LEAs*, London, Batsford.

LINDBLOM, C.E., (1959) 'The science of muddling through', *Public Administration Review*, 24, 2.

MIDGLEY, J., (1984) 'Fields of practice and professional roles for social planners: An overview' in MIDGLEY, J., and PIACHAUD, D., (Eds) *The Fields and Methods of Social Planning*, London, Heinemann.

MSC/LAA POLICY GROUP, (1985) *Work Related NAFE — A Guidance Handbook*, London, MSC/LAA.

RANSON, S, and TRAVERS, T., (1986) *The Revolution in Education and Training*, Longman, London.

REID, W.A., (1975) 'The changing curriculum: Theory and practice' in REID, W.A., and WALKER, D.F. (Eds), *Case Studies in Curriculum Change*, London, Routledge & Kegan Paul.

SHAW, K.E., (1975) 'Negotiating curriculum change in a college of education' in REID, W.A. and WALKER, D.F. (Eds) *Case Studies in Curriculum Change*, London, Routledge and Kegan Paul.

SIMKINS, T., (1986) 'Patronage, markets and collegiality: Reflections on the allocation of finance in secondary schools', *Educational Management and Administration*, 14, 1.

WEICK, K., (1976) 'Educational organizations as loosely coupled systems', *Administrative Science Quarterly*, 21, 1, March.

9   Relationships and Integration

The framework outlined in Chapter 6 showed that the process of assessing the needs of the 16–19 age group can be analyzed along certain dimensions. Of importance here is the concept of the local educational system, made up of the different institutions and agencies concerned with the delivery of services and provision for this age group. These will make their own separate assessments of what are the needs of the 16–19 age group and what courses are required. As Chapter 6 demonstrated, one important dimension in understanding needs assessment is the type of interaction that occurs between these components and whether the different assessments can be tested against each other. It is therefore important to analyze the relationships and interaction between these different bodies in the post-16 network to investigate whose definition of need is influential and how these get taken up in planning.

The Relationship Between Clients and Providers

The ideal of professionalism in education implies that it is the task of the teacher to assess and respond to the needs of the clients — student, parent, or employer. This is seen to imply a responsiveness by the institutions to the needs they identify (Robinson, 1978). The question arises of the nature of the relationship between provider and client and how this affects needs assessment.

Students

The first set of interactions is between the students who receive post-16 education and those staff in schools and colleges responsible for identifying their needs and determining provision. This section starts by reviewing from research material the type, scope and characteristics of the relationships which are used by institutions to assess student needs. As Chapter 6 has indicated, student needs are assessed in a number of different ways. Some are direct and others are inferred from activities that serve another purpose.

Recruitment process

Recruitment was used as a first step in the selection and then finding out the needs of potential students. In schools this process began as early as the end of the third and during the fourth and fifth years when staff help students identify their aspirations through such mechanisms as tutorials, careers guidance and questionnaires asking for preliminary intentions as to the courses to be followed. Parents expressed their views at careers evenings. The available provision was made known to students through brochures stating the range and combination of courses. In some cases questionnaires were distributed to students as a way of ascertaining their wishes. In the college sector recruitment assumed a special and more important role because of the break at 16. In general, staff of sixth form or tertiary colleges visited the pre-16 institutions to publicize what was available and college 'open days' were held to allow students to visit departments and sample courses. Procedures were less elaborate for part-time students in the colleges who tended to find out about courses through prospectuses and advertisements or through their employers. The main event in the recruitment of full-time students was the interview held with the student to ascertain suitability for a course of study. This was an encounter between staff and student, where views could be exchanged although it also required a completed application form and reports from the student's school. An individual's needs were commonly negotiated between staff and student and the permutation of available courses selected accordingly. The recruitment process was therefore primarily concerned with matching needs to existing provision. However, because of falling rolls institutions in many of our authorities competed with each other for students. Staff recognized the importance of marketing their provision and of trying to respond to new demands as they perceived them. Yet staff interviewed noted that there could be a dilemma between providing objective guidance to students which might entail a change of institution and also serving the interests of their own institution through maintaining recruitment. Thus, the way in which recruitment procedures were applied was an important influence on the selection of the clients to be served by the institution (Greenley, 1980).

Pastoral care

The system of pastoral care and careers guidance was also viewed by staff as a further opportunity for assessing student needs. Institutions varied in how this was structured and in the responsibilities of tutors. In schools, the reports on students could be used to highlight dissatisfaction with a course and allow staff to recommend a programme of individual progress. However, reports were used by staff in different ways and not always for individual review. In the colleges, part-time students did not have the same amount of pastoral care as those studying full-time. Careers guidance for the post-16-year-old also varied between the different categories of students. This was provided both by the institution's own careers staff and by a more specialized input from the careers service, although the latter varied in the priority it gave to the post-16 age group. Students intending to continue to higher or further education tended to receive most help. In the college sector those on full-time courses received more help than those on part-time vocational courses. Apart from the formal system of careers guidance provided in institutions, it was recognized that members of staff in departments would give guidance and this was particularly so with the vocational departments of FE colleges.

All of these assessment procedures were controlled by the professionals. Therefore much depended on the ability of staff to forge relationships with students and the students' ability to raise questions about their own needs. One criticism made in some institutions in our research was that tutorial time was too limited and its use depended on the willingness of the student to seek help. Another problem was the role and status of those providing careers guidance and pastoral care and how far they were, in fact, used by the rest of the staff in the institution.

Teaching process

Apart from specialist support that might be given to students, staff recognized that teaching provided an indication of the needs of students. The teacher-student relationship could be used to identify particular needs which could then be dealt with by 'fine-tuning' provision. Examples mentioned were extra tuition or particular types of work experience, but these depended on staff judgments of what was required. Staff also believed that individual needs were already determined when a student entered an institution and that it was difficult for these to be changed. It might be feasible for a student to change course early in the year but increasingly difficult as the year elapsed. It was felt that in many cases if students found they had chosen a wrong course, then they left the institution. In some institutions student councils promoted exchanges with staff. These might provide an alternative view of needs that was less dependent on the prognosis of the professional. However, where these existed they tended to play a limited role and were concerned with peripheral matters rather than explicitly discussing educational needs or satisfaction with provision.

The relationship between the student as a client and the professional was therefore negotiated on an individual level and could develop in different ways (McKinlay, 1980). The form of this was similar in all the institutions in our case studies. The clients were dependent upon the professionals for assessing their needs. Yet in most cases the students had to refer themselves for guidance even though their general progress was monitored by staff. Another feature of this relationship was that it involved a combination of specialist and general roles and a student could apply for guidance both from their subject teacher and from the pastoral or careers guidance staff. The problem for the institution was how the different information could be aggregated in responding to student needs, an issue which is taken up later in this section.

Employers

The issue of whether employers are clients of education is difficult to answer. Certainly the FE colleges have traditionally seen themselves as serving the needs of employers through the development of vocational courses. (Gleeson and Mardle, 1980; Theodossin, 1986). There have been recent attempts by central government to ensure that education, and particularly the schools sector, develops closer contacts with employers and makes its provision more related to the needs of industry. A number of different types of contact exist between the different levels of the local educational system and employers and the following section outlines how they contributed to needs assessment.

Direct contacts

Schools and colleges in the research behaved differently in the way they related to employers. In schools there were a range of direct contacts involving particular staff meeting and talking with employers but these served a range of purposes and not just a way of assessing employers' needs. The provision of work experience had increased in most schools and staff invested considerable time in organizing placements. On occasions staff contacted employers to collect reactions to new courses, particularly new one-year pre-vocational courses. One example from the research concerned a school that had brought in employers to discuss the format of a CPVE course and give it endorsement. Some schools also organized special events such as a conference or forum to discuss a specific issue such as the teaching of mathematics which established contact with either a broad range of local employers or those in a particular type of industry. In contrast schools operating the TVEI scheme tended to have created more structured contacts, as employers were included in the mechanisms of evaluating courses run as part of TVEI. Another form of individual contact came through schemes to allow teachers to spend time in industry and industrial staff to spend time in the schools. In colleges, the range and experience of contacts was larger (Theodossin, 1986). Staff in the departments with a vocational tradition emphasized them as a way of finding out what employers wanted; but their involvement was often low and unrepresentative. Some colleges had carried out surveys of employers to find out their views about their own training needs, although these varied in the response rate.

Indirect contact

Other forms of education-employer contact involved selected employers acting on behalf of other employers. School governing bodies were one such mechanism by which employers could be represented, although their participation varied between authorities. The role of governing bodies tended to be unclear and variable; they provided a mixture of support and advice, while exercising authority over some part of the school's activity and negotiating with other parts of the education system. College governing bodies had advisory committees with employer representatives which were organized either around a particular occupation or around the span of work of a college department. In most cases the function of these bodies was to review provision, provide feedback on courses, and consider new course proposals. In some colleges they received information on course recruitment, examination results and employment destinations. However, they tended to meet only on a termly basis and their functions and composition were determined by the college. Staff views varied from seeing them as providing a useful source of advice about courses to performing a more passive role. Those employers interviewed regarded them as one possible source of influence that could be exerted upon the colleges.

Employer representation might also be possible on some of the consortia that existed. But as will be seen later in this chapter, they were mainly concerned with the coordination and rationalization of existing provision rather than acting as a forum to negotiate assessments of need. A further forum for employer contact was through the school-industry liaison committees where they existed. These brought together senior staff from schools and colleges in an area, local employers, trade unionists, careers service staff and officers from the LEA. Their purpose was to provide a means of contact and to promote curriculum projects and work experience. In the one example encountered in the research those involved felt it was a means of cultivating general contact between education and employment and did not discuss the detail of or review local educational provision.

Careers service

Apart from these direct and indirect forms of contact with employers there were also relationships that used an intermediary, particularly the careers service. This is discussed briefly here and is taken up later in this chapter. In all authorities studied the careers service had started to develop closer relationships with employers, not just in dealing with vacancies but also in seeking to learn their views and requirements for transmission to other bodies. Careers officers were generally allocated a number of employers. Careers officers were also represented on some of the advisory and liaison committees considered above. However, the main problem with the careers service's role as intermediary was that the service might be bypassed by the other channels of contact that existed. The educational institutions had their own contacts with employers and, for example, might deal directly with employers about vacancies.

LEA contact

Although the majority of education-employer contacts were at the institutional level, some existed at the LEA level in order to influence authority policies. Our national survey of LEAs' policy making showed that many authorities had developed consultative bodies between education and industry or participated in wider authority meetings concerned with employment matters. Yet as LEAs covered large areas, employer representation was bound to be selective and there was a tendency for only the larger employers to be represented. In our case study authorities, councillors and officers also had their own contacts with industry. Local authority departments such as those for employment, economic development or planning were also in contact with employers and possessed sources of information about employer needs.

Conclusions

There were a number of relationships between employers and education, varying in their functions and roles. In the main these had been initiated from the education side rather than employers. Much depended on the views of senior staff about what they wanted from these contacts and these views varied widely both between and within institutions. Employers as clients had to use the available mechanisms. Employers' representatives interviewed in the research wanted a closer relationship with education but there were difficulties in how far they could contribute to formulating educational provision. The available mechanisms served a number of different purposes, from providing information about education to reviewing courses, as well as simply exchanging ideas. Employers' views therefore entered at different points in the education system. It was uncertain from the research how far the employers' views received were representative of all local employers. Inevitably employers tended to speak from an individual perspective within their own sector of employment. The tendency was for the larger rather than the smaller companies to enter into relationships with education. Staff in the institutions studied reported difficulty in gaining a comprehensive viewpoint and in aggregating the frequently conflicting views.

The Manpower Services Commission

The arrival of the MSC on the educational scene meant that the FE colleges had to take into account their needs as clients. The MSC was obliged to provide a YTS place for all minimum age school-leavers who sought one. The MSC planning relied on forecasts of numbers from the careers service and on its advice on the number and type of schemes to provide. The MSC and managing agents purchased YTS education and training so there were a number of relationships with the education system.

At a formal level there was liaison between MSC and LEA officers which had become more productive as YTS had developed (Challis *et al.*, 1984). It has also been stimulated by the work-related NAFE development plans. These formal mechanisms were concerned with coordinating YTS arrangements and discussing policies. It was customary for there to be one chief education officer on each Area Manpower Board which reviewed local arrangements and related MSC policies to local arrangements. But it was felt by those involved in AMBs that their role was primarily advisory.

At a local level, managing agents of employer-based schemes had a 'customer' relationship with the colleges and were in a position to indicate what they wanted by way of education and training. Yet, as with all customers, there was a tendency for the managing agents to purchase their requirements from what was provided. Managing agents tended to carry out their negotiations over YTS with individual departments, although attempts were made to provide some type of central mechanism for administering and reviewing overall college provision for YTS. This was deemed necessary because YTS represented a major reorientation of provision, both in its aims and in the type of student entering the colleges. It was felt in many colleges that internal coordination of YTS provision was essential. Attempts by managing agents to monitor the provision received by the trainees sometimes encountered resistance from college staff. MSC was engaged in the formal monitoring of college provision and in some cases it had suggested improvements by way of 'informal pressure' particularly where it was felt that provision was too academically oriented and geared to examination requirements. Some MSC officials felt that colleges varied in their willingness to change their provision to make it appropriate for YTS trainees. It was also recognized that if colleges did not become more responsive to the needs of the YTS, then there were private agencies which could provide training. Thus in terms of being a client, the MSC had the resources to purchase provision from the colleges which enabled it to bargain over provision. Some of the colleges in the research stated that it was difficult to change their provision to meet MSC requirements because of the way that official policies fluctuated in response to national direction. Colleges were also hampered through their own deficiencies in forward planning.

Conclusion: The Relationship Between Clients and Providers

The relationship between the providers of education and the clients was thus of a different form depending on the balance of power between them. The main variable at work can be seen to be the dependency of one on the other for information, resources and legitimacy which produced different patterns of relationship (Scharpf, 1978). This is illustrated in diagrammatic form in Table 10 for students, employers and the MSC.

In education the individual student has traditionally been regarded as the prime client, resting on the view that it is the task of the teacher to assess needs and develop provision accordingly. The student is assumed to be in a passive position and the assessment of need is of a normative kind with little contribution by the client. This can be seen to have changed as institutions have improved their ways of assessing needs, particularly when there is more competition between them and the client has attained more power in society (Wirt, 1981). However, it is still true that in many cases the student has to initiate the contact. With employers the relationship with education is of a more uncertain kind depending on the extent to which the providers seek out employers' views, and the resulting structure of contacts that has been established. These contacts have almost totally been created by education as a way of receiving the views of employers and perform other purposes than just identifying their needs. It is the educationalists who determine which employers should take part, the functions of such bodies or contacts and, more importantly, the use of the knowledge

TABLE 10: *RELATIONSHIPS BETWEEN CLIENTS AND PROVIDER*

Client	Dependency on provider	Structure of relationship	Resources possessed by client
Students	High	* Individual interaction with professionals	* Individual demand/choice of courses * Collective demand
Employers	Medium	* Varied forms of contact. Contact determined by providers	* Employer legitimacy * Knowledge of employers' needs * Sending employees on courses
MSC	Low	* Indirect through managing agents	* Purchase of provision or withdrawing provision

gained. The emphasis on securing employers' views can be seen primarily as being to gain endorsement from employers for existing provision and knowledge of their requirements.

The relationship with the MSC is of yet a different kind. It has been initiated by central government, and colleges have been placed in the position of having to respond in changing their provision. The resources possessed by MSC in this relationship are those of finance and the threat of withdrawal. Hitherto the planning of YTS used to be carried out separately from the rest of post-16 provision. The education service has been drawn in to contribute to YTS planning rather than the MSC contributing to total educational provision and training. However, since the involvement of the MSC with the planning of work-related NAFE, local discussions about YTS have related more to other parts of post-16 education and training.

The Relationship Between Providers

The local educational system is made up of different providers with different interests. They each make assessments of the needs of the 16–19 age group but the way that these may be taken up and used in planning is a complex process and depends on the relations that exist between the providers. Looking at the system in total there are a number of key characteristics. The first is that education and training are provided by institutions separately assessing needs responding in terms of the scope and orientation of their provision. Secondly, the LEA's influence on provision has traditionally been limited; in the main its role has been to ensure that institutions received the necessary resources to make provision. Until the 1970s there was a common and entrenched view amongst participants that institutions should exercise a high degree of autonomy in making provision. However, the onset of financial, political and demographic changes have brought a greater awareness of the need to coordinate across the system to ensure effectiveness and efficiency in meeting needs. These ideas were most visibly spelt out in the Macfarlane Report but have also been continued in some of the reports from the Audit Commission (1986) and in the DES Circular, *Providing for Quality* (DES, 1987). These principles of autonomy, coordination, efficiency and effectiveness may conflict in relationships within the local education system. They are important because they condition the way in which needs assessment is undertaken and how planning of provision is conducted.

Coordination at LEA Level

The local education authority is not a monolithic body but is made up of various interests — different officers, advisers, elected members, and others, the various agencies such as the careers and the youth and community services. The relationships between interests is important in considering how needs are assessed at this level and how policies become framed. One of the important questions, then, is how these different bodies were coordinated in their activities.

Organization of the education department

Education departments can be seen as organizations with the function of producing, administering and implementing policies on education. Their structure affects their response to issues and problems. In general they have traditionally been organized functionally, with sections responsible for the different areas of work carried out — schools, further education, special education, and then with specialist sections for finance and buildings and development. Policy making and management for the post-16 age group is often split between the sections for schools and further education as shown by our survey of LEAs. In those authorities where this traditional division existed, the research indicated different views about its effects. One view was that the organization of the department along these lines led to a lack of coordination in dealing with the issues affecting the post-16 age group and as a consequence there was no clear view of the priorities in 16–19 provision. The sections were seen to be introspective and aware only of their own responsibilities. They tended to collect information relevant to their own concerns and there was no central collection of information about provision and the identified needs of students. This was similar to the findings of the Macfarlane Report (DES, 1980), which stated that authorities were not organized in a way that enabled them to provide effective coordination of 16–19 provision. A less pessimistic view was that although there was a split in responsibilities, there were mechanisms to ensure that the sections were aware of each other's developments. These included regular officer contacts, the senior officers' management team meetings and informal contacts. In some of the authorities studied, the split in functions was defended because it was seen to be a natural break and any other split, such as between pre- and post-16 concerns, would merely present difficulties of coordination at another key point in the system.

A number of the case study LEAs had appointed specific officers to provide coordination of post-16 policies. However, their influence depended on the seniority and status of the post. In one case study LEA, a third tier officer had been appointed with specific responsibility for the coordination of post-16 policy reporting directly to a deputy chief education officer. In another LEA this responsibility was added to that of an officer in the FE section but for this individual there were problems with the time available to perform this function. In others, a deputy CEO had the task of providing an overall view. The same problems of coordination were evident in the organization of the advisory service and in some authorities there was an adviser with the function of 16–19 coordination. Added to these specific posts, some LEAs had established working groups of officers and inspectors to coordinate the various initiatives in the post-16 field.

One of the case study county LEAs had introduced a post-16 division with responsibilities for all policy for this age group, whether provision was in schools or colleges. This was seen as surmounting the traditional schools/FE divide. Yet difficulties of coordination were still recognized; the school sixth forms were still administered by the schools division and they were financed under different regulations from those governing colleges. The policies on transport were budgeted in different ways. Moreover, at member level, school policy came under the Schools Sub-committee and college policy under the FE Sub-committee. The importance of the structure of the education department lay in the extent to which it affected policy making and the visibility of the needs of the 16–19 age group within the administrative process.

Education Committee structure

In most LEAs the structure of sub-committees reflected the split in responsibilities in the organization of the education department. This was again seen to lead to problems of coordination and in particular to competition between sectors in the preparation of the education budget. The survey of LEA policy making arrangements showed that a small number of authorities had a sub-committee with overall responsibility for 16–19 education but this had only an advisory function. On the question of the relationship between officers and councillors, the pattern in the case study LEAs was for officers to produce policies and the elected members to respond to these rather than themselves being proactive in developing their own policies and definitions of need.

Education department relationships with the rest of the local authority

Another important relationship is that between the education department and other bodies in the local authority. The relationship with the careers service is dealt with later in the chapter. Contact with the youth and community service was mainly on specific issues such as social problems involving the 16–19 age group. The youth and community service did have its own definitions of the needs of the 16–19 age group. However, these were rarely used in planning provision by education officers or advisers. The education department was also involved in relationships with other local authority departments; mainly social services, employment, finance, chief executive's department or planning. These were either of a structured form as a result of an authority's system of corporate management, or had developed to deal with ad hoc problems. For example, educational provision for those with special needs involved contact with the social services department. In most of the authorities studied, issues of employment were being dealt with through interdepartmental working groups of officers or elected members. There were some examples of information from other departments being used for planning purposes but in general this was limited. On matters concerned with needs, the education department tended to remain semi-autonomous in its own domain (Jennings, 1984). However, the picture was different on issues concerning resources, where education departments were facing pressures from finance departments to reduce expenditure (Hewton, 1986).

Relationships Across the Local Education System

The importance of coordination was also seen in the relationships between the LEA and its institutions. These had come about as a result of a combination of different influences — resource constraints, the competition between institutions providing post-16 education, and the growing interdependence of institutions arising from new initiatives such as CPVE. The greater leadership role of the LEA in the planning of 16–19 provision was also significant. This was influenced by the nature of the relationships between the authority and its institutions. The patterns differed in the various authorities studied as a result of specific factors such as size and geography. Of particular importance to understanding this relationship is the notion of the 'administrative culture'. This refers to the style and complexity of relationships between the LEA and the institutions, and the views about these held by the various participants in the local education system (Kogan *et al*, 1984). The main dimensions of this administrative culture are factors such as LEA administrative procedures on resources, the nature of institutional accountability to the LEA, and the existence of multiple channels of contact, all of which affect the degree of autonomy possessed by institutions. The degree of political involvement in determining provision is another factor. However, in all the case study LEAs this was low, although there is evidence that in recent years political involvement has increased in some LEAs.

LEA-institutional communication

The first relationship is the pattern of communication between the LEA and the institutions. This affects the implementation of LEA policies and influences the extent that definitions of need are transmitted across the local education system. The relationships found in the case study authorities can be characterized along a continuum in terms of their degree of formality and their scope. The research showed that at the most formal end were those LEAs which produced and disseminated policy guidelines on 16–19 provision. These were seen by officers to provide guidance on such issues as the scope and orientation of provision, the demarcation of courses between institutions and how courses might be provided. Potentially guidelines could indicate the priorities accorded by the LEA to the various needs of the 16–19 age group. However, in the case study authorities where guidelines existed, both officers and the staff of institutions recognized that they were only advisory in character and were difficult to implement. Instead they acted as symbolic statements about how provision should be distributed between institutions.

Authorities also used a number of different types of meetings in their relationships with institutions. These covered a range of different issues but might also be used to provide a dialogue about what needs existed and how they were to be met. It was common for these to be held with the heads of the different types of institutions. Thus in one county authority in our research with a mixed system of institutional arrangements, there were separate meetings with the heads of schools, the principals of the sixth form colleges and the FE college principals. These tended to discuss issues related to their own sphere of concern and 16–19 education might be only one issue within many. In another authority with largely a tertiary college system, there was a principals' conference composed of authority representatives and the principals of the colleges. This served a number of functions including communicating the views of the LEA and identifying central and local views of need. It was also responsible for receiving the proposals for new courses. However, there were clearly conflicts of interest between the participants. Decision making was characterized by reluctance to alter the consensus between participants. This authority was also promoting an open consideration of priorities and objectives but there were mixed views of whether this style of collective decision-making could work.

Working parties

The meetings considered above were only partly concerned with assessing needs and discussing provision, yet they brought in all the heads of the institutions. Another mechanism used by some authorities was a working party composed of LEA officers and advisers, occasionally elected members, and representatives of the heads of institutions. These were generally set up to discuss 16–19 provision and had an advisory role, in some cases reporting to an education sub-committee. It was felt by some of the participants that the existence of such bodies gave a high profile to the needs of the 16–19 age group in the policy making process.

Role of advisers

Advisers also provided a way of communicating between the authority and its institutions. Advisers monitored provision across an authority and stimulated initiatives. In some cases there was an adviser with specific responsibility for post-16 provision but elsewhere advisers were organized on an area or subject basis. Yet their relationship with the institutions varied in the research, particularly whether they were consulted or became involved in developments or changes in provision as was shown in the previous chapter. They could communicate LEA policies to the institutions yet in practice their low frequency of direct contact with the institutions meant they could only play a reactive role.

Governing bodies

Another point of contact between authority and institutions was the school or college governing bodies. In some authorities these were seen to be significant because they brought together politicians, officers, employers and institutional staff in the context of the institution's performance and development. They could allow the representatives from the LEA to receive views about local needs and in turn tell the institutions about the constraints and about the authority's policies.

The Role of the Careers Service

The careers service was involved in creating relationships across the educational system and therefore could act as an intermediary. Potentially careers officers saw themselves as combining two functions; providing guidance to students in ascertaining their individual needs, and providing information and advice about the collective needs of students including those expressed by employers. The kind of information they collect has been reviewed in Chapter 7. The careers services were involved in a number of different relationships with various bodies in the local education system. Some careers officers interviewed saw themselves as having four different clients — the individual student, the institution, employers and the LEA.

Relationships with institutions

Careers officers were involved in providing guidance to students and the time allocated to this activity in institutions was normally two days a week. Careers services varied in the way that they were organized and in particular the degree of specialization in the activities of officers, Similarly there was the question of the priority they gave to advice to the post-16 age group and this varied between authorities. The traditional way of relating to the student was through the careers interview, although there was a trend away from blanket interviewing to developing different forms of guidance. Opportunities for guidance varied between the different categories of students, with less time being devoted to part time students in the colleges. Much depended on the way that the institution used the careers service in terms of giving it priority and publicity. The main contact with the institution was through the teacher or lecturer responsible for careers education. The important factor here was the ability of the individual careers officer to liaise and communicate with the tutors and the heads of departments. Yet uncertainties were apparent about guidance; careers officers felt that they had to provide objective guidance but with competition so strong they ran a risk of offending the institutions.

Careers officers also believed that they could legitimately participate in the development of the curriculum through their knowledge of the employment market. However, this role was less certain and varied considerably between the institutions in our research. In some institutions careers officers were consulted about changes in the curriculum but this was by no means common and much depended on the attitude of senior staff towards their contribution and the personal relationship established. Careers officers' contribution to curriculum change was mainly in the development of vocational courses which had implications for employment.

Contacts with employers

All the careers services in the case study authorities were devoting more time to maintaining contacts with employers and transmitting their views to education. This was felt by careers officers to be an important function of the careers service at the present time. Relationships with employers were achieved through a number of different channels. It was normal for careers officers to be allocated either a geographical patch or employers related to their own sphere of interest. Individual contact with employers served different purposes; recruitment, learning their activities, publicizing the activities of the careers service, or, familiarizing them with new developments in education. Employers varied in how they saw the role of the careers service and the use they made of its services. In some cases there was extensive contact, whereas other employers used their own direct contacts with institutions or recruited through some other channel. The careers service might determine the collective needs of employers through such devices as conferences, careers meetings or industrial liaison committees where employers and educationalists were present, although the use of these events varied between authorities. The difficulty experienced by careers officers lay in identifying the needs of employers with any degree of precision. The forums mentioned above might be unrepresentative, as there was a tendency for certain types of employer, particularly the smaller ones, not to participate. This highlighted the question of how the views of small employers could be obtained. Another problem was that there were frequently conflicting views amongst employers about their own requirements and their expectations from education. It was felt that some of these might be unrealistic, such as the entry requirements for particular jobs, and this raised the problem of how to educate employers.

Relationship with the education department

The relationship between the careers service and the education department differed between authorities. In management terms the principal careers officer normally reported to a third tier education officer responsible for further education and the service reported to the FE sub-committee or in some cases a joint sub-committee for education and employment. Contacts with the education department included regular meetings with senior officers and participation in consultative meetings, course approval mechanisms, and in some cases institutional coordination. The careers service dealt with the MSC on the planning of YTS and provided it with information. Yet the range of contacts varied between LEAs depending on the status of the service in the authority and the use made of its knowledge by officers and advisers. The careers service regularly supplied information on destinations and employment trends to the education department and to elected members. The use of this information varied as was seen earlier. In some of the authorities studied, officers felt that they received enough information from the careers service and there was the danger of 'information overload'. Much of this information, anyway, could not always be used directly in planning. In general the careers service responded to, rather than initiated, relationships with officers and advisers.

Influences on the careers service role

The careers service played a mediating role in the local educational system which reflected a movement away from its traditional placement and guidance function (Ranson and Ribbins, 1986). There were indications from the research that the work of the careers service was showing signs of division between the assessment of individual needs that was undertaken by junior or specialist staff and the assessment of collective need that was increasingly performed by more senior staff. The careers service could potentially bring together the different participants in 16–19 education and act as an intermediary. But because of its location in the education system its effectiveness as an intermediary varied and there were a number of factors which reduced its influence. The work of the careers service was conditioned by how others see it and their own decisions about what use to make of its services. The expertise of the careers service lay in its ability to provide an interpretation of both the individual and collective needs of students and employers. Yet this was also carried out by the other bodies in the educational system to different degrees. Moreover, they each had their own connections which could be used and might bypass the careers service.

Therefore the role of the careers service was no more than advisory in its relationships with all parts of the system and much depended on the personal relationships that were developed by individual officers. There was less dependency on the information and expertise of the careers service by the other bodies. Its expertise was limited as it did not possess the monopoly of information. Its relationships were frequently uncertain and it had to exploit the networks in which it was involved.

Institutional Coordination of 16–19 Provision

Types of coordination

The development of institutional coordination had been attempted in many authorities. The pattern varied between the authorities studied depending on such factors as the size of the authority, geographical considerations, the type of institutions, the extent of falling rolls and the administrative culture of the particular LEA.

The patterns of coordination found in the survey of LEAs can be analyzed according to their scope, the degree of formality in their operation, the participants involved, the functions carried out and relationship with the LEA. These are shown in diagrammatic form in Table 11.

Informal cooperation The first type was the *informal cooperation* between institutions, either between schools or between school and college. This had arisen out of the action of local heads and the main activity was in sharing minority courses.

Consortia At a more formal level was the *consortia system* where relationships were more structured and formal and these tended to be organized for a geographical area. The LEA had an involvement in setting up consortia either in a particular area or across the whole authority. Activities varied from sharing courses to a common timetable for all the participating institutions.

Area coordinating groups The third type was the *area coordinating group* and this involved a body acting as an intermediary between the schools and colleges or the consortium in an area and the LEA. Its purpose was to review provision across its area and provide coordination. This body was normally composed of the professionals together with LEA officers but in some cases included representation from other associated bodies, such as the careers service, the youth and community service and in a few cases councillors and employer representatives. The range of functions was larger and could include coordinating both 'A' level and pre-vocational provision, making decisions on the allocation of new courses, publicizing

TABLE 11: A CLASSIFICATION OF INSTITUTIONAL COORDINATION OF 16–19 PROVISION

Type	Contact Between Institutions	Functions	Participants	Relationship with LEA
A. Informal Cooperation	Informal: School — school School — college	• sharing of minority subjects for example, 'A' Levels • joint timetabling of certain blocs	Senior staff of institutions — head, sixth form head, heads of department	Informal
B. Consortia	More formal: schools — school school — college — sixth form centre	• joint provision of minority courses • sharing of staff • publicizing provision • may control some resources • occasionally joint sixth form	Senior staff of institutions, may include LEA representation	More formal — but varied in LEAs split between prescription and autonomy

| C. Area Coordinating Committees | Formal
• inter-institutional consortium — Area Coordinating Committee | • overview of provision
• advisory function and mechanism for detailed planning
• publicizing provision | Broader composition — can include: school and college staff, careers service, youth and community service, LEA representatives, governors, industry, Trade Unions, rarely MSC | More formal — report to central body |
| D. LEA Central Direction | LEA control exerted over institutions | • setting guidelines on provision
• demarcation of provision
• development of new provision | LEA staff, may include consultation with heads | LEA prescription |

167

provision, providing joint sixth form activities and coordinating applications for courses. In one of the case study LEAs the area coordinating group were used by the LEA as a forum to discuss the authority's 16–19 policy and act as a means of contact with officers.

Central direction   The final type of institutional coordination was *central direction* by the LEA. Most LEAs engaged in monitoring the range of provision across the authority but some exerted a wider range of controls including setting guidelines on appropriate provision, the demarcation of provision and in some cases setting up centres of provision such as providing music courses across an authority. In the case study LEAs there was a problem in implementing these guidelines as the institutions possessed autonomy and were able to resist prescription. This raised the problem of what levers could be used by the LEA to stimulate coordination or change.

Relationships between collaborative groups and the LEA

The relationship between consortia or area coordinating groups with the LEA differed in our case study authorities. In some cases they had been set up by the authority which prescribed their composition and functions. They then had to work within guidelines prescribed by the authority. In others they had evolved in a less structured way and had developed their own format and style of operation. One issue emphasized by those involved was the degree of autonomy possessed by these bodies. The research showed a number of instances where the expectations of the LEA differed from those of the institutions participating. In most authorities the LEA wanted the consortia to rationalize existing provision and increase the coordination between the member institutions. For example, in one Metropolitan district authority the authority wanted 'A' level provision to be rationalized whereas one of the consortia saw collaboration as a way of extending pre-vocational courses. The main resources possessed by the LEA to influence the institutions were its formal authority, persuasion and the threat of the withdrawal of resources from those which did not participate.

Relationship between institutions and the collaborative groups

The relationship between the participating institution and the collaborative group displayed a number of common features in the case studies. In general, participation in the group served the institution's own interests, enabling it to continue making 16–19 provision. The extent of, and commitment to, participation by an institution depended upon the views of its senior management, the history of collaboration and the viability of the institution concerned. Motivation to collaborate varied between institutions and according to the balance between positive and negative factors. Positive factors included the requirement to participate, the involvement

168

by the LEA, the possibility of keeping sixth form students and sixth form teaching, the strengths of joint working and professional solidarity. Factors which weakened the willingness to participate were the fear of a reduction in institutional autonomy, a possible reduction in student and public identity, the lack of necessity to participate, the intra-institutional problems of collaboration and the increase in administration that resulted from collaboration. This balance could shift over time according to the institutions' perceptions of whether there would be benefits or losses from participating.

In planning, institutions had no choice but to take the existence of the consortium into account. Collaboration did not affect the way that needs assessment was carried out, although it did mean that demand became even more important in planning courses because of the imposition in some LEAs of a minimum teaching group size for courses within the consortium. The consortium did not possess any authority over the participating members except those presented by convention and the use of social sanctions and it was still possible for member institutions to limit the extent of their participation and indeed transgress the rules laid down within the consortium.

The operation of such bodies did allow the views of institutions to be aggregated and for there to be a wider discussion of the needs of the 16–19 age group, which might also include inputs from the careers service and other participants. In a few examples the consortium carried out its own investigation of student demand, but in general it relied on the views of the participating institutions about what student needs existed.

Institutional coordination and needs assessment

Institutional coordination was concerned with making provision more cost effective and efficient as well as providing a way of assessing needs across institutional boundaries. As such it served both the interest of the providers and consumers of post-16 educational provision (Weiss, 1981). Its significance was in showing the decline in institutional autonomy and the necessity for institutions to collaborate in their provision (Cordingley, 1985; Mundy and Elliott, 1979). The effect of this upon needs assessment was experienced by the institutions studied in different ways. One effect was for them to become more competitive in their recruitment as increasing student numbers would reduce the need to collaborate over provision. Another effect was to make institutions more specialized in their provision so that they were only meeting a limited number of educational needs.

Coordination and Relationships Within Institutions

If there were difficulties encountered in coordination across the local educational system, then there were also similar problems within educational institutions. Chapter 8 indicated that planning by institutions was a complex process involving different parts. The need for internal coordination arose for several reasons. First, educational institutions are diffuse organizations composed of different subject teaching areas, levels of management, and pastoral and curriculum areas and these will have their own interests and practices (Handy and Aitken, 1986). This was particularly acute in, for example, the college sector where departmentalism was seen by many of those interviewed to pose problems of internal communication and coordination of different practices and policies. Secondly, it was felt that responding to a changing environment required clear goals so that changes could be managed and overall policies produced. This showed the importance of leadership and internal consensus over provision. A third factor was that many of the new educational developments in the post-16 sector required some degree of cooperation between different departments, for example, so that new courses could be devised.

In schools the introduction of CPVE involved different subject departments. Similarly, the introduction of YTS in the FE colleges posed the same problems of developing common policies for teaching and providing these courses. The urgency of these problems varied between institutions but relationships between different parts of the institutions and their coordinating mechanisms exhibited a number of common patterns.

School coordination

In the schools sector a number of important relationships affected the way that provision was made and needs assessed. The first were the relationships between staff on the pastoral side and those in the subject departments. One issue was how the assessments of need made by those staff responsible for pastoral care influenced the determination of provision. There was a problem that, for example, the insights about individual need gained through careers advice might not be utilized. This was partly resolved through record keeping, by regular contacts between tutors and subject teachers and by the role of the head of sixth form. However, much depended on adequate internal communication. The relationship between departments also affected coordination within the school. Departments might be allowed responsibility for their own teaching policies and recruitment procedures for particular courses which differed within the institution. Staff also identified with their own subject and there were distinctive views about the nature and aims of provision. Competition for post-16 students between departments in some schools studied was as significant as that between schools.

Decisions about changes in provision came from different levels in the institution. Departments might have their own views about new provision which were then fed into the institution's decision-making system. The formal pattern of coordination came from the school's decision making mechanisms. These included bodies such as the senior management team, heads of department meetings, and the heads of year meetings. These bodies varied between schools in terms of their exact influence and how far they ensured that coordination was achieved. The head of the sixth was also important in providing an overview of provision and procedures. This was particularly so when institutions participated in a consortium and in one case where this happened in the research the heads of sixth played a major role in both internal negotiations and in negotiations between schools regarding the extent and scope of collaboration over provision. Ultimately it was the headteacher who provided coordination and leadership. This role varied between schools depending on the specific culture of that school and the way the head interpreted his or her role. There were examples in the research where heads and senior management played a major role in influencing curriculum change from a 'top down' perspective by providing leadership and using the resources of the post to stimulate change. In one school pre-vocational courses had been initiated by its senior management who had overcome the resistance from staff in departments. Change was therefore a result both of the formal structure of decision making and informal patterns of negotiation.

College coordination

Colleges were beset by similar problems of coordination, in many cases more prominent than in schools because of their larger size and complexity. Departmentalism was felt by some to enforce rigidity particularly in adapting to new demands. In a large college the interests of academic, vocational and service departments were distinct. They varied in their own ways of working, their views on the needs they were meeting and of their distinctive forms of provision. Their methods of recruitment and monitoring might differ. As with schools there were problems in relating the college careers advisory and student advisory services to the activities of the departments. Departments varied in what use was made of their expertise and information, and a vocational department might have its own contacts with employers and so choose not to use this college function.

In most colleges the basic planning unit was the department with its different subject sections. The value of departmentalism was that it allowed those staff most closely in contact with the students' needs to frame provision. Initiatives might be started at this level and then submitted to higher levels. It was felt by staff in a number of the colleges studied that senior management was having to play an increasing role in coordination. This was undertaken through such devices as heads of department meetings, Academic Board and senior management team meetings. The development of new provision might involve different areas of a college which necessitated an overall college approach to be undertaken. This required a systematic procedure for the development of courses, in most cases involving senior management, and was seen as indicative of the increasing centralization of management and planning in colleges. Some colleges had introduced a matrix structure designed to provide a greater coordination of activities in the college and reduce the rigidities of departmentalism. Yet with this type of structure senior management faced the same problems in shifting resources within the college and aggregating new initiatives.

Obviously the role of the principal was an important influence upon the nature of the organizational climate which governed the character of the relationships in the college. For example, in one tertiary college studied the leadership of the principal and senior management was based more upon charismatic than formal authority, stressing informal and flexible structures and decision-making. The principal had set up a development group open to any member of staff to advise him of new developments. There was also a marketing group which acted in the same way. A college newspaper was provided to help coordinate activities within the college. Consideration of the internal relationships in educational institutions is important in understanding the main characteristics of the processes of needs assessment. Of particular importance were the relationships between the providers of education. These governed how definitions of need were made, who was responsible for making them, and whose definitions counted in determining what provision should be made. This highlights the value of seeing the assessment of need as located within an organizational framework which is characterized by different values, interests and power relationships.

Conclusion: Issues in Coordination

The analytical framework outlined in Chapter 6 demonstrated that three important dimensions of needs assessment were: the location of that assessment; the participants involved in making the assessment; and the pattern of interaction between these participants. This chapter has outlined some of the main relationships between clients and providers and between providers in the local educational system and the patterns of coordination of policy making and service delivery. It is now possible to put forward a number of conclusions about these relationships and ways of explaining the patterns found.

Different Purposes of Coordination

The first general point is that the relationships between the various participants served a number of different purposes. These included the communication of policies, the exchange of information, management purposes, evaluating provision, as well as making an assessment of needs and transmitting information about needs between providers. Needs assessment might not figure in these relationships. For example, the recruitment process could be used primarily as a way of determining demand for institutional or LEA planning rather than as a way of assessing the needs of individual students. Some of the relationships involved needs assessment as a by-product of these other more significant activities. There were, of course, some relationships which were explicitly designed to provide information about needs. However, the problem with these multiple purposes was that needs assessment could be neglected and only have a minor contribution to make. This was shown in the case of the consortia studied in the research, where there were structured relationships between participating institutions yet there was no specific assessment of the needs of the locality apart from the perspectives from the institutions. Moreover, the different purposes of the relationship were also influenced by the views of those involved in them. In some cases there was consensus about the aims and purposes resulting in a collegial style of relationship. In others there were different views expressed which resulted occasionally in conflict.

Extent of Relationships

A second general point is that the extent of relationships varied between bodies. For example, local education authorities varied in the scope of their relationships with bodies outside the education system — employers, other local authority departments, and community organizations. Similarly, educational institutions varied in the extent to which they entered into relationships with other bodies. These different contacts affected the scope of possible inputs to needs assessment.

Degree of Formality

A third characteristic of the relationships within the local education system was in the variation in their degree of formality. For example, there were informal relationships between staff members and employers' representatives as well as more structured relationships such as advisory committees or school-industry liaison committees. The importance of formality in relationships was that this might affect the status of the relationship and hence give it more prominence. Conversely, formality in arrangements could also reduce the amount of interaction by reducing them to 'talking shops'. Informal relationships were sometimes preferred by staff because they were less binding on the participants and could result in greater flexibility and more rapid responses. Very often formal and informal relationships co-existed, with informal mechanisms being used to supplement formal contacts.

Who Exerted Influence?

There was also the key question of who exerted influence in these relationships and how this ultimately affected the process of needs assessment and educational planning. Here it is useful to refer back to the various theories outlined in Chapter 5 as possible explanations of the nature of relationships within the education system. Bush (1986), reviewing various models of educational management, argues that no one model can adequately explain the different features of the processes of education management and instead different models concentrate on particular aspects but not the whole picture. Our approach in this book has been eclectic in the use of various theories to explain needs assessment in post-16 education.

The formal structure of the education system provided a context for the way that relationships occurred. The principle of hierarchy has been noted earlier as important in the government of the education system. This has assumed greater significance both with the growing interest from central government in the needs of the post-16 age group and what provision should be made as well as the influence of the local education authority in resource control. At institutional level the power of the head or principal is important in determining the educational ethos of that institution and its main priorities. Our evidence shows that although the processes of needs assessment took place within the broad structure of hierarchy, this is insufficient by itself as a theory to explain the complex patterns of relationships. It fails to take into account the underlying basis of the relationships.

The literature on interorganizational relations provides a basis for analyzing the relationships. This developed from attempts to explain the interactions between the various institutions of government and particularly their coordination. Its theoretical underpinning rests on the application of exchange theory (Blau, 1964). This theory held that the pattern of relationships was based on the exchanges that existed between separate bodies associated in a common service network. The whole process of interorganizational relations is shaped by the pattern of resource ownership and control. Resources in this context included not only finance but also authority, information, expertise and the status possessed by the participants. Exchange theory has been used in a number of different settings but particularly in explaining inter-organizational relations (Rhodes, 1979; Benson, 1975; Crozier and Thoenig, 1976; Archer, 1979). The pattern of relations alters over time as the rules of resource ownership change and so the power of the various participants will increase or decrease.

Applied to the relationships between different groups in the local educational system this can be used to explain our general findings. It was the senior professionals and managers who were most influential in their definitions of need. They controlled the main lines of decision-making in the institutions by virtue of their expertise and formal authority. The Local Education Authority's influence rested on its exercise of resource control, its formal authority and position in the local educational system. The interests of students and employers varied in how far they were considered and taken up in planning provision. Their resources were more limited. In the case of students their participation on courses was important in the climate of falling rolls and institutional competition. Employers' views were felt by the service providers to be of more importance than in the past, partly because of national pronouncements but also because of their legitimacy in determining and evaluating provision. The careers service was, as we have seen, an intermediary in the system but it lacked the resources to influence decision making either at institutional or LEA level and it was therefore dependent on negotiation. The contribution of other groups in the process of needs assessment was more limited because of their lack of resources and access to decision making.

The relationships in needs assessment were shaped not only by the changing interests of the participants but were ultimately influenced by the overall structure of power in the local education system. This focuses attention on the broader influences within and upon the local educational system. As Chapter 2 showed it is also important to emphasize the role of central government in influencing the determination of provision through its control of resources and examination requirements and its general ability to influence the relationship between the LEA and its institutions. These factors have been particularly marked in post-16 education and training.

Educational relationships therefore reflect changes in the distribution of power in society (Salter and Tapper, 1981). Offe has argued that the state in a period of crisis has to intervene in education to maintain the capitalist system's economic infrastructure (Offe, 1975). It plays a greater role in policy formation through developing rules which determine the nature of goals, the range of potential issues and proposed solutions. This illustrates what Lukes has termed the third dimension of power whereby in this case the state can determine public consciousness in such a way as to ensure that the state's concerns are unchallenged (Lukes, 1974).

The question arises of what is the desirable structure of relationships in needs assessment within the local education system as a way of improving this process. One issue from the research is the relationship between centre and periphery (Schon, 1971). This has been shown to be important in needs assessment for the 16–19-year-olds through the degree of autonomy in defining and responding to needs that should be possessed by institutions vis a vis the LEA. Our conclusions on what might be the desirable relationships are taken up in the final chapter.

References

ARCHER, M., (1979) *Social Origins of Educational Systems*, London, Sage.

AUDIT COMMISSION, (1986) *Towards Better Management of Secondary Education*, London, HMSO.

BENSON, J.K., (1975) 'The inter-organizational network as a political economy', *Administrative Science Quarterly*, 20, 2.

BLAU, P., (1964) *Exchange and Power*, New York, Wiley.

BUSH, T., (1986) *Theories of Educational Management*, London, Harper & Row.

CHALLIS, R., MASON, C. and PARKES, D. (1984) *The Local Authority and YTS, Interim Report*, Sheffield, MSC.

CORDINGLEY, P., (1985) 'Crossing sector boundaries', *Educational Management and Administration*, 13, 3, autumn.

CROZIER, M., and THOENIG, J.C., (1976) 'The regulation of complex organized systems', *Administrative Science Quarterly*, 21, 4.

DES, (1980) *Education for 16–19 Year Olds*, (The Macfarlane Report), London, HMSO.

DES, (1987) *Providing for Quality: The Pattern of Organization to Age 19*, London, HMSO.

GRUNOW, D., and HEGNER, F. (Eds) (1980) *Welfare or Bureaucracy: Problems of the Theory and Practice of Day Release Education*, London, Routledge & Kegan Paul.

GREENLEY, J.R., (1980) 'Organizational processes and client selectivity in social welfare services' in GRUNOW, D., and HEGNER, E. (Eds) *Welfare or Bureaucracy: Problems of Matching Social Services to Clients' Needs — Research on Service Delivery, Vol II*, Oelgeschlager.

GRUNOW, D., and HEGNER, F. (Eds) (1980) *Welfare or Bureaucracy: Problems of Matching Social Services to Clients' Needs — Research on Service Delivery, Vol, II*, Oelgeschlager.

HANDY, C., and AITKEN, R., (1986) *Understanding Schools as Organizations*, Harmondsworth, Penguin.

HEWTON, E., (1986) *Education in Recession: Crisis in County Hall and Classroom*, London, Allen & Unwin.

JENNINGS, R.E., (1984) *Going Corporate in Local Education Authorities*, Aldershot, Gower.

KOGAN, M., et al, (1984) *School Governing Bodies*, London, Heinemann.

LUKES, S., (1974) *Power: A Radical View*, London, Macmillan.

MCKINLAY, J.B., (1980) 'Professionalism and the imbalance between clients' needs and the organization's interests' in GRUNOW, D., and HEGNER, F. (Eds), *Welfare or Bureaucracy: Problems of Matching Social Services to Clients' Needs — Research on Service Delivery, Vol. II*, Oelgeschlager.

MUNDY, J.A., and ELLIOTT, M.J., (1979) 'The development of consortia for 16+ provision in the face of falling enrolments', *Sheffield Polytechnic Papers in Education Management*, 12, September.

OFFE, C., (1975) 'The theory of the capitalist state and the problem policy formation' in LINDBERG et al, (Eds) *Stress and Contradiction in Modern Capitalism*, Lexington, MA, Lexington Books.

RANSON, S., (1980) 'Changing relations between centre and locality in education', *Local Government Studies*, 6, 6.

RANSON, S., and RIBBINS, P., with CHESTERFIELD, L., and SMITH, T., (1986) *The Management of Change in the Careers Service*, Birmingham, University of Birmingham, INLOGOV.

RHODES, R., (1979) *Research into Central-Local Relations in Britain: A Framework for Analysis*, London, SSRC.

ROBINSON, T., (1978) *In Worlds Apart*, London, Athlone.

SALTER, B. and TAPPER, T. (1981) *Education, Politics and the State: The Theory and Practice of Educational Change*, London, Grant McIntyre.

SCHARPF, F.W., (1978) 'Interorganizational policy studies: Issues, concepts and perspectives' in HANF, D., and SCHARPF, F.W. (Eds) *Inter-Organizational Policy Making: Limits to Co-ordination and Central Control: Modern Politics Series, Vol. 1*, London, Sage.

SCHON, D.A. (1971) *Beyond the Stable State*, Harmondsworth, Penguin.

THEODOSSIN, E., (1986) *In Search of the Responsive College*, Bristol, Further Education Staff College.

WEISS, J.A., (1981) 'Substance V symbol in administrative reform: The case of human services coordination', *Policy Analysis*, 7, 1, Winter.

WIRT, F., (1981) 'Professionalism and political conflict: A developmental model', *Journal of Public Policy*, 1, 1, February.

Part 4:
Nature and Possibilities of Needs Assessment

10   The Characteristics of Needs Assessment

The preceding four chapters set out the framework we used for examining how educational needs are assessed and then discussed three key aspects of the subject — the information available for needs assessment; its contribution to planning; and the effects of relationships between different parts of local education systems. This chapter draws these different perspectives together in light of the earlier discussion of context, types of provision, explanations of need and the nature of education, to bring out the major characteristics of needs assessment as currently applied in English education. The approach adopted in earlier chapters is continued, with separate attention given to the three educational components most involved, the institutions, careers services and LEAs, before turning to cumulative and general features that pervade local systems of education as a whole.

Characteristics of Institutional Assessment of Need

Importance of Existing Provision

The way in which schools and colleges approached needs assessment appeared, perhaps not surprisingly, to be dominated by their existing provision. Assessment of individual need was mainly concerned with matching individuals to the courses that were available, while assessment of larger groupings was concerned with whether what was provided appeared to be succeeding in meeting needs. With falling rolls, new requirements and increased competition, schools and colleges faced a harder and more uncertain environment. It was vitally important to maintain demand. Systems theory suggests that they would react by giving attention to the way in which their outputs are received. There were signs of this in the importance attached to evaluating their success in terms of recruitment, results and destinations. An associated reaction would be to gain a greater control over inputs to education by marketing what they have to offer. Students and employers can only feel or express a need for what they know about. It was our experience that schools and colleges were indeed giving more attention to recruitment procedures and liaison with employers. This must help needs assessment. The more knowledge of the available opportunities clients possess, the more precisely they can attempt to satisfy their needs. However, there is a risk that an emphasis on recruitment puts numbers before needs.

There were fewer signs of institutions adopting a third possible strategy by attempting to predict environmental demands or shape them in new ways. Less effort was devoted to discovering whether new needs existed and devising appropriate responses. This can be explained from the standpoint of educational government in that despite enjoying considerable freedom in determining their own way of working, institutions are not completely free agents. Their operation is constrained by decisions made elsewhere; by central government, by the LEA, and by examination boards. Institutions are obliged to meet these demands and there are precious few resources left available for free use. The TVEI scheme does provide considerable resources for schools, and since this study was undertaken it has been made available to all secondary schools. It remains to be seen how far TVEI will be experienced as a stimulus or as a constraint to institutions in meeting needs. The lack of autonomous responses to need also reflects the nature of the education process. 16–19 education is delivered in packages, still predominantly one or two years in length, designed to take students to a particular educational standard. Entry to these packages is conditioned by the previous packages students have taken and standards they have achieved while at school. Once embarked upon a course of study, the need to complete it is generally assumed. There are a number of ways that enable students to take stock, such as the tutorial relationship, poor recorded performance, a report or a careers interview, but there is a limit to the extent that the packages can be adjusted to individual circumstances. Attention, then, is devoted to making better use of the provision that exists, not to changing its nature. In general, and always excepting the MSC, existing clients did not appear to be pressing for change. They defined their educational needs according to the packages that schools and colleges provided. To the public these determined an institution's character and reputation and conditioned their choice.

Although individual institutions varied in their practice, schools and (even more) colleges did appear to be more open to definitions of need made by employers. This can be explained both in terms of current policy emphases in education (DES/DE, 1985) and because responding to employers' need carries weight in terms of potential resources. Schools, for example, stand to gain resources if they participate in TVEI. If colleges can attract more custom from employers it means more students and thus more cash and staffing.

Variation in Practice

A further characteristic of institutional needs assessment was the considerable variation in practice that existed both between and within schools and colleges; some provided pastoral care one way, some another; some participated in industrial liaison mechanisms, others did not. This is consistent with the traditional freedom that is given to educational institutions to determine their own way of working (Kogan, 1975) and with the fact that services are provided by professionals who are allowed freedom in the way in which they work (Shipman, 1984).

Importance of Professional Interpretations

Professional definitions of need were extremely influential. All mechanisms for assessing individual needs involved interaction between clients and professional workers — teachers, careers officers. These allow, or may allow, clients the opportunity to express their own views of needs. The mechanisms are, however, provided and organized by the professionals and their purpose is to arrive at a professional definition of the action the client should take. Although teachers were concerned with the less tangible benefits of education, such as 'maturity' and 'preparation for life', examination success and entry into employment or higher education were seen as the immediate needs they must try to satisfy. Although some of the means of assessing collective need also involved interaction with clients, such as advisory committees or course evaluations, those most generally used and seen to be most influential, such as demand, examination results and student destinations, did not. Needs, if they were considered at all, were inferred from information that was collected for management and planning purposes. And even where mechanisms enabled clients to directly express their views, as with student surveys or employers' conferences, these views required interpretation by educationalists when, and if, they were applied to planning. In short, although the clients' views of needs might be received, their impact on provision was filtered by the judgment of the educationalists.

Incremental Contribution to Planning

The contribution of needs assessment to educational planning emerges as predominantly ad hoc; closer to an incremental than to a rational pattern of decision-making. For example, the products of individual assessments of need did not regularly or routinely feed into collective assessments. Individual assessments were largely made by junior staff, by teachers or tutors, or specialists, such as careers teachers and careers officers. Collective assessments were largely the province of institutional managers; headteachers, principals, deputies, heads of department and course leaders. They might, or might not, come together in staff or course planning meetings. Individual assessments of need were not, in any case, readily amenable to wider analysis and reflection. Information concerning assessments of individual need was primarily qualitative. It was not necessarily recorded or transmitted to the part of the institution concerned with planning.

Some of the information available for collective assessment displayed the same characteristics, although the institutional managers who were most involved with it were also the planners. Where information could be expressed quantitatively, as for demand or examination results, it received greater use and appeared to carry more weight. Educational institutions, dominated by annual or biennial cycles of provision and having to ensure certainty and coherence for the present population of students, found it difficult to respond flexibly and rapidly to new definitions of need.

Personalities and Roles

At both the individual and collective levels, assessment of needs depended heavily on personalities; on the ability of a student to express his or her needs, of a tutor to raise his or her judgments, of a headteacher or principal to decide that a suggestion or a statistic called for some action. Assessment also depended on the existence of roles; on the designation of staff as tutors, careers teachers or industrial liaison officers. Headteachers, principals and heads of department, occupying formal positions of authority, were enormously influential in needs assessment. There was a general acceptance and an expectation that they would provide leadership (Regan, 1977). They were felt to determine the emphasis in institutions and departments, to be the source of new approaches and ideas and to set the organizational climate which could encourage or discourage staff questioning whether provision was meeting needs. In one respect the role of institutional managers was seen to have increased in importance, as responsibility for new patterns of coordinated working had largely fallen to their lot. This concentration of power reflects the nature of the educational environment, especially the increased importance of external influences. Decision-making in schools and colleges has become concentrated at the centre which is the location of those roles that relate to influential external bodies. But centralization does not necessarily entail the creation of effective systems for identifying and assessing needs.

Characteristics of Careers Services Assessment of Needs

Limited Contribution to Collective Assessments

Overall, the careers services' methods of assessing needs provided opportunities for gaining insight into the needs held by the clients of education — pupils, students and employers — and those perceived by the service providers — staff working in schools and colleges. Careers services used this knowledge diagnostically when giving guidance to individuals. Using Bradshaw's definitions (Bradshaw, 1972), they matched felt needs with normative definitions of the opportunities that were available and that appeared to be within the students' capabilities and best interests. But the insights gained by careers services appeared to contribute little to the assessment of collective educational needs and the shaping of educational provision. This was true at the LEA level and even more apparent with reference to schools and colleges.

The reason for this limited contribution appeared to lie in the role of the careers service and the way it was perceived by other parts of education systems. First, it was seen as providing a service to pupils and students, but also to institutions to enable them to provide both careers education and individual guidance. The work of the careers service was thus conditioned by decisions made by the service users; for example, by the priority the headteacher gave to careers work or by the pattern of organization adopted by a college. Poster (1976) observed that there were few areas of school management where role definition was quite as confused as in the respective tasks of the schools careers staff and the authority's careers guidance officers. The scope for careers work depended on negotiation between careers services and semi-autonomous institutions. Careers service staff, themselves, lacked the power fully to determine their own role. It follows from this that there will be a wide variation in the way in which the service functions. In some cases the careers service was available to all students, in others to few. In some cases careers officers were brought into institutional mechanisms for assessing collective needs, such as advisory committees, in others they were not. Some LEAs appeared to put considerable store on a careers service input to their planning, drawing senior officers into discussions of course provision and institutional forecasts and including them in conferences and working parties to discuss new initiatives; others involved them far less.

Second, within local education systems, careers services were seen as primarily concerned with gaining employment rather than with education. It was suggested that the presence or absence of an employment aspect conditioned the involvement of careers service personnel in educational planning. Although the careers services we encountered did employ specialist careers officers to provide information for students expected to proceed into higher education, we found cases of schools and colleges directing pupils and students wishing to enter employment towards careers officers, while providing their own guidance for those who wished to remain in higher education. Institutions which had their own 16–19 provision were more likely to have developed their own, often informal, processes of educational guidance for 16-year-olds. Although this reflected the availability of relevant sources of guidance, it also represented self-interest.

A third related reason for the relative lack of influence of the service lies in the fact that careers officers were not regarded as possessing a monopoly on guidance. They were one of a number of influences on occupational choice and this must reflect on their professional status. Studies of employers' recruitment practices show how they may place a higher premium on local advertising or direct contacts with schools and colleges, than on the careers service (Ashton *et al*, 1982). This certainly held true for some of the employers we interviewed. Similarly it is well known that pupils and students may look to help from family or peer group contacts and that institutions may place great store on the ability of teachers and tutors to advise their students. Careers guidance for post-16 students, in particular, depends upon the extent to which individuals wish to make use of the service. The limited contribution of the careers service to assessments of collective need may, then, reflect a view by other participants that their knowledge is partial or that they have little to contribute that is not already known.

A fourth explanation comes from the way in which the careers service was organized. Schools and colleges are hierarchical as well as professional organizations. In discussing the characteristics of need assessment in institutions earlier, we suggested that assessments of individual need were largely the province of relatively junior or specialist staff whilst assessments of collective need were undertaken by senior managers. The role of careers services in providing individual guidance was clearly perceived but it brought careers officers into contact with their opposite numbers in schools and colleges — tutorial staff and careers specialists — not with the senior educational managers concerned with making collective assessments of need. Thus the brokerage role of the careers service, integrating the various views of need held by students, employers and educational institutions and promoting change, was less clearly perceived and had fewer opportunities for expression. On our evidence, if a careers input to collective assessments of need was being provided this either reflected the personality of the careers officer concerned and his, or her, ability to develop a relationship with senior educationalists, or came from the local or district manager who had made contact with education managers by participating in advisory or industrial liaison committees. Careers service participation in LEA planning appeared similarly to reflect personal relationships between careers staff and LEA officers and advisers and the local status accorded to the careers service within the LEA.

Increased Contribution to Needs Assessment

There were signs that the influence of careers services in needs assessment was increasing. This can be partly attributed to changes in the way careers services have interpreted their own role; moving from a placement service, to one that is concerned with guidance, counselling and affecting the opportunities available for young people (Ranson *et al*, 1986). Increased influence also stemmed from changes in the environment which educational systems inhabit; specifically, it stemmed from the growth of youth unemployment and its high status on the political agenda and from the emphasis on work-related education. Careers services had responded by becoming more involved in the labour market and by developing closer relationships with employers. They had become concerned with the needs of industry and employment as well as those of young people (Carter, 1966). Involvement with the labour market gave careers services resources of knowledge and contacts that were increasingly valued by education. They were seen to know about employment and employment had become a matter of concern to education. Careers services could advise on likely provision of work experience or predict whether a course would prove attractive to employers. Careers service participation had been built into new initiatives such as TVEI. Our survey of educational planning by LEAs indicated how some authorities had included careers service representatives within consortia or district arrangements for coordinating educational provision. And the value is not confined to education. Much of the careers service's role was concerned with guiding school leavers into MSC schemes. Its analyses of local employment possibilities and forecasts of pupil destinations contributed to planning YTS provision. Indeed our research suggests that the potential demands on the service exceeded its available resources.

Characteristics of LEA Assessment of Needs

The means applied by LEAs to assess needs are mainly concerned with the needs of groups of students or potential students. This reflects the educational structure. LEAs are responsible for the management and administration of education rather than directly providing it to individuals.

Evaluating Provision

LEAs' concern with the assessment of needs was primarily evaluative. Was local provision succeeding in meeting needs? It is an important part of any LEA's work to monitor the efficiency and effectiveness of educational provision. Many of the respondents at the LEA level endorsed the views expressed by staff in schools and colleges that the latter were best placed to recognize local needs and that institutions required sufficient freedom to design their provision accordingly. Under this scenario the LEA's role was reactive, arbitrating and supporting institutional demands. But LEAs had taken the arguments of the Macfarlane Report (DES, 1980), reiterated in the recent circular (DES, 1987) and reinforced by the requirement to plan non-advanced FE in collaboration with the MSC, that efficiency and effectiveness required a coordinated system. Constraints in public expenditure, fresh thinking in respect of 16–19 education and the introduction of new policies and initiatives presented local educational systems with new demands. LEAs had to evaluate how their institutions were coping and be prepared to promote new ways of working. As the resources available to institutions became more tightly constrained and their traditional ways of working more threatened, so the power of LEAs increased. In terms of exchange theory, discussed in Chapter 5, their resources of finance and of information and guidance gained in value. The requirement for institutions to coordinate their provision recast their power vis à vis LEAs, reducing their autonomy.

In the local authorities we observed, LEAs appeared to be given freedom to arrive at their own definitions of need and priorities. However, this freedom was seen as more apparent than real. Definitions of need were externally imposed upon LEAs by decisions made by the DES and other central government departments and agencies, in particular by the MSC, and by the universities and examination boards. LEAs were restricted by the resources available to local government.

It also appeared that in general LEAs had little capacity, or perhaps little incentive, to undertake their own direct assessments of needs. As discussed in Chapter 7, the means they used were largely indirect, with needs being inferred at second-hand from information collected as part of the on-going management and administrative role. Needs were gauged from knowledge of recruitment patterns, of course provision and from institutional forecasts. In so far as this information served other purposes, particularly resource control, there was a possibility that its implications for needs was treated as secondary. LEA officers, advisers and politicians pointed to the prevailing influence that resource considerations had come to exercise over policy-making in recent years.

In justice, it must be added that the information that would enable LEAs to directly assess needs was in short supply. As has already been argued, employers and students tend to present their needs in terms of the educational provision that is already available.

Professional Interpretation

LEAs also relied heavily on the insights into needs gained by their officers, advisers and politicians. These were seen to depend upon individual values, experience and contacts. Personal viewpoints and the consensus of the educational establishment did influence policy-making. Because so much of LEAs' assessment of need was indirect, it required interpretation and this gave scope to personal knowledge and opinions. An adviser, for example, might express considerable reservations regarding a school's proposal for course development as a result of his or her contacts with the institution. The importance attached to officers' and advisers' insights thus reflected the lack of alternative sources of hard evidence to guide policy-making. It also reflected the traditional high status afforded to professionals within education (Shipman, 1984; Kogan, 1986). But it had the effect of pushing assessment of needs towards the incremental model of decision-making. Professional contributions appeared haphazard and certainly varied from one authority to another. They depended on the way in which LEAs were organized, on the working arrangements for collecting and considering information, on the style of working favoured by senior officers and on the impact of personalities.

Limited Overview of Needs

The importance of professional interpretation went some way to explain our observation of the considerable variation between the way in which one authority went about assessing needs, compared with another. As independent organs of government, local authorities enjoyed considerable freedom in shaping their organization in the way that appeared most appropriate to local circumstances (DE, 1972). Yet they did appear to share a common problem in finding it difficult to gain a comprehensive view of 16–19 needs. First, because they occupied the apex of local educational systems, LEAs collected and received many messages. These were difficult to compare or aggregate, or to use for determining priorities in making provision. Second, despite the arrangements that LEAs had made to coordinate the administration of 16–19 provision, it remained divided institutionally between schools and FE, by central government agencies, by legal requirements, by the purposes it served and by arrangements for local political control. This made it difficult to gain an oversight of needs.

The Nature of Needs Assessment

We now turn to the cumulative effects of the way in which needs assessment was undertaken in local education systems, its general characteristics and their implications.

Reactive Character

Needs assessment appeared strongly conservative. It was reactive rather than proactive in nature. This was a reflection of the way in which needs were most commonly assessed against the template of existing provision, rather than what *might* be provided. Chapter 8 drew attention to the way in which the process of educational planning was shaped by the provision that already existed. Thus the various means used for assessment, set out in the framework in Chapter 6, were weighted towards diagnosing how to meet, or evaluating the satisfaction of, needs that had already been identified. Less attention was devoted to approaching needs in reverse order; finding out what needs existed and then considering their implications for provision. Surveys and evaluations of client opinions were not unknown, but they were not common practice. When they were used, it was generally on an ad hoc basis rather than being systematically tied in to the planning process. But the imposition of definitions of need on local education systems by new central government policies had caused some movement in this direction. The obligation to introduce new courses had led LEAs and institutions to find out whether ascribed needs did, in fact, exist.

This reactive character has a further aspect. It meant that needs were largely assessed in terms of already recognized and accepted client groups, such as academic or vocational students, YTS trainees, different occupational categories of employed or the unemployed. This could neglect needs that cut across or were not currently reflected in provision for existing groupings.

Needs assessment, then, largely conforms to the classical model defined by Kaufman, as described in Chapter 4 (Kaufman, 1972). Programmes are developed to meet goals without much attention to how far they satisfy needs. But recent central government initiatives developing work related education would be classed as the deductive model, since they relate educational programmes and change requirements to defined goals. The third of Kaufman's models, the inductive approach which develops goals and programmes from clients' expectations, is less in evidence. This, however, is the way in which needs assessment might be expected to be applied were 16–19 education to become more market-orientated.

Dependence on Existing Relationships

Needs assessments reflected the relationships between different components of local education systems. There are a number of bodies with a stake in the education of 16–19-year-olds — LEAs, the MSC, managing agents, employers, careers services, youth and community services, schools and colleges — and the arrangements for provision vary between and within different authorities. Relationships between the different bodies obviously varied, depending on the administrative culture and traditions, on circumstances and the style of working adopted by senior figures. Some of the latter preferred to use informal approaches and procedures wherever possible, others relied upon formal mechanisms. However, there were a number of common features.

The different bodies, and indeed disciplines and individuals within them, had their own interests in 16–19 provision. The way in which individuals, be they teachers, advisers or employers, saw the needs of this age group reflected their values, experience and aspirations. Consequently, as Chapter 8 showed, planning and the implementation of policies involved an element of negotiation between the different parties. One particularly sensitive area of negotiation, present to a greater or lesser extent in all the authorities we studied, was the balance between allowing institutions freedom to meet needs as they saw them and adhering to common national and LEA perceptions of needs. This points to a political model of educational government (Bush, 1986) and is a reminder that educational provision reflects the dynamic interaction and conflict between different interests with their own purposes and resources of power.

As was brought out in Chapter 9, relationships between different bodies served many purposes. They could, on occasion, transmit and negotiate views of needs but this was only part, and often a minor part, of the traffic. This is obvious in the case of relationships between LEAs and their schools and colleges which are heavily concerned with administration. But it was also true in respect of relationships between institutions and employers, which were concerned with marketing provision, arranging student work placements, recruiting new employees and providing industrial teaching projects, as well as with exchanging views on educational needs.

A further common feature was that educational organization had not kept pace with developing views of 16–19 provision. Thus relationships had to be created to enable organizations that had been devised to meet one set of needs to meet another. Colleges had to accommodate a wider cross-section of the age group than before, as a result of YTS programmes. Schools and colleges had to work together to provide CPVE courses and the TVEI scheme. LEAs and institutions had to work collectively to make the most effective use of scarce resources. Since organizations could not be totally reshaped to meet the new demands, new sets of relationships had to be grafted on to the old. Coordination has become fashionable but because coordinating relationships have to make use of existing organizational patterns and roles that have their own well-established concerns, they are particularly prone to the conflict of interests mentioned earlier.

Normative Character

In general it was 'the experts' who defined what was, or was not, an educational need. The values and beliefs of the service providers were particularly important and influential (Smith, 1980). Although senior managers were seen, and expected, to provide the lead in defining what, and how, needs should be met, it must be a strength of the education service that it provides room for staff at all levels to advance their own assessments of need. This emphasizes the importance of the collegial model of educational government and provides a reminder of the strength of professional interests based upon common purposes and values, and upon expertise. But this gives needs assessment a strong normative bias. This was particularly the case with regard to definitions of the needs of individual students and employers. Service providers were less influential regarding the needs of those on YTS or TVEI courses, but here MSC had its own normative views of what was required and the power to influence decisions.

Of course some quantitative information was used widely in needs assessment. For example, information on recruitment, forecasts, destinations and examination results. This information was valued as being objective in character and less a reflection of professional advocacy. It served informative and predictive purposes (Carlisle, 1972), and was seen to provide a useful common starting point for assessing needs. However, the statistics still required professional interpretation and their application to needs assessment depended upon professional recognition of a problem.

Incremental Character

Needs assessment appeared highly incremental. This was partly explained by the importance of professional viewpoints. Needs assessment remained an area for the entrepreneur. It was everyone's concern and nobody's. In a general sense all educationalists were concerned with the needs of their clientèle and how far these were being satisfied. Some took their concerns further and tried to influence provision; others did not. Probably most educationalists were selective. They followed up their concerns with some people and in some situations. Thus insights accumulated and might stimulate further and more explicit enquiry. Although needs assessment represented a large component of certain roles, such as those of head-teachers, principals, advisers, senior LEA officers, directors of education and members of education committees, this was in general terms and was combined with other responsibilities. We did not encounter (and were not informed of the existence of) any roles or units that had the identification and assessment of needs as their sole concern. Professional viewpoints contributed haphazardly and ad hoc to needs assessment. This goes some way in accounting for the variety of practice and its incremental nature.

And, as has already been stressed, the means used for needs assessment were a motley collection, disparate in their purposes, processes and in the information they supplied. Assessment of collective needs relied heavily upon information that was used for other purposes, and was governed by the existing work processes and transmission routes that suited these purposes. This could obscure the relevance of the information for the consideration of needs.

Because this study adopted a broad definition of needs and needs assessment, it has considered a range of different activities at different levels of specificity. The different messages about needs were difficult to aggregate and compare. From this broad perspective, needs assessment did not provide a focus for planning and evaluation. Rather it provided a constant element within these activities that might, or might not, receive emphasis and was subject to negotiation between different service interests. As suggested likely in Chapter 4, needs were indeed treated ambiguously (Witkin, 1984); perhaps as representing a desired state of affairs, more often as a way of remedying a problem. But the incremental nature of needs assessment reflects the character of educational planning discussed in Chapter 8. Planning was tied to client demand and subject to negotiation between different interests. It did not work from explicit educational objectives that could form the subject of explicit needs assessment techniques directed at particular, or potential, client groups. Perhaps it is unrealistic to expect anything different. Bush (1986) points out how institutions occupying a turbulent environment (and currently these must include education) have little time or opportunity to engage in a rational process of choice. Rationality rarely occurs in practice. Decisions have no clear focus. Instead problems, solutions and participants interact and choices somehow emerge from the confusion.

Unequal Character

Finally, needs assessment appeared to be unequal. Despite the variation in the way in which institutions, agencies and LEAs applied different mechanisms to assess needs, some clients and categories of clients consistently received greater attention than others. Among those who benefited most were: full-time students on academic courses, commonly well catered for with recruitment procedures, pastoral care and careers guidance; those industrial firms that were willing and able to work with education; and, those students or employers who were prepared to take some initiative in assessing their own needs. In theory YTS students should also be included among the favoured, since the assessment and reassessment of their needs was intended to occur continuously throughout their training programmes. However, the views we gained regarding YTS provision suggested that at present practice frequently falls short of intentions. Among the least favoured were: part-time students, whose needs were widely treated as being defined by their choice of course; students and employers who were diffident in expressing their views; and, all those pupils and students with teachers and tutors who did not see needs assessment as part of their work and gave it scant attention.

An even greater degree of inequality was apparent in the way that mechanisms of needs assessment concentrated upon those who were participating in education. Few mechanisms were applied to the non-participants; the unemployed who were not attending any form of education or those who dropped out of YTS programmes. Indeed the mechanisms of needs assessment commonly used were hardly suitable for non-participants, who were difficult to contact and monitor.

Provision-led Assessment

The table below (Table 12) summarizes the principal features of needs assessment as currently practised. Needs assessment is grounded in the work processes and relationships of local education systems. It thus reflects their characteristics and is shaped by administrative structures and service conditions (Rein, 1973). This confirms Smith's findings that clients are 'slotted-in' to categories of need created by administrative procedures and professional ideologies (Smith, 1980). Need is defined by demand but this is demand as defined by existing services and existing service interests. Education is not unique in displaying this form of needs assessment (Spicker, 1987) and although attention has been drawn to some of the limitations that result, this reflected character may also be a source of strength. Because the means used for needs assessment harmonize with the working and decision-making processes in their immediate environment, they attract consensus and are the more readily used. Means of needs assessment that ignore the realities of relationships, interests and work

TABLE 12: MODES OF WORKING IN NEEDS ASSESSMENT
AS CURRENTLY PRACTISED

Predominant Modes	Predominant Characteristics
Conservative) Reactive) Incremental) Pluralistic) Professionally dominated) Negotiative)	Determined by existing relationships and interests, existing client groups; existing provision and work processes. Exhibiting a mixture of 'top-down' and 'bottom-up' strategies. Not easily innovative. Unequal in its application.

processes are likely to invoke resistance and therefore less likely to impact on provision.

Changing Attitudes to Needs Assessment

We found that attitudes towards needs assessment were changing. As discussed in Chapter 2, the context of 16–19 education was seen to be undergoing tremendous change. The stimuli were partly external: new definitions of the educational role by central government, limitations on resources that made it necessary to determine priorities, new methods of providing 16–19 education that competed with LEA provision. They were also internal: produced by falling rolls, by competition between institutions and growing experience of a variety of different types of provision. We found wide agreement that 16–19 education had to be broadened, both in its provision and in its clientèle. There was less certainty concerning what the nature of provision should or could be, or the future role of existing institutions. As one head of department put it, 'you can't take what you provide for granted any longer'. Change was constrained by lack of resources and, as the chapter on planning discussed, it was difficult to know if top-down or bottom-up strategies were most effective and in what conditions. Although the extent varies, local education systems are pluralistic (Kogan, 1975). They have, therefore, to adopt a political approach to decision-making that allows for the expression and negotiation of different interests. This said, there does appear to be incentive for adopting greater rationality in undertaking needs assessment.

In all parts of local education systems there appeared to be increasing interest in discovering what was required, considering how it could be provided and in evaluating the success of provision. More attention has been given to using the available mechanisms to learn about needs, such as scrutinizing demand, reviewing course provision, activating and expanding links with employers, improving recruitment processes and making greater use of monitoring procedures. But, as has been stressed in the preceding pages, these mechanisms were not necessarily designed with needs assessment in mind. Although there were no signs that English education is about to imitate American experience in making needs assessment the explicit starting point for service planning and evaluation, both the growing incentive to market provision and the sharper definition of educational goals by central government have brought needs into greater prominence. We found evidence that LEAs were giving more consideration to needs in their planning, in the use they made of information and, in particular, in the coordination of their provision.

Our study suggests a number of ways to take advantage of this increased interest. Needs assessment could make a greater contribution to educational planning. A number of possibilities are set out in the final chapter.

References

ASHTON, D., MAGUIRE, M. and GARLAND, V., (1982) *Youth in the Labour Market*, London, DE.

BRADSHAW, J., (1972) 'The concept of social need', *New Society*, 30 March.

BUSH, T., (1986) *Theories of Educational Management*, London, Harper and Row.

CARLISLE, E., (1972) 'The conceptual structure of social indicators' in SHONFIELD, A., and SHAW, S., (Eds) *Social Indicators and Social Policy*, London, Heinemann.

CARTER, M., (1966) *Into Work*, London, Penguin.

DE, (1972) *The New Local Authorities: Management and Structure*, London, HMSO.

DES, (1980) *Education for 16–19 Year Olds* (The Macfarlane Report), London, HMSO.

DES, (1987) *Providing for Quality: The Pattern of Organization to Age 19*, London, HMSO.

DES/DE, (1985) *Education and Training for Young People*, Cmnd 9482, London, HMSO.

KAUFMAN, R.A., (1972) *Educational System Planning*, Englewood Cliffs, NJ, Prentice Hall.

KOGAN, M., (1975) *Educational Policy Making: A Study of Interest Groups and Parliament*, London, Allen & Unwin.

KOGAN, M., (1986) *Educational Accountability*, London, Hutchinson.

POSTER, C., (1976) *School Decision-Making*, London, Heinemann.

RANSON, S., and RIBBINS, P. with CHESTERFIELD, L. and SMITH, T., (1986) *The Management of Change in the Careers Service*, Birmingham, University of Birmingham, INLOGOV.

REGAN, D. (1977) *Local Government and Education*, London, Allen & Unwin.

REIN, M., (1983) *From Policy to Practice*, London, Macmillan.

SHIPMAN, M., (1984) *Education As a Public Service*, London, Harper & Row.

SMITH, G., (1980) *Social Need: Policy, Practice and Research*, London, Routledge & Kegan Paul.

SPICKER, P., (1987) 'Concepts of need in housing allocations,' *Policy and Politics*, 15, 1, January.

WITKIN, B., (1984) *Assessing Needs in Educational and Social Programs: Using Information to Make Decisions, Set Priorities and Allocate Resources*, San Francisco, CA, Jossey-Bass.

11 Improving Needs Assessment

The concepts of needs and needs assessment have been deliberately defined broadly in this book. Need was seen as a discrepancy between an existing and a desired condition which could be remedied by education. Needs assessment was defined as the different ways in which such discrepancies might be identified and taken up in decision-making and planning within local education systems. The broad approach to the subject offered strong advantages. It drew attention to the different interests that have their own views of educational needs. It alerted us to the possibility that needs may conflict and be perceived by one party but not by another, or seen by one party as requiring one remedy and by another as calling for a different solution. It also enabled an examination of the variety of ways in which those involved in education identify discrepancies and use their insight to affect provision. An understanding of the place and treatment of needs in education would inevitably have been restricted, and further from reality, if more prescriptive definitions of needs and needs assessment had been adopted.

Our examination of current practice has shown ways in which the assessment of needs might be improved and make a greater contribution to educational planning. The chapter begins with these suggestions. In putting these forward two lines of argument have been taken.

1 *Better use can be made of the mechanisms for needs assessment that are already available.* It would be tempting to advocate the wide introduction of new techniques of survey and analysis, such as can be found in the American literature on needs assessment, but it has to be doubted whether local education systems have the capacity to extend their work in this way or whether the results would justify the effort.

2 *Needs and needs assessment justify attention in their own right.* The potential benefits from education are reduced if needs are regarded as already decided by the age of 16, or as fixed by the

provision that already exists or by the present pattern of client demand. Opportunities for education to respond to changing needs may be lost if the latter are continually inferred at second hand, from information collected for other purposes.

We have not attempted to enter the debate as to whether one form of educational provision is more successful in identifying and meeting needs than any other. In our view this depends more upon the attention that needs assessment is given than on educational structure. This holds true regardless of the fundamental changes in the organization and provision of education that may result from the 1987 Education Bill. The two principal recommendations reflect our belief that needs assessment should be both broad and eclectic in the methods employed and explicit. They are interrelated. Greater priority for needs assessment would make possible more productive use of the available mechanisms. For convenience, however, the suggestions for improved practice are grouped separately under the two headings.

The chapter concludes by briefly contrasting existing practice of needs assessment with a more rational approach that gives greater prominence to needs in educational planning.

Making Better Use of Existing Mechanisms

Using Professional Assessment to Greater Effect

Attention has been drawn at a number of points to the importance of assessments of need made by educationalists. This was a feature of practice in schools and colleges and of LEAs. It applied to junior staff concerned with teaching and counselling individual students and to advisers and senior managers — LEA officers, headteachers, principals, deputies, heads of department, year heads, course coordinators — who were concerned with evaluating and planning provision. At all points considerable reliance was placed on professional interpretations of need. Yet professional assessments were subjective, not necessarily explicit, and their contribution to planning was haphazard. Insights might or might not be recorded in a form that allowed their consideration by others and might or might not contribute to decision-making. We encountered examples of procedures that had been introduced by educational managers to standardize different aspects of professional need assessment. Tutors were required to evaluate and record their tutees' satisfaction with their education or to use the biannual reports to review their progress and determine future emphases. Absences were monitored and reasons recorded. Contacts with employers and their purposes were recorded centrally and reviewed by an industrial liaison officer. Teachers and lecturers evaluated and recorded their students' judgment of a course of studies. Course teachers or departmental staff met together for a formal review of the examination results that their students had achieved. Procedures for recruiting students were formulated and agreed between schools and colleges, and responsibilities allocated for their maintenance. College representatives had to describe proposed course developments and the reasons for them, to representatives from other colleges in the authority and to LEA officers and advisers. Advisers evaluated the success of particular courses in meeting needs and officers and advisers systematically reviewed the pattern of courses provided by the LEA's institutions.

No doubt such procedures formalized what some professionals in most authorities did anyway. Their presence was often criticized as adding to 'red tape' and as contributing to the increasing burden of administration in education. But this research project has consistently shown that because the assessment of need involves different views of what is required, different participants and a range of different institutions and agencies, it must be complex and requires administration. The wider use of procedures that formalize professional assessments recognizes their importance and enables them to make a more certain contribution to decision-making (Schon, 1971).

Professionalism does not always sit easily with management. The latter may be seen as imposing hierarchical authority and rigid definitions of responsiblity that are contrary to professional characteristics of authority and responsibility stemming from knowledge and the task to be performed. Thus professional assessments of need are more readily obtained where management in institutions and LEAs encourages those with relevant knowledge and/or interest to contribute to decision-making, regardless of seniority or hierarchical status. This is not solely a matter of designing evaluative and decision-making procedures with a wide membership in mind. Over the last quarter century education has generally moved a long way in making opportunities for professional staff, as well as their managers, to have some involvement with decision-making (Kogan, 1975; Bush, 1986). It is more a matter of creating an organizational climate that encourages wide participation and treats it as part of the professional role rather than as an irrelevant addition (Hoyle, 1975). This encourages professionals to accept that providing more explicit and expert contributions towards systematic needs assessment is a vital part of their work.

Using Formal Mechanisms to Bring Different Interests Together

In our study such mechanisms as college advisory committees, schools/industry liaison committees and LEA/employers committees were seen by many of our respondents to be valuable in bringing together senior institutional managers, senior LEA officers and advisers and possibly careers services staff, with employers. They provided a forum in which employers could express their own needs and evaluate their satisfaction with existing provision, and transmit their opinions to educationalists who had the necessary authority to make a definitive response. For their part, the educationalists could explain new developments, test new proposals and learn something of what employers wanted and how they valued what was currently available. Not all believed these mechanisms useful and there were a number of criticisms. The mechanisms varied in the attention they were given by educationalists. It was generally hard to gain a representative cross-section of employers and the mechanisms served other purposes than the transmission of educational needs. Where their advisory role was taken seriously, they were seen as a useful way of determining needs and the means by which they might be met. This meant giving advisory bodies access to information regarding both employers' future intentions for recruiting and training their work force and details of educational provision and achievements.

The ability of formal advisory mechanisms to supply information on needs has been doubted (Theodossin, 1986). From our standpoint they have merits in allowing the possibility of interaction between different interests and focusing attention explicitly on needs. We would thus support the efforts of central government to create mechanisms to enable education to learn employers' needs (DES/DE, 1985). The lion's share of the effort in creating a relationship appears to have fallen on education. It is possible that educationalists might be able to tap in to a wider and more representative forum of employers if they were able to make greater use of employer-initiated mechanisms. The example of industrial training boards, with their own training officers, was suggested, as were chambers of commerce and rotary clubs. But any grouping of employers is likely to display a concentration of some interests and an absence of others. If schools, colleges, careers services and LEAs wish to gain a wide spectrum of views, they should review their contacts with employers and undertake their own consultations to fill in the gaps.

It was noticeable that students did not participate in these formal mechanisms. The reasons can be readily suggested. Education is an individual matter. Students may be regarded as passive recipients of education. Educationalists are in daily contact with students and may believe that they are well aware of their needs. Student needs are defined by educationalists, employers, politicians and laid down in course require-ments and syllabi. And, other mechanisms, such as student unions and school councils, may provide an opportunity for learning student needs. Nonetheless there may be a case for sixth forms, and college departments or course areas to follow examples in higher education and set up formal course advisory committees. These would enable educationalists and students to relate the provision to different views of needs and test out new ideas.

Inclusion of Needs Assessment Within Recruitment and Guidance Procedures

It was striking how recruitment and guidance mechanisms varied. There was variation within institutions, between institutions and between authorities. 16–19 education has become more complex but has also become more competitive, with different institutions seeking to maintain their numbers, and all these numbers represent in terms of resources, in face of a reduced total population. In these circumstances students require help with their education and career choices but institutions may be motivated to put their own interests first. Many staff, too, feel that they are not equipped to provide the necessary help. Students, parents or employers have either made their own choices in applying to an institution or taking a course, or they have sought specialist help, such as provided by careers teachers, careers officers or student counsellors. The classroom teacher or lecturer's job is to help students make the most of the choice. Yet it remains a fact that recruitment procedures and pastoral care arrangements largely depend upon teachers or lecturers who are allocated this work as one part of their duties. Some staff find the work congenial or discover they have an aptitude for it, others do not. Some staff are conscientious in providing help, others give it little attention.

We believe that student guidance and recruitment procedures should include some explicit consideration of what needs exist and whether these are being, or are likely to be, met. Our findings thus reinforce what others have urged regarding the importance of careers education in schools, of the provision of timely and clear information describing the available opportunities and the provision of advisory and supporting mechanisms to back-up the work of teachers and tutors (CPRS, 1980; DES, 1980; Locke and Bloomfield, 1982; DES, 1987). Here again, procedures can help. The recruitment process can provide opportunities for institutions to describe what they have to offer and allow prospective students to sample it, as well as enabling a student to discuss what he, or she, is seeking from education with a member of staff. An example was provided in Chapter 7. A tutorial curriculum can be constructed in terms of different activities that a tutor should undertake with tutees during the year, such as induction, evaluation of progress, enquiry regarding satisfaction of needs and consideration of career choice.

Procedures cannot cover all eventualities, nor should they. The process of education still depends upon the individual relationship that is formed between the teacher and the taught. Students will seek help from those staff they find to be sympathetic and interested. Assessment of need is part of every teacher's role and every teacher should be aware of the supporting mechanisms that can be used if he, or she, is at a loss. This is particularly important for part-time students who are generally less obviously served in terms of specialist help and advice. Yet inadequate guidance pre-16, or the actual experience of education, of training or of employment, causes many part-time students to reassess the decisions they made at 16.

Existing provision for guidance can also be used more flexibly. A careers teacher or officer in a college who is prepared or allowed to adapt his or her working hours to include the lunch hour or an evening session, may reach a much wider range of students than one who is only available during the standard teaching day. Professional hunches about needs can be tested by small scale market research. We encountered an example of a college Business Studies Department surveying the views of both employers and students regarding the impact of changing office procedures for secretarial courses. A school had sought the reaction of both parents and local employers regarding the introduction of a new pre-vocational course. A student may be steered towards a combination of academic and vocational subjects rather than being given the traditional choice of concentrating in one area or the other.

But the extent to which more sensitive guidance procedures can effect greater flexibility in education is clearly limited. LEAs and their institutions cannot cater for the nuances of individual need. They are limited by their resources and by courses that follow national criteria. They are limited by public expectations and the strength of academic traditions. They are limited by the organization of provision which is largely annual or biennial. If the need for a change is identified and if the institution or consortium has something more appropriate available, transfer may be impossible until the course commences in the next academic year. The way forward here may lie with the development of modular and self-programmed learning. This is occurring, as with courses developed for the new vocational certificate in Scotland that allow the combination of general and specialist modules and in connection with TVEI courses, but it is by no means the common pattern of teaching.

Inclusion of Needs Assessment Within Evaluation Procedures

Because education is so much the product of interaction and negotiation between different interests, its results are uncertain. Evaluation is crucial to allow for development and correction (Hyder, 1984). At all levels local education systems are engaged in evaluating their provision. But this, too, is distinguished by its variety. Chapter 8 drew attention to the different purposes served by evaluation, the different criteria that were applied and the range of information that could contribute. Evaluation was more formative than summative in character. It was continuous rather than a closing stage in a rational planning cycle. It depended heavily upon professional interpretation and values. Where clients were involved it was largely in response to professional purposes and initiatives. The information used in evaluative mechanisms might or might not relate to needs. Where they did so, the information was frequently implicit and required some trigger or initiative for the messages to be taken up.

Without advocating prescriptive models of planning that take needs identification and satisfaction as the sole objective, we believe that the issue of whether provision is satisfying needs could, and should, figure more prominently and explicitly in evaluations. This could apply at the institutional level for staff or governors engaged in evaluating individual student progress, the success of courses or the total package of provision. Demand is determined by too many extraneous factors to serve as a sensitive proxy for student satisfaction. At the LEA level, the satisfaction of need should be ranked as high in importance as the quality and cost effectiveness of teaching in monitoring institutional performance.

Because education is a professional activity, then professional evaluations must be important. But since education is not provided for the benefit of the educators, there is a strong case for actively seeking clients' own opinions of what is provided. Clients' views are received at present, but they are usually heard through professional transmission and interpretation. Clients' felt needs should be given a higher and more explicit status in evaluation. Given that their responsibilities extend to all young people within an authority, LEAs specifically might seek, as some already do, to broaden their evaluations by including the viewpoints of those apparently least satisfied. This means attempting to gain the views of 16–19-year-olds and employers who do not participate in education and of those who have sampled it and withdrawn. Extraneous perspectives, drawing on comparative information and experience, can also serve to broaden an LEA's evaluation of its satisfaction of needs. Members of HMI have an important contribution to make in this area, as do professional networks and media.

Increase Careers Services Contribution to Educational Planning and Decision Making

Careers services appear to have been accepted within local education systems as a source of advice on employment matters, but not on educational provision. Yet the careers service has a strong interest in educational provision. In its work with 16–19-year-olds it is as concerned with educational as with employment opportunities. When account is taken of YTS, the majority of 15 and 16-year-olds seen by careers officers in secondary schools will continue with some form of participation in education. Indeed it is often left to the careers service to inform pupils of the range of local educational opportunities that are available at 16+, and they regularly guide employers in this respect. Careers services are also directly involved in 16–19 education through the arrangements made for providing guidance to students in sixth forms and colleges.

Careers services also possess knowledge of students' needs that, we believe, could inform education. As was shown in Chapter 7, the guidance process enables them to learn how pupils and students view their own needs. This knowledge may appear superficial compared with that possessed by teachers and lecturers who have formed deeper relationships over a long period of time, but the numbers seen by careers officers and the concentration of the guidance process on identifying needs and their satisfaction, mean that patterns may become apparent. Pupils and students may also feel able to talk more freely to an informed and interested outsider, than to their own teachers. And since careers services are not concerned with marketing institutional provision and future course survival, they are likely to be less self-interested than institutions in their advice. Contacts made with employers to recruit or place students may similarly lead to knowledge of what industry wants, or believes it is getting, from education.

These insights could aid educational planning. At present their contribution appears to be a matter of chance. It depends upon personalities and personal relationships, and the extent to which those concerned with educational planning in institutions and the LEA perceive that careers officers can have something useful to say about education as well as employment.

On our evidence the careers service is increasingly being included in the formal mechanisms that bring employers and educationalists together, such as college advisory committees and school/industry liaison committees. This enables the service to contribute and test its own insights of both employment and education, which are likely to be wider than those available to other participants. It would be valuable to find a means for careers services to report back to schools and colleges and the LEA, the broad pattern of needs they encountered each year and any significant mismatches between aspirations and available opportunities. This information could aid educational planners in evaluating their provision and could be of direct help in shaping careers education. Clearly such information would have to be handled sensitively to avoid being seen as criticism and destroying cooperation between educationalists and the careers service. At the institutional level we met examples where the careers officer, or officers, working most closely with a school or college presented an annual report of activities to the headteacher or principal. Perhaps this practice could be widely extended, the report indicating in tabular form the main areas of aspiration and the extent to which they were satisfied, together with a comment on the match between aspirations and opportunities. If this information was presented in a standardized format for each institution, it could then be collated for the LEA as a whole. Such an initiative could well stimulate further and fuller discussion of the extent to which education was meeting students' and employers' needs.

Directing Needs Assessment to Unmet Needs

Our study suggests that particular client groups receive less attention or have poorer access to means of needs assessment than do others. This is the case for:

(i)   students or pupils at school who require a greater opportunity to express their evolving and changing view of their own needs during the course of education and their satisfaction with what is provided;

(ii)   part-time students who, in addition, require greater access to facilities that will help them diagnose their needs;

(iii)   16–19-year-olds not participating in education whose opinions regarding their needs require to be learned by educationalists and who require access to guidance facilities;

(iv)   small employers who require the opportunity to express their own view of their educational needs and their satisfaction with existing provision, and require access to facilities that will help them diagnose their needs.

To a large extent this neglect reflects the difficulty of creating an educational dialogue with those who are uninterested or who have little available opportunity. Some institutions and LEAs have invested considerable effort in attempting to learn the needs of young people or employers who are not participating in education (Davies and Scribbins, 1985). Table 13 sets out what have been suggested to us as the most effective means of applying or extending needs assessment to these less privileged groups.

These client groups contain members of wider social groupings; as defined by sex, presence of handicap, economic class, race or location. Some of these groupings have been characterized as disadvantaged in their access to education (Mortimore and Blackstone, 1982; Sammons, 1983). Needs assessment must be sensitive to social attitudes and beliefs if it is to help rectify educational discrimination and disadvantage. One example we encountered was of a tertiary college that was prepared to encourage Muslim women to participate in further education by ensuring the absence of males from their learning area.

It was suggested in the previous chapter that institutions, and the same would be true of LEAs, did not give as much attention as they might to identifying changes in their wider environment. This reluctance is characteristic of education (Ratsay, 1980). Given the number of changes that it is currently having to accommodate, some reluctance to seek for more is understandable but this makes it hard to predict new demands or opportunities. For local education systems environmental monitoring means being aware of social and economic changes that are likely to affect education. The more they can do this, the better they are able to discover

TABLE 13: *EXTENDING NEEDS ASSESSMENT TO MEET UNMET NEEDS OF CLIENT GROUPS*

	Methods	*Responsibility*
Students and Pupils	Surveys, sampling or consultation, (pre and post 16–19 as well as during 16–19 education). Careers service information on aspirations. Greater attention to needs within pastoral care. Course advisory committees.	*Institutions*, in undertaking surveys and consultations, giving explicit attention to felt needs and setting up mechanisms. *Careers service*, in monitoring and aggregating student aspirations. *LEAs*, in monitoring institutional quality.
Part-time Students	Surveys, sampling or consultation. Employment visits by college industrial liaison officers. Access to continuing careers guidance. Routine guidance during college recruitment. Pastoral care provision.	*Institutions*, colleges in undertaking surveys and consultations, and providing guidance facilities. *Careers services*, in providing continuing support. *LEAs*, in monitoring institutional quality.
Non-participants	Publicity, media coverage, marketing provision. Surveys, sampling or consultation. Analysis of school records. Outreach work. Easy access to guidance facilities.	*Institutions*, pre-16 schools, in ensuring available 16–19 provision is known, 11–19 schools in monitoring those who leave education at 16. *Careers services*, in providing continuing support. *LEAs*, in providing publicity and undertaking investigations into reasons for non-participation.
Small Employers	Publicity, media coverage, marketing provision. Visits by school or college industrial liaison officers. Access to guidance facilities.	*Institutions*, in providing industrial liaison. *Careers services*, in providing information. *LEAs*, in providing specific information and guidance facilities for small industries.

and prepare to meet new needs and to discard provision that is no longer relevant.

Environmental monitoring involves drawing on the knowledge of educational professionals and politicians. It also requires explicit analysis of the available information, such as employment trends, demography, population movement and social characteristics, student destinations and costs of different forms of provision. Evaluations of student, employer and professional satisfaction with existing provision are also relevant. It requires identifying what is *not* known and seeing if the answers can be found or guessed. LEAs and institutions do some of this already, but analyses are not necessarily aggregated or directed to identifying needs. Environmental monitoring appears to be most successful where it is made the responsibility of a specifically constituted working party or developmental group that can draw upon individuals with the necessary knowledge and enthusiasm.

LEAs should, we believe, take the prime responsibility for environmental monitoring, working through careers services and other local authority departments. They would then have to take up the implications of what was found in monitoring the work of their institutions and developing educational provision. Also, institutions should themselves pay attention to monitoring their own environment.

Attention to Needs and Needs Assessment in its Own Right

Analyzing the Available Information

Both Chapters 7 and 8 suggested that local education systems potentially have information available about needs and their satisfaction. The problem was more that it was not analyzed in ways that were relevant to needs assessment. Indeed it was not readily available for analysis, being contained within information that was gathered for management and resource control or within the heads of professionals located in institutions and agencies across authorities. As a result assessing needs occurred haphazardly, depending on the information available at the time and who was around to provide an interpretation. Not surprisingly, information on demand, which was widely circulated and to some extent spoke for itself, was seen to be one of the most important sources of needs assessment in all parts of local systems.

We believe that there must be a good case for explicitly analyzing the available sources of information to see what they tell about needs, and for aggregating and comparing the different messages. Analysis is likely to point up contradictions, the different interests involved and the necessity for further investigation. It is likely, for example, that information will be found to be limited in respect of the needs of those not participating in education or of students' felt needs. Information on employment sought by students might be found to bear little relationship to courses provided and neither might match with destinations achieved or employer recruitment patterns. Such knowledge should have important implications for educational provision. Analysis is a job for LEAs to perform and one that they are now having to undertake in planning non-advanced further education in partnership with the MSC. LEAs have to promote needs assessment as part of their responsibility for monitoring and evaluating their educational provision. It might require a full-time officer or part-time work by a group of officers drawn from different divisions of the department. Indeed in some LEAs, officers with responsibility for 16–19 education are already performing such a role, although it is unlikely to be explicitly recognized. This officer, or unit, would act as a focus for information bearing on needs. Deciding just what was, or was not, relevant would require careful thought. However, the officer, or unit, could make the case for initiating specific studies or inquiries to fill in gaps of knowledge. This could also provide the focus for the environmental monitoring function, discussed above.

Needs Assessment Reviews

Undertaking explicit needs analyses of the available information would help increase the contribution of needs assessment to educational planning. But it would still be largely emerging as a by-product of other processes; an after-thought rather than a central concern in its own right. The latter is only likely to occur if needs assessment is made part of regular management and administrative procedures that apply across local education systems.

One possible approach would be to institute a formal needs review mechanism. This would contain three stages.

Stage 1 — Institutional and agency reviews

Institutions and LEA agencies would be required to produce an annual *Needs Assessment Statement* for the LEA. This statement would indicate the educational needs of 16–19-year-olds that institutions and agencies believed they were meeting, and any that were within their purview but which they were unable to meet. The precise information sought and its format would be a matter for LEAs to determine according to their requirements and situation but it might well include the following headings.

For institutions

Existing course provision and numbers of students taking courses.

Perceived needs of the students taking existing courses, in terms of broad categories — academic vocational, pre-vocational, maturation, employment, social, etc.

Available information on destinations of students leaving the institution.

Available information on employers' needs.

Identification of planned changes in provision and the needs these are intended to meet.

Needs perceived by the institution and within its remit that it is unable to meet, together with reasons for this inability.

Statement of institutional priorities.

For the careers service

Pupil and student destinations.

Employers' recruitment patterns.

Employers' views of their requirements from educational provision.

Perceptions of needs, in broad categories, that are being met by educational provision.

Perceptions of needs, in broad categories, that are unmet by educational provision.

Identification of likely changes in the employment market.

Statement of service priorities.

The above headings are only suggested to illustrate what might be required. Some of this information is already being collected as part of the planning process for work-related non-advanced FE. Clearly statements should not be lengthy. Perceptions of needs met or unmet should generalize from collective experience rather than enter into the detail of individual cases. The process of formulating annual statements would require coordination and guidance by the LEA.

Within schools and colleges the creation of the annual statement would focus attention on the identification of needs and the extent to which they were being satisfied. It would stimulate institutions to evaluate whether their provision was meeting needs and help them determine priorities. It might represent the culmination of a process that required departments or course teams to explicitly evaluate their provision, thereby increasing the opportunities for practitioners to contribute their insights. It might also include the perceptions of any of the formal advisory mechanisms, or those contained in a career services report, that were advocated earlier in the chapter. The statement would be passed to the governing body for consideration and contribution. Governors would find it a valuable source of information for exercising their own oversight of provision and in making the annual report of activities required in the recent Education Act

(Education (No. 2) Act, 1986). Where institutions are working together, as in a consortium, they might produce a collective statement.

Although the statement need not be detailed or elaborate, it would add to the administrative burdens faced by schools and colleges and these are already experienced as heavy. But it would also add considerably to the status of needs assessment in educational planning. Needs would become more explicit. The case for institutions being given freedom in the way that they worked could be shown to rest on the presence of identified local needs.

The production of such statements by institutions and agencies would also aid LEAs in managing local education systems, so it is suggested that they should be passed to the relevant administrative division of the education department for consideration. First, they would improve LEAs' ability to respond to local demands; learning how needs are seen at the periphery (Schon, 1971). Second, they would be remedial; helping LEAs make judgments on where support was required and indicating issues that required monitoring or further investigation. Third, they would help LEAs shape the character of educational provision; indicating perceptions and approaches that departed from, or ignored, desired objectives.

Stage 2 — LEA reviews

It would also be valuable if LEAs produced a similar statement of the needs that they, themselves, were meeting or unable to meet, and provided this for consideration and contribution to the education committee. Again, the following headings are provided as an illustration of what might be included in such a statement.

Perceptions, in broad categories, of needs being met by provision.

Perceived shortfall in provision to meet existing needs.

Identification of planned changes in provision and the needs these will meet.

Indication of employers' needs.

Identification of any factors in the local or national context likely to cause changes in provision.

Needs perceived by the authority and within its remit that it is unable to meet, together with reasons for this inability.

Statement of LEA priorities.

Preparation of the LEA statement might be a function of the officer or unit responsible for analyzing information on needs advocated earlier. It would thus draw upon the analysis of information routinely collected by LEAs and upon any special investigation that had been undertaken on the initiative of this officer or unit. It would also draw upon the views of the different divisions and agencies within the department, thus including assessments made by the careers and youth and community services. Assessments made by divisions and agencies within LEAs would have been informed by scrutinizing the annual statements passed to them by institutions or groups of institutions. The existence of these latter would, in any case, provide LEAs with information explicitly concerned with needs and reduce the necessity of teasing out the implications for needs from information collected for other purposes. Where LEAs engaged in formal advisory mechanisms at the authority level, these might also contribute their perceptions of met or unmet needs.

The LEA's *Statement of Needs Assessment* would inevitably provide a subjective view of needs and their satisfaction and its creation would require interpretation and justification. But once created it would aid educational planning. First, it would help determine priorities. It would provide an overview of needs met and unmet which could be analyzed in terms of client groups for the whole of the 16–19 population, or by the constituent areas or institutions within the authority. Second, it would help in preparing for the future, in considering the impact of new developments and demographic change, and in budget preparation and negotiation.

It could also inform discussion with the DES and other central government departments and agencies. In particular, it would provide an explicit and relevant basis for the planning of non-advanced FE with the MSC.

Stage 3 — Negotiating Reviews

The annual statement of needs produced by the LEA would represent both an assessment of what 16–19 education was achieving and a forecast of how it was intended to develop in the future. It would provide strategic guidelines for the local system. The LEA's statement should, therefore, be circulated to institutions and agencies for their consideration. Consideration should include comparisons with their own statements. This might reveal significant differences in provision or intention. Where these existed, it would provide a signal for further exploration by LEA officers and advisers. Differences might well be justified by local circumstances or policies. Yet they might denote problems in terms of access to, or deployment of, resources, failure to identify opportunities on the existence of different ideas of educational purpose. Production of annual statements of need would clarify differences in perception between LEAs and their institutions and agencies at an early stage, and provide a basis for such differences to be discussed.

The suggested review process, which is depicted in diagram form below (Figure 4), would contribute to the purposes of the review of 16–19 provision suggested to LEAs by the DES in their recent circular (DES, 1987). It would, however, be a continual process, designed to enable needs

FIGURE 4: NEEDS ASSESSMENT REVIEW PROCESS

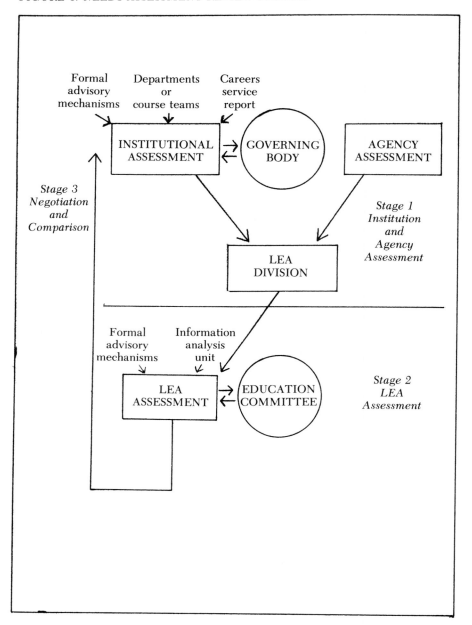

assessment make a more rational contribution to educational planning and decision-making. It does not seek to apply new techniques but rather requires different parts of local educational systems to focus their attention on needs and use the infomation they already possess to that end. This is not to argue that there is no case for applying different techniques. Analysis of the available information and the introduction of a review process would be likely to indicate gaps in knowledge or suggest ideas about needs that required further evidence. In such cases, existing means of obtaining information might well be inadequate. Even if LEAs do become less directly involved in determining the nature of education in the future, they should retain a regulatory role to ensure that what is being provided is adequate. This should surely include the degree to which needs are being met, and the overseeing of independent institutions would be more efficient if based on an explicit, formal process as outlined above.

An Alternative Model for Needs Assessment

The Existing Model

The discussion in Chapter 10 concluded that as currently practised, needs assessment mirrors the nature of local education systems. It was characterized as incremental in its contribution to educational planning and decision-making. It is conservative in the way in which it reacts to existing provision, existing client groups, and existing work processes. It is pluralistic and the product of negotiation, in that it reflects the importance of professional contributions and the distribution of power between different organizations and different interests. As a consequence it is unequal in its application and not readily innovative. Our recommendations were directed towards improving needs assessment within the current educational context.

An Objective-led Model

Although we did not encounter it in our research, it is possible to suggest an alternative, more rational, conception of needs assessment. This alternative can be described as objectives-led assessment. It is based upon the assumption that educational provision is determined by the achievement of explicit objectives which satisfy political and professional value choices. If, for example, central government's, an LEA's, or an institution's prime objective was to promote social justice, the means of needs assessment could then be directed towards groups that appeared to be the most deprived in terms of receiving educational provision. These might be defined by extent or quality of participation in education, by sex, by race, by

TABLE 14: MODES OF WORKING IN AN OBJECTIVE-LED MODEL OF NEEDS ASSESSMENT

Predominant Modes		Predominant Characteristics
Proactive	)	Determined by educational objectives of central
Rational	)	government, the LEA, or institution which
Elitist	)	decide whose needs are assessed and given
Centralized	)	priority.
Purposive	)	Centralized, exhibiting 'top-down' strategy.
Conflictual	)	Could be innovative.
		Unequal in its application.

class or by place of residence in the authority. Information would be collected on their social, economic and educational characteristics and on their patterns of involvement with, and participation in, education. Professional views of their needs would be obtained as would the opinions of the different groups, themselves. The needs of the disadvantaged would become a focus in monitoring and planning educational provision. If, by contrast, the prime objective was to promote economic development, needs assessment would concentrate upon different employment groups. These might be defined by employment or unemployment, by category of employment, by level of employment and by form of qualification or training. Information would be collected on employment trends and characteristics, on student qualifications and on their destinations and subsequent employment careers. Again professional views of need would be important but so would those of employers of all types.

Table 14 summarizes the principal features of this alternative conception of needs assessment. Comparison with Table 12 in the preceding chapter indicates the contrast with existing 'provision-led' practice. Were needs assessment to become 'objectives-led', its contribution to educational planning would become more focused and more rational. It would be proactive in seeking out needs in relation to the identified objectives. It would not be shaped by the existing provision nor by negotiations reflecting the pattern of relationships and power of different educational interests. The assessment would be more purposive and not influenced by existing work routines. Professional viewpoints would remain important but not necessarily dominant. Needs assessment would be elitist rather than pluralistic, determined from the centre by power holders in central government, the LEA, or institution. It might, or might not, prove a radical influence and could engender innovation. Needs assessment would be explicitly unequal in its application, concentrating on the particular objectives to be attained. This model of needs assessment equates with Kaufman's deductive model (Kaufman, 1972), deducing and evaluating educational programmes according to defined goals. Central government initiatives to develop cost-effective and work-related education have already moved some way in this direction.

This conception of needs assessment is problematic given the present incremental and pluralistic nature of education, although it may be prophetic. It suggests the presence of a hierarchical rather than a political model of educational government. Judging from the current state of education, were such an approach to become the norm it would become a source of conflict. The clarification of objectives and their central position in planning would act as a focus for opposition and discontent. Views of needs that did not equate with the objectives set might well be ignored and there would be a danger that all needs would be pre-defined in terms of the approved objectives, overlooking the individual and the local.

Considering a different role and status for needs assessment moves into the sphere of educational government and far exceeds our brief. But it does underline the complexities, choices and uncertainties that are involved in deciding how best to assess educational needs and in relating assessments to provision. This study has been concerned to understand how needs are defined in practice and how they then affect educational provision. The research will have succeeded in its purpose if it has shed light on this process and on the issues involved.

References

BUSH, T., (1986) *Theories of Educational Management*, London, Harper & Row.

CENTRAL POLICY REVIEW STAFF, (1980) *Education, Training and Industrial Performance*, London, HMSO.

DAVIES, P., and SCRIBBINS, K. (1985) *Marketing Further and Higher Education*, London, Longman.

DES, (1980) *Education for 16–19 Year Olds* (The Macfarlane Report), London, HMSO.

DES, (1987) *Providing for Quality: The Pattern of Organization to Age 19*, London, HMSO.

DES/DE, (1985) *Education and Training for Young People*, (Cmnd 9482), London, HMSO.

EDUCATION (No. 2) ACT (1986).

HOYLE, E., (1975) 'Leadership and decision-making in education' in HUGHES, N. (Ed.), *Administering Education*, London, Athlone Press.

HYDER, M., (1984) 'Implementation: The evolutionary model' in LEWIS, D. and WALLACE, H., (Eds), *Policies into Practice*, London, Heinemann.

KAUFMAN, R.A., (1972) *Educational System Planning*, Englewood Cliffs, NJ, Prentice Hall.

KOGAN, M., (1975) *The Politics of Educational Change*, London, Fontana.

LOCKE M. and BLOOMFIELD, J. (1982) *Mapping and Reviewing the Pattern of 16–19 Education*, Schools Council Pamphlet 20, London, Schools Council.

MORTIMORE, J. and BLACKSTONE, T., (1982) *Disadvantage and Education*, London, Heinemann.

RATSAY, E., (1980) 'Environments, linkages and policy making in educational organizations', *The Canadian Administrator*, 19, 7.

SAMMONS, P., (1983) 'Patterns of participation in vocational further education: A study of school leavers in Inner London' in GLEESON, D., (Ed) *Youth Training and the Search for Work*, London, Routledge & Kegan Paul.

SCHON, D., (1971) *Beyond the Stable State*, London, Temple Smith.

THEODOSSIN, E., (1986) *In Search of The Responsive College*, Bristol, Further Education Staff College.

Appendix: Methodology of the Research

Research Methodology

The research was undertaken in two stages employing different methodologies. The first stage commenced with a survey of all LEAs in England regarding the documentation on their policies for the 16–19 age group. This was followed by a questionnaire, similarly sent to all LEAs in England, to explore their methods of planning post-16 provision, their policies on institutional arrangements for this age group and views on the needs and provision made for these students. The response rate for both these exercises was just over 75 per cent. In addition interviews were held in eight selected authorities to follow up some of the issues from the study of documentation and the responses from the questionnaires. The intention of this first stage of the research was to develop general findings on the patterns of LEA policies and planning systems in 16–19 provision in order to select detailed case studies. From this exercise an interim report was produced summarizing and analyzing the findings (Whitaker, 1985).

The second and major part of the research comprised six case studies, three large scale case studies looking at the needs assessment within whole LEAs and three smaller studies of selected issues in post-16 provision — the role of a tertiary college, the role of a careers service in planning 16–19 provision and the role of a consortium of providers of post-16 education. The case study mode was selected because it was felt that this was most appropriate to meet the aims of the research. (Adelman et al, 1984; Yin, 1984; Miles and Huberman, 1984). In particular, it would allow the dynamic of LEA and institutional processes and relationships to be studied. The main method of gathering data was through semi-structured interviews with selected role holders. This provided comparable data together with the ability to be flexible in exploring further issues as they arose. These interviews were recorded in note form and then typed for internal team use.

The fieldwork was similar in each of the large scale case studies in that areas of questioning were decided by the research team prior to interviewing. For the most part interviews were single but some role holders in the LEA were interviewed on a number of occasions to seek interpretation of the research findings and coordinate its progress. In these studies officers, councillors and advisers were interviewed within the LEA. Interviews were also undertaken with officers in LEA agencies such as the careers service and youth and community service. A small number of interviews were conducted with officers in other local authority departments. In the institutions selected for study, interviews were held with senior managers including the head or principal and heads of sixth forms or departments mainly concerned with post-16 provision and development. In each of these studies local officials of MSC were interviewed and the secretary of the Regional Advisory Council. Finally interviews were held with a small sample of employers selected to provide a broader interpretation of employers' views of educational needs and provision. A second method of research employed in the large scale studies was the observation of meetings in the LEA. These were selected in an opportunistic way. The third method was the study of documentation from the LEA and from institutions. This was to provide information on formal policies as well as background information prior to interviews.

The fieldwork in the small scale case studies was undertaken in a similar way. Because the sites of the research study were different, the type and range of role holders interviewed varied between studies although the focus of interviews was similar.

The fieldwork was carried out by two researchers so there had to be some method ensuring comparability. The same range of techniques were used in all studies. Coverage in terms of the interviews undertaken followed the principle of reputational sampling — making contact with those who were seen to be important to other people and a more systematic coverage of a range of incumbents of formal roles who were felt to have a legitimate involvement in the assessment of needs and in determining post-16 provision. The organization of the fieldwork was carried out in a similar way by two researchers and team meetings provided a way of checking on the direction and coverage of the various case studies. The early interviews in the LEA were concerned with discovering general influences on post-16 provision and key issues. The remainder of interviews were concerned with the processes through which assessments of needs were made and how these affected the determination of educational provision. Validation of the findings was approached in a number of different ways. Cross checking was carried out in each of the case studies through the application of the different techniques — interviews, recurrent interviews in some cases, the observation of meetings and through the study of documents. The method of 'triangulation' could therefore be used to test the responses from the various interviewees. Finally, as a guard to check the reliability of the findings and interpretations made by the researchers in each case study, a case study document was produced which provided the basis for discussion with senior officers.

The Selection of the Case Studies

The selection of the large scale case studies followed a number of stages. The intention was to select these case studies after the survey of documents and the results from the questionnaires sent to LEAs in order to learn their planning and provision. This exercise produced three sets of factors which were felt to be likely influences on the way that LEAs assessed the needs of the 16–19 age group. These primary factors included the institutional arrangements for making provision (traditional or mixed), and the range of policy inputs (high or low) defined by the extent of participation and level of information used in planning. Secondary factors included the level of LEA direction over coordination of 16–19 provision, the type of planned change in the institutional arrangements, and the type of LEA. Subsidiary factors were the nature of party political control, the level of age participation rate in post-16 education, the size of the authority, the presence of urban or rural characteristics and other socio-demographic variables. It was decided to select one LEA with traditional institutional arrangements and high inputs to planning; one LEA with a mixed form of arrangements and high inputs and one LEA with traditional institutional arrangements and low inputs to planning. A list of possible LEAs was submitted to a meeting of the DES Steering Committee for the research project and members also indicated their own choices. The three chosen authorities varied in terms of their size, political complexion, geographical considerations and social class characteristics.

For the small scale case studies the team used their own knowledge of relevant examples and also relied upon advice from steering committee members and HMI. To some extent cases were chosen because they were judged to be examples of 'good practice' as defined by practitioners.

The negotiation of research access was undertaken by the team members who explained the aims of the research and the likely demands in terms of fieldwork for the authorities and institutions. Only one of the large scale case study authorities refused access and another with similar characteristics was chosen in its place.

Within the case studies institutions were selected for study and this relied on both pre-defined criteria, as well as advice from senior officers to obtain a cross section of organizational arrangements and types of provision. In all thirty-six institutions were studied.

Description of the Case Studies

Case Study 1

This county authority was located in the south of England and bordered a major conurbation. Its population was mainly concentrated in a number of medium-sized towns. A particular feature of this authority was its prosperity as reflected in the low rate of unemployment and the high proportion of managerial and professional employees. The authority was under Conservative control. It had one of the highest staying on rates in post-16 education with a high proportion of students following academically related courses for entry to higher education. The LEA had a mixed system of institutional arrangements — 11–16 schools, 11–19 schools, sixth form colleges, and FE colleges — varying between different administrative areas of the authority.

Case Study 2

This was a large rural county in the south of England. Its population was dispersed, with a series of medium sized towns serving the surrounding villages. The employment structure was based on agriculture, the service sector and tourism with a below average rate of unemployment. The authority was Conservative controlled. There was no single institutional pattern in the county for providing post-16 education; in the urban areas there were tertiary colleges and in the sparsely populated areas school sixth forms provided the academically oriented courses with the urban tertiary colleges providing vocational education. In addition one urban area had a sixth form college and a large FE college.

Case Study 3

This authority was a Metropolitan District located in an urban area in the north of England. It was heavily influenced by the increase in unemployment which had arisen through the decline in the traditional industries. The city was characterized by a wide range of socio-demographic characteristics but there was a below average rate of staying on for post-16 education. The authority was Labour controlled and had been a high spender on educational provision. The LEA had made a conscious decision to retain the traditional system of post-16 arrangements through sixth forms and a FE college but had instituted a policy on institutional coordination.

Case Study 4

This was a study of a careers service in a county authority located in the south of England. The area had been one of population and economic growth and there was a high staying on rate in post-16 education and the presence of employment opportunities. The county had a mixed system of institutional arrangements and in two areas there was still selection at the age of 11. The two careers offices selected for study were in the east of the county in medium sized towns. One was in a new town in an area of economic growth whilst the other was in an older industrial area with a significant concentration of ethnic minorities.

Case Study 5

This was a study of a tertiary college in a county authority in the north of England. The college served an area of about fifteen square miles and was the major provider of 16–19 education for seven 11–16 schools. It had around 1000 full-time students, mostly in the 16–19 age group and some 11,000 part-time. The college was organized on five sites. The population of this area was mainly concentrated on two urban centres. It was characterized by an average county percentage of skilled and non-manual workers but a slightly above average county rate for semi and unskilled workers. There was a significant Asian community. The traditional employment structure of the area had changed due to the collapse of the traditional industries.

Case Study 6

This study was of a collaborative group comprising a consortium of six 11–19 schools and an FE college located in a county authority in the Midlands. The town in which it was based differed from the rest of the county. It had a large working class population and there had been one major source of industrial employment that had closed down in the late 1970s. The rates of social and economic deprivation were higher than the rest of county and there was a below average staying on rate in post-16 education. The scheme of collaboration had been in existence since the early 1970s. The schools in the scheme were experiencing the effects of falling rolls.

Appendix

References

ADELMAN, C., *et al*, (1984) 'Rethinking case study' in BELL, J., *et al*, (Eds) *Conducting Small Scale Investigations in Education Management*, London, Harper & Row.

MILES, M.B., and HUBERMAN, A.M., (1984) *Qualitative Data Analysis*, London, Sage.

WHITAKER, T., (1985) *Educational Planning: LEAs' Assessment of Educational Need for the 16–19 Age Group*, Middlesex, Brunel University.

YIN, R., (1984) *Case Study Research: Design and Methods*, London, Sage.

Name Index

Subject Index

Page numbers in italics refer to Figures and Tables.
Passim is used where scattered references occur over a number of pages.
Abbreviations are used where these are cited in the Glossary.